The Price of Permanence

environmental history and the american south

SERIES EDITOR

James C. Giesen, Mississippi State University

Erin Stewart Mauldin, University of South Florida

ADVISORY BOARD

Judith Carney, University of California–Los Angeles

S. Max Edelson, University of Virginia

Robbie Ethridge, University of Mississippi

Ari Kelman, University of California–Davis

Shepard Krech III, Brown University

Megan Kate Nelson, www.historista.com

Tim Silver, Appalachian State University

Mart Stewart, Western Washington University

Paul S. Sutter, founding editor, University of Colorado, Boulder

The Price of Permanence

NATURE AND BUSINESS IN THE NEW SOUTH

William D. Bryan

The University of Georgia Press
Athens

Parts of chapter 1 appeared in a different form as "'Constructive and Not Destructive Development': Permanent Uses of Resources in the American South" in *Green Capitalism?: Business and the Environment in the Twentieth Century,* edited by Hartmut Berghoff and Adam Rome (Philadelphia: University of Pennsylvania Press, 2017).

Paperback edition, 2020
© 2018 by the University of Georgia Press
Athens, Georgia 30602
www.ugapress.org
All rights reserved
Set in 10.5/13.5 Adobe Garamond Pro by Graphic Composition, Inc.

Most University of Georgia Press titles are
available from popular e-book vendors.

Printed digitally

The Library of Congress has cataloged the hardcover
edition of this book as follows:

Names: Bryan, William D., author.
Title: The price of permanence : nature and business in the New South / William D. Bryan.
Description: Athens : The University of Georgia Press, 2018. |
 Series: Environmental history and the american south |
 Includes bibliographical references and index.
Identifiers: LCCN 2017058465| ISBN 9780820353395 (hardcover : alk. paper) |
 ISBN 9780820353388 (ebook)
Subjects: LCSH: Southern States—Environmental conditions. |
 Environmental policy—Southern States—History. |
 Environmental responsibility—Southern States—History. |
 Economic development—Environmental aspects—
 Southern States—History. | Business enterprises—
 Environmental aspects—Southern States—History.
Classification: LCC GE155.S68 B79 2018 | DDC 333.720975—dc23
 LC record available at https://lccn.loc.gov/2017058465

Paperback ISBN 978-0-8203-5878-9

For my parents

CONTENTS

List of Illustrations   ix

Foreword, by James C. Giesen   xi

Preface   xv

Acknowledgments   xxi

CHAPTER 1 Nature's Bounty   1

CHAPTER 2 Cultivating Permanence   33

CHAPTER 3 Utilizing Southern Wastes   68

CHAPTER 4 The Costs of Permanence   111

CHAPTER 5 Tourism's New Path   142

CONCLUSION   175

Notes   183

Index   217

ILLUSTRATIONS

From Darkness to Light 6
"Bird Court" 22
E. Lee Worsham 27
Cottonseed being unloaded at a Mississippi railroad station 62
Champion Fibre Company's mill in Canton, North Carolina 70
Charles Holmes Herty 85
Florida pine trees tapped using the Herty system 87
Phosphate dredge, crusher, and washer of South Carolina's Central Mining Company 89
His Inspiration 96
Refuse burner, Great Southern Lumber Company in Bogalusa, Louisiana 107
Hydroelectric dam at Parr Shoals, South Carolina 120
Helen D. Longstreet 160

FOREWORD

In 1891, the local newspaper in Big Stone Gap, Virginia, argued it would be a good idea to blow a local dam "sky high." Many residents agreed, believing that the structure, built to harness the flow of the Powell River to power a textile mill, was bad for their health. The stagnant water blocked by the dam was a nuisance, many believed, as it was the source of disease and general ill health around the town. It didn't help that the mill owner was an outsider, unaffected by the supposedly toxic environment of his own factory while he lived far away in Chicago. From that city he argued, in turn, that the dam was not a nuisance to the environment at all and claimed instead that his investment in the town and his mill's employment of locals was nothing but a boon to the remote Appalachian locale. It was in many ways a classic conflict over industry and capital, on the one hand, and local controls over the natural world on the other.

Yet, as Will Bryan demonstrates throughout *The Price of Permanence*, local decisions about resources were hardly the simple matter of use versus conservation that historians have so often portrayed. Indeed, Big Stone Gap officials voted to destroy the mill and free the flow of the river—to return the landscape to what locals thought was its natural state. The absentee owner's textile factory shut down soon after. But what allowed locals' decision not just to spurn "foreign" capital investment but to actively shut down existing operations was not the result of an impulse of environmental protection. Rather, it was capital itself. Had the region not been in the middle of a coal-mining boom, Bryan tells us, these Virginians would not have been in a place to shut down a different kind of business.

This book is full of such stories, historical lessons that complicate our common understanding of both conservation and New South boosterism. Readers will find here many of the stock characters of the post–Civil War southern renaissance—would-be local steel magnates and carpetbagger industrialists—but here they are surrounded by, even dependent on, the region's vast natural resources. So while this book paints the portraits of these business leaders in much finer detail than readers of southern history may recognize, it is the coal, water, and farm crops of the region that make this explanation of southern conservation fresh and important.

As with so much of the work of environmental history, and particularly southern environmental history, surprises abound. The best environmental history takes a traditional historical narrative and turns it slightly so that readers might see the past from a slightly new point of view. Many times this new perspective changes not just how readers understand outcomes, but it can also alter fundamental understandings of causation. In other words, the environmental history lens can change our understandings not just of what happened, but it can change the basic questions that we ask. That is the case with this volume.

Will Bryan argues here that the greedy, resource-devouring capitalists that drive most accounts of the New South were actually far more interested in the future of those resources than we have previously believed. Enter the idea of permanence. Those with political power in places like Big Stone Gap were not interested only in jobs to the detriment of human and ecological health. Rather, in example after example, Bryan demonstrates how southerners sought permanence over the quick buck (or quick hire). These resources were, after all, one of the few assets that southerners had following the war, and those people in power protected access to them in telling and surprising ways. The forests were depositories of resin and lumber, pulp and paper. The soil was an engine for valuable cotton and tobacco. Even the animals of the backcountry were important sources of income from hunters and tourists. But all of these assets needed to be meted out rather than conquered. And as Bryan argues, this management was a "stunning success," at least to those on top.

Permanence meant something other than success for those who were not in a position of power over the region's water, animals, minerals, and soil. African Americans in particular found their fates inextricably tied to the white elite's control over resources. Indeed, the permanence of natural resources depended on what whites saw as a malleable and inexhaustible supply of labor. Boosters began selling not just the resources of the environment to court outside capital but cheap, controllable labor as well. Bryan is quick to point out the ways that African Americans sought to thwart this control, sometimes successfully. Of course, as the book's title suggests, permanence came with a cost, and its role in the continuation of Jim Crow was only one price the South paid. For the full story of that cost, you will have to read on.

The Price of Permanence continues the Environmental History and the American South series' effort to push the boundaries of this subfield. As the reader will see, the book offers many insights and pushes many arguments that those familiar with the field will find compelling. Indeed, conservation, that subject that lies at the heart of world and U.S. environmental history, has been insufficiently covered in the southern context until now. Likewise, southern historians comfortable with decades-old treatments of New South industrial expansion will find their perspectives significantly shifted when they view the subject from Bryan's environmental position. Thanks to *The Price of Permanence* we now have a better understanding of how conservation played out in a region so often castigated for not caring about it at all.

James C. Giesen

PREFACE

When I began researching the relationship between nature and economic development in the American South, I did not expect to find people calling for the conservation of natural resources so that they would be permanently available for future generations. I had spent my entire life in the region, and the legacies of southern environmental degradation were still evident in deep gullies cutting through fields, the familiar smell of chemicals spewing from paper mills, straight rows of slash pine in industrial forests, rivers laden with heavy metals, and even the red clay that had replaced once-fertile soils at my home. Yet as I read more about the New South, I found that in the decades after the Civil War southern businesspeople and public officials were preoccupied with the idea that there could be "permanent" ways of using the region's dwindling natural resources. Rather than advocating a get-rich-quick strategy premised on simply selling resources to the highest bidder and exploiting them to depletion, southerners debated the most "permanent" ways to use and conserve their resources so that they would be available indefinitely, and southerners worked to implement these measures in a developing region struggling with the legacies of the Civil War.

The idea of permanence did not square with what I had learned from southern historians who see development at any cost as the New South "credo."[1] For more than six decades scholars have caricatured southerners as so desperate for economic growth after the Civil War that they rapaciously consumed the region's abundant resources. In this narrative the urgent need for jobs overrode any sense of stewardship that southerners had toward their environment. Despite recent studies of ecological changes occurring over hundreds of years of human habitation, the complicated path that led to these changes is often reduced to a choice to prioritize profits over environmental quality. In this simplistic tale of environmental declension, the common wisdom is that "the concepts of conservation and environmental protection were too esoteric to stand up against the region's seemingly insatiable desire for more industrial payrolls" and that "rivers, trees, the soil, all could be taken for granted—jobs were the truly precious commodity in an economically deprived Dixie."[2]

Permanence also did not square with what I learned from environmental historians who have never seen the South as a major player in the American conservation movement. As scholars have moved away from seeing conservation through the boosterish lens of its early historians, they have shed new light on its complex social, political, and even global facets. Recent scholarship on conservation has demonstrated how federal and state officials often clashed with local communities, how Progressive Era visions for conservation simplified complex ecosystems to maintain stocks of valuable natural resources, how diverse constituencies contributed to the ideals of conservation, and how conserving resources had exploitative social effects on ordinary people. Yet the stakeholders most identified with conservation debates—federal officials, nature lovers, scientists, wealthy tourists, and Native Americans—were not key players in the New South, leading historians to write the region almost entirely out of the story of American conservation.

As I struggled to come to terms with this disconnect between my perceptions of the region's history and what I had discovered, I had to confront a number of questions. What were the roots of ideas about permanence? How did southerners work through multiple visions for what permanence meant and how to achieve it? How effective were they at building a permanent economy? How did permanence shape economic development in the years after the Civil War? How did it fit into the narratives of environmental declension that formed my understanding of southern environmental history? Answering these questions convinced me that tired scholarly debates about the New South and the conservation movement looked fresh when viewed as struggles over environmental permanence, and this approach rewrites both literatures in important ways.

For southern historians, *The Price of Permanence* moves beyond persistent caricatures of business leaders and public officials as so desperate for economic growth that they had little concern for the environment. Ever since C. Vann Woodward characterized the words of Henry Grady as "one long hymn of invocation to preemption and exploitation" of the region's resources, scholars have deviated little from this simplistic take on southern boosters.[3] Yet natural resources were one of the most important assets in the wake of the Civil War, and regional leaders continually debated how to make the most of them. If we take these debates seriously, we can move beyond one-dimensional characterizations of boosters and see how important their ideas about long-term uses of resources through conservation were to shaping development strategies in the years after the Civil War.

The Price of Permanence also provides a new way to understand racial dynamics in the post–Civil War South. Although scholars have written at length about the widespread racial discrimination and violence that pockmarked the New South, they have not considered how the emergence of Jim Crow related to conflicts over natural resources that occurred as southerners worked out their economic future. But attempts to build an economy that would use resources in permanent ways were never just about maintaining abundant stocks of natural resources. White business and municipal officials benefited from racial discrimination, and their efforts to build a permanent economy were bound up with their efforts to ensure the permanence of the racial hierarchy. Because the enterprises that boosters deemed permanent were largely dependent upon cheap labor, these industries provided a way to prevent radical change and social unrest, maintain the exploitative employer-employee relationship, and allow businessmen to keep a tight grip on the South's economic, political, and social development. In this way, permanence was a critical tool wielded by southern businessmen and public officials to maintain the exploitative racial hierarchy and cut off access to valuable resources for black southerners. Jim Crow, which was dubbed the "permanent system" by white elites, even shared the same vocabulary as conservation.[4]

Permanence was not uncontested, however. Businessmen and public officials often clashed with stakeholders who had far different dreams for what was most likely to provide durable foundations for a new economy, which resources to develop or conserve, what groups should benefit most and least from development, and how to implement change in a region where land and resources were often privately owned. Even people without a formal claim to resources had a stake in these questions and participated in struggles over the best uses of the South's natural bounty. Framing permanence as a contested process shows how ideas about long-term uses of resources undergirded many different visions for the New South and suggests how black and white groups of "other southerners"—to use Carl Degler's phrase—shaped economic development and resource use after the Civil War.[5]

The Price of Permanence also sheds light on the region's relationship with the rest of the United States during the Gilded Age and Progressive Era. Despite claims that the end of the Civil War would usher in a time of reconciliation and reunion, scholars show that the South had a schizophrenic relationship with the rest of the nation. While boosters appealed to the North for investment and immigration, they also crafted particular memories of the past and visions for the future that decried the South's colonial relationship with northern capitalists. The South's distinctly regional labor market, its legacy of poverty, the agricultural bent of its economy, and even the freight-rate differential between North and South further worked to keep the region isolated. Despite this distance, southern boosters supported national conservation measures and embraced a philosophy of conservation that emanated from officials in the North and West, hoping that a permanent economy would make the region independently prosperous. Understanding how the South fit into the national conservation movement moves us beyond viewing national reunion as a process that played out only as southerners struggled over how to memorialize the Civil War.

This book also provides a new perspective on the origins of twentieth-century environmental degradation. By the New Deal, lumbering, mining, exhaustive cultivation of soils, and industrial pollution had taken their toll on the southern environment. Most scholars chalk this up either to the region's poverty or to the probusiness, antiregulation views of its leaders. *The Price of Permanence* locates this environmental degradation in the wave of economic development spawned by the ideals of permanence. Permanent enterprises may have used certain resources efficiently, but they also intensified resource use generally and created a bevy of other environmental problems. Manufacturing paper promoted forestry but polluted skies and waters; slash pine created industrial forests that simplified complex ecosystems; commercial fertilizers temporarily boosted soil fertility at the expense of long-term soil health; portland cement eased pressure on forest resources but resulted in significant air pollution. These problems simply did not figure into the developmental calculus of the businesspeople and public officials most enthusiastic about permanent development. Permanence was also myopic and privileged strategies for maintaining stocks of profitable resources for business uses at the expense of overall environmental quality. Only by looking past simplistic explanations of environmental problems, then, can we understand why such terrible degradation occurred just as New South leaders were embracing the ideals of conservation that were becoming popular throughout the nation.

For environmental historians, *The Price of Permanence* uses the experience of the South to provide a fresh perspective on the goals and strategies of all American conservationists. Although historians have moved beyond early scholarship that characterized conservation as a contest between businesses and the state, they have not fully explored the role that businesspeople played in shaping the conservation movement in the United States. Developmental imperatives were always an important part of the vision of conservationists—a point Gifford Pinchot and other conservation leaders made clear. By focusing on businesspeople, this book sheds light on the "use" part of conservationists' "wise use" mantra. This brings out the complexities of the conservation vision nationally, not just in the South.

The Price of Permanence also suggests how malleable conservation could be and shows how it fueled different strategies for managing resources. Southern business leaders found much to admire in federal efforts to conserve resources, but they ultimately hoped to maintain resource stocks through private measures, not federal regulation. Rather than "seeing" and administering natural resources like a state, these boosters hoped to secure conservation by exercising corporate authority. In short, the types of corporate conservation popular below the Mason-Dixon Line gave conservation a twang that distinguished it from the rest of the nation.[6]

To examine how the struggle for environmental permanence shaped the New South, it is necessary to depart from traditional environmental and southern histories both in geographic scope and in chronology. The South is undoubtedly a diverse place—socially, economically, ecologically—and whether it holds together as a coherent region has animated a great deal of debate.[7] While there are important differences between southern regions, *The Price of Permanence* shows that the idea of permanence spanned multiple ecosystems within the political and cultural boundaries of the South. Throughout the eleven states of the former Confederacy and in Kentucky, businesspeople, boosters, and public officials all saw environmental permanence as a strategy that could lead to long-term economic growth, whether they were struggling to envision the future of tobacco, cotton, naval stores, iron, or even tourism.

This book also departs from the typical chronological boundaries of the New South era. For nearly sixty years, scholars have debated whether the New South was really new and what period is best described by this label. Competing definitions of the bounds of the New South range from C. Vann Woodward, who focuses on the years between 1877 and 1913, to Numan Bartley, who argues that there was no New South until after World War II.[8] This book begins in 1865, when the future of the region was an open question and new possibilities for using resources were considered in a meaningful way. This was also a period when private businessmen and state and municipal officials played the key role shaping economic development. This book concludes with the New Deal, when the federal government became a major new player in the South's development, dramatically changing the dynamics of the search for environmental and economic permanence. In this way, *The Price of Permanence* cuts across multiple conceptions of the New South to see how the conservation of natural resources shaped the long arc of development after the Civil War.

When I started working on the New South, I never expected that my research would lead me to think about sustainable development—a concept that has been popular only since the early 1980s and still has little momentum in the South. Although advocates of sustainable development now speak the language of ecology, sustainability is just the newest strategy for using resources in ways that will keep them available for future generations. Indeed, the idea that there could be permanent uses of resources mimics contemporary enthusiasm for sustainability. Sustainable development and permanence are both predicated on finding developmental solutions to environmental problems that do not require radical changes in corporate behavior. Because of these commonalities, understanding why corporate leaders embraced permanent uses of resources a century ago can help to explain the popularity of sustainability with business leaders today. It can also suggest the ways that sustainable development fails to address the issues that are at the heart of so many environmental problems.

Developing areas globally face the same dilemma as postbellum southerners: how to balance environmental quality and long-term stewardship of natural resources with the desperate need for jobs and economic prosperity. As debates about sustainability shift to the developing world, the experience of the South is useful. In many respects, the post–Civil War South—with its regional labor market, low average incomes, manual labor founded on exploitative racial ideologies, and colonial economic status—resembles the developing world more than the rest of the United States. Rather than taking the American path, where capitalist intensification and the transition to free labor upended the social order and brought a group of new entrepreneurs to power, the South mimics the "Prussian path," where capitalist growth was driven by continued repressive manual labor and traditional social relations. The Prussian path is just as capitalist as the American path, but it is a useful reminder that the South's postbellum development deviated from the rest of the nation in important ways.[9] Understanding the choices that southern business and political leaders made as they worked to rebuild their economy after the Civil War, then, can shed light on how other developing areas balance conflicting priorities of jobs, social justice, and environmental quality as they work to build their own stable and long-lasting economic foundations.

ಬ

Wallace Stegner has described people as either "boomers" or "stickers." Boomers are "those who pillage and run" and use profit as their mark of success, while stickers are "those who settle, and love the life they have made and the place they have made it in."[10] For decades southern businesspeople and public officials have been seen as the quintessential boomers. But in the decades after the Civil War, these boomers sought to refashion themselves into stickers. *The Price of Permanence* is the story of how they did it, whether they succeeded, and the effects of this transformation on southern people and landscapes.

ACKNOWLEDGMENTS

I am lucky to have been surrounded by a wonderful community of scholars and friends who have strengthened my work and made the process of writing this book so enjoyable. I am especially grateful for the guidance of two scholars and mentors. I will never be able to fully thank Adam Rome for all that he has done for me both in graduate school and beyond. Adam is a model scholar and advisor. He is generous with his time and encouraging with his critiques. He commented on every part of this project, and it is far better because of his input. I am proud to be one of his students. Bill Blair graciously stepped in to chair my dissertation committee in the latter stages of this project, and he provided direction as I was writing and revising. Bill helped me to hone the argument of this book in key ways, worked with me to secure crucial support during graduate school, and has given me welcome counsel on scholarship, career, and life. His shrimp and grits brought me back home, even in Pennsylvania.

At Penn State I was fortunate to work alongside other faculty and graduate students who strengthened my work and provided encouragement and good cheer. I am grateful to Robert Burkholder, Solsiree Del Moral, and Mark Neely—a stellar sounding board and dissertation committee. I learned about the New South from Nan Woodruff, and my work on this topic owes a great deal to her work and teaching. Dan Letwin gave me the opportunity to present my research to his classes and always provided insightful feedback during our conversations. Eric Novotny came through with valuable research assistance whenever I needed it. I am also grateful to Gary Cross, Tony Kaye, Sally McMurry, Mike Milligan, and Crystal Sanders for their support during my graduate career and since. My graduate cohort and my officemates in Pond Laboratory provided an ideal scholarly and social community, and I would like to thank Bill Cossen, Katie Falvo, Andrea Gatzke, Lauren Golder, David Greenspoon, David Hensley, John Hoenig, Jeff Horton, Antwain Hunter, Chris Hyashida-Knight, Matt Isham, Kelly Knight, Kevin Lowe, Paul Matzko, Rachel Moran, Tim Orr, Andrew Prymak, Lesley Rains, J. Adam Rogers, Evan Rothera, Emily Seitz, Jonathan Steplyk, Juan Tebes, Sean Trainor, Alfred Wallace, Eric Welch, and Tim Wesley.

The staff of the Bill and Carol Fox Center for Humanistic Inquiry made my year at Emory University one of the most productive and enjoyable of my career. I am especially thankful to Keith Anthony, Collete Barlow, Martine Brownley, and Amy Erbil. The other Fox Center fellows provided stimulating conversation during weekly lunches, and pushed me to think about my work in completely new ways. I would especially like to thank Jeremy Bell, Seth Perlow, and Amanda Wright.

Many other scholars have graciously provided input on this book. Paul Sutter has assisted me in innumerable ways since I started graduate school, from providing feedback on my work to introducing me to other people working in my field. Mark Hersey read and commented on drafts of several chapters and provided valuable advice throughout the course of this project. Jim Cobb and Elliott West provided direction for expanding key parts of my argument during a seminar arranged by the Richards Civil War Era Center at Penn State. Bert Way has read and talked through work with me on a number of occasions, and he has been welcoming as I have settled in Atlanta. Jamil Zainaldin has gone out of his way to support my work and help me find opportunities for public engagement. At Emory, Tom Rogers and Astrid Eckert provided feedback at a critical stage. Steve Anderson, Jason Howard, Eben Lehman, and Jamie Lewis all helped to make my time researching at the Forest History Society fruitful. I have been lucky to learn from a wonderful community of scholars in Atlanta who read and commented on parts of this book while providing good cheer. Thanks to Brian Banks, Casey Cater, Rachel Ernst, Felix Harcourt, Deanna Matheuszik, Allyson Tadjer, Jay Watkins, and Carolyn Zimmerman.

I presented research from this project at a number of conferences, and I am indebted to my fellow panelists, chairs, and commentators, including Nicole Cox, Eric Dinmore, Jon Free, Monica Gisolfi, Christine Keiner, Merritt McKinney, Amanda McVety, Tom Okie, Aaron Sachs, and Matthew Vitz. The Center for Ecological History at Renmin University of China and the Rachel Carson Center for Environment and Society brought me to Beijing for the "Manufacturing Landscapes" conference. All the participants provided valuable comments, and I would like to especially thank Tim LeCain and Don Worster. The Center for the History of Agriculture, Science, and the Environment of the South at Mississippi State University invited me in 2014 to present parts of my work at its symposium, where I had a wonderful opportunity to learn from leaders in the field. The participants of the University of Delaware's history workshop helped me think through an important part of my argument, and I appreciate Adam Rome's invitation to speak.

The seeds for this project were planted while I was an undergraduate at Furman University, where I spent a semester researching and writing about conservation and industrial pollution in the New South. Steve O'Neill supervised that thesis and introduced me to southern and environmental history—in the classroom and floating down the Reedy River in his canoe. I am grateful for his continued guidance and friendship. Gary Malvern also provided warm support for my historical endeavors and has been an invaluable sounding board on scholarship and life.

I received generous financial support that allowed me to research and write this book. I am grateful to the George and Ann Richards Civil War Era Center, Penn State's Department of History, the Institute for the Arts and Humanities at Penn State, the Penn State Alumni Association, the Bill and Carol Fox Center for Humanistic Inquiry at Emory University, and the Forest History Society.

I have eagerly followed the Environmental History and the American South series since I was in graduate school, and I am humbled to now count myself among the contributors. Jim Giesen has been a model editor, and I appreciate the time he put into his perceptive and humorous line-by-line feedback on my manuscript, which has undoubtedly made it a stronger book. Mick Gusinde-Duffy, the staff at the University of Georgia Press, and the two anonymous readers have all provided valuable feedback, and they have patiently put up with all of the foibles of this first-time author.

I am lucky to have had Mary Bryan beside me for the final years of work on this project. Her loving support and encouragement through the long process of writing and revising kept up my spirits, and I am thankful that she has made my life so joyful. My parents have provided more support than I will ever be able to thank them for. My interest in history began on family vacations, but my parents have always allowed me to follow my own path and encouraged me along the way. For their unflagging love and support, this book is dedicated to them.

The Price of Permanence

CHAPTER 1

Nature's Bounty

IN 1913 Robert Lowry, an Atlanta banker, joined the chorus of postwar boosters fawning over the natural resources of the South. Lowry's editorial for the *Atlanta Constitution* was right out of the playbook of such well-known boosters as Henry Grady and William "Pig Iron" Kelley, who for decades had argued that the South's abundant natural resources were key to fueling economic growth that would undergird a "new" post–Civil War South. Echoing Grady and Kelley, Lowry insisted that in north Georgia "nature has smiled upon us with a magnificent climate, with a gorgeous verdure, with beautiful and powerful streams, with mountain storehouses and minerals of all kinds." These resources would help southerners remake their region into an urban, industrial society, erasing the plantation South with a wave of factories and smokestacks. Despite his glowing description of these resources, however, Lowry cautioned southerners not to see them as unlimited. He observed that communities where "nature has bestowed her vast riches in abundance" tended to be "wasteful and wantonly destructive of natural assets," even though these should "prove a permanent source of maintenance and wealth to succeeding generations." Lowry worried that southerners had started down this destructive path. But the South did not have to be a cautionary tale, and he sketched out a vision for the future that promised perpetual economic growth—growth that was possible by "permanent" uses of natural resources through conservation.[1]

Despite his interest in conserving resources, Lowry was not an idealistic nature lover. He was a hard-nosed businessman. As the president of a bank, he was not opposed to industrial development and did not believe resources should be kept from use. Yet Lowry argued that certain enterprises were better than others, and he urged businesspeople and municipal officials to be more discerning about what industries they sought out. Long-term development required weighing the suitability of each enterprise based on whether it stewarded resources. As Lowry explained, he "favor[ed] a conservative use of natural resources, which results in constructive and not destructive development." Constructive development, which he also referred to as "legitimate development," meant using natural resources in long-term ways. Rivers, minerals, game, forests, and soils all needed to be left in "better shape" for future generations. This did not mean less development. Lowry hoped southerners would find more efficient ways of using natural resources and cut down on industrial wastes, allowing production to continue without having to rein in resource use. Lowry's end goal was permanence—both economic and environmental—and he concluded that "the development of these resources [of the South] should be of a permanent and not a temporary nature." By taking this path, "the natural resources of this wonderful section, in which our thriving city of Atlanta is located, can be turned into permanent productive sources of wealth for this and all future generations."[2]

For Lowry, conserving resources was just a commonsense business strategy. Environmental permanence meant permanent profits, and Lowry couched his argument in a language that businesspeople could understand. He counseled southern business leaders to consider their natural resources as "virgin capital," which would bring on bankruptcy if depleted. Provided that "each generation will conserve the capital of the country and ... make that capital earn more and live within their income" through efficient production, Lowry predicted that "agriculture, forestry, mining and manufacturing can go on in this country for centuries and centuries to come." He urged southerners to "heed the cry of conservation, preserve our capital and increase its volume and earning power by the application of business and scientific principles and the rules of ordinary economy." Only then would the region realize the "commercial prestige and importance, to which these natural resources justly entitle her."[3]

Robert Lowry was a typical New South booster. Born in Greenville, Tennessee, he came of age during the Civil War. He migrated in 1861, when he was twenty-one years old, to the bustling metropolis of Atlanta, where he started a bank and wholesale grocery. By the late nineteenth century Lowry Banking Company was one of the most prominent businesses in the city, and Lowry played a leading role shaping Atlanta's post–Civil War boom. He was elected to the Atlanta City Council in 1870. He served on the city's Board of Education for more than two decades. He was a trustee of Grady Hospital. He was an official for the world-renowned International Cotton Exposition of 1881 and the Cotton States and International Exposition of 1895. He founded and served as president of the Atlanta Home Fire Insurance Company. He was a receiver for the Central of Georgia Railroad. He owned a stake in the Atlanta Consolidated Street Railroad System. One of his contemporaries noted that "every object that looks to the good of the whole people of Atlanta he will be found using his money, energy, and influence to further" and concluded that Lowry "believes in building up and patronizing home industry ... to develop the vast resources of Georgia."[4] Lowry was, in short, a "new man"—the archetype of an up-and-coming generation of leaders intent on rebuilding the South through industrial and urban growth.[5]

Lowry may have been cut from the same cloth as Henry Grady, but his "cry for conservation" does not fit with well-worn caricatures of boosters as development-crazed industrialists who had little interest in the health of the South's environment. Instead, Lowry's enthusiasm for permanent forms of development suggests that not all southerners saw profit and environmental quality as mutually exclusive goals. Natural resources were the South's most valuable asset in the wake of the Civil War. Business leaders like Lowry were desperate to create durable economic growth, even if that meant finding and implementing "permanent" uses of the region's natural resources through conservation. This was not a radical doctrine. Permanence was simply a way to promote economic growth without having to rein in the use of valuable natural resources. It also fit with the desires of New South boosters, typically white business and political elites, to preserve the racial status quo. In short, conservation was never antithetical to the New South mantra of economic development. It was a key part of this creed.

Lowry's vision for "constructive development" also does not fit with long-standing views of the American conservation movement, which treat conservation as a chiefly state-sponsored program. While conservation was closely linked to state power in parts of the country—especially the West—this framework provides little insight into the peculiar brand of conservation practiced by southerners. Conservation below the Mason-Dixon Line was not orchestrated by the professional bureaucrats who oversaw federal programs in the late nineteenth and early twentieth centuries. It originated from business leaders like Lowry. The South has long been viewed outside of the mainstream conservation movement, but this suggests that scholars have simply been looking in the wrong places to find evidence of conservation in the region. Rather than state or national parks, government-managed forests, or state-level conservation agencies, historians should look to the South's businesses—often the very businesses responsible for the worst environmental problems—to understand the complex relationship between conservation, economic development, and environmental quality in the New South.

෴

The most pressing question facing Americans at the end of the Civil War was what to do with the South. Emancipation and four years of war swept away the South's plantation economy and upended its slave-based social structure. Two-thirds of its net wealth was gone, cities were in ruins, farmland lay idle, monetary and banking systems were in turmoil, state governments faced crippling debts, there was little functioning industrial infrastructure, and railroads looked more like "iron neckties" than transportation arteries.[6] There were many different visions for the future, but it was clear that a "new" South would have to replace the region's antebellum plantation society. Ben Allston, a former Confederate and ruined South Carolina rice planter, expressed the prevailing mood when he declared that "we must . . . begin at the beginning again. We must make a new start."[7]

This was an unprecedented task—one that no other part of the United States had attempted on this scale. It required reimagining not only the economic structure of an entire region but also its labor systems, legal codes, social hierarchies, and political ideologies. How these issues were resolved had implications for the entire United States. According to John King, president of the Georgia Railroad and a delegate to the state's 1865 constitutional convention, "the prosperity of every material interest in the free States depends upon the successful development of Southern resources."[8]

Despite this unique challenge, American policy makers and businesspeople were optimistic that the region had the right stuff to become prosperous once again. As King's comment suggests, confidence about the future was fueled by the perception that the South had abundant stores of untapped natural resources that would trigger economic development. While industrial activities had depleted timber, minerals, and other industrial resources above the Mason-Dixon Line, the single-minded cultivation of staple crops seemingly spared the South's nonagricultural resources. In the first issue of *DeBow's Review* published after the war, regional spokesman J. D. B. DeBow explained that "whilst the Northern and Western States . . . exhibited miracles of progress and development, the South, with vast natural resources for mining, manufactures, and agriculture, advanced in but the slow ratio of its natural increase." DeBow concluded that "immense dominions, capable of contributing untold treasures to the commerce of the world, remained hermetically sealed."[9]

The end of the Civil War unsealed these "immense dominions." After 1865 southern resources became one of the most gripping topics on the national agenda. These resources were studied by businesspeople, farmers, public officials, journalists, tourists, armchair travelers, and others interested in the plight of the postbellum South. Evaluations of southern resources were everywhere, it seemed. After considering what elements could contribute to the region's "future progress," author John Calvin Reed of Georgia concluded that "she retains her genial climate, her kindly soil, and her many natural resources," which "far more than compensate for all her losses."[10] As industrial development began in earnest in the 1880s, a Galveston newspaper similarly commented that during the Civil War the region "lost four thousand millions, but her greatest wealth remained intact—her manhood and her vast domain of undeveloped mineral and agricultural resources."[11] The *Boston Herald* hypothesized that "the Southern States would have been more than the rivals of the northern commonwealths in material wealth" had slavery gone "extinct" earlier and concluded that "Nature has given to the people of that section many advantages which we do not enjoy, but until very recently the social condition of the people made them indifferent to their opportunities and incapable of utilizing them."[12] These groups cast the Civil War as an important turning point—less for striking down slavery than for opening up the South's abundant natural resources to commercial exploitation.

In the last two decades of the nineteenth century, a parade of authors, newspaper correspondents, businesspeople, and public officials exhausted nearly every synonym for "abundant" as they struggled to describe the South's resources, characterizing them as "bountiful," "matchless," "profuse," "inexhaustible," "opulent," "vast," "unlimited," "immense," "boundless," and "illimitable," to name just a few.[13] State and municipal officials from virtually every community in the region published glowing estimates of local resources, Chamber of Commerce members promoted their municipalities in advertisements and speeches, academics studied latent raw materials, novelists wrote fictionalized accounts of southern attempts to develop natural resources, and editors of trade journals joined hands with corporate officials to crow about all they could do with these raw materials. The American public devoured thousands of accounts discussing the natural resources of the New South, and literature describing "southern resources"—both fiction and nonfiction—became a genre of its own. After visiting the Gulf in 1885, novelist Charles Dudley Warner summed up the general mood, noting, "The mind of the South to-day is on the development of its resources, upon the rehabilitation of its affairs."[14] The Civil War may have made the South into a "ruin[ed] nation," but on paper it appeared anything but ruined.[15]

The South's natural resources looked even more valuable in a global context, and promoters favorably compared its resources with other parts of the nation or the world. No one was more tireless than Richard Hathaway Edmonds, editor of the popular *Manufacturers' Record* and one of the region's most outspoken boosters. In 1890 Edmonds argued that the South's climate, soil, minerals, timber, waterways, seacoast, and healthfulness proved that "nature seems to have done her best for this favored land." He affirmed that "no one can carefully study the remarkable combination of resources which the South enjoys without being convinced that, in natural advantages, the section stands far ahead of any other country in the world." Developing these resources would

From Darkness to Light.
A print issued for the 1895 Atlanta Exposition, showing a personified New South rising from the ruins of the Civil War—thanks to the cornucopia of abundant resources that was one of the South's few assets after 1865. CREDIT: Hamilton E. Grant. L1979-40 12, 19th and Early 20th Century Labor Prints, Southern Labor Archives, Special Collections and Archives, Georgia State University Library.

lead to what Edmonds called the "South's Redemption," a phrase C. Vann Woodward later used to describe the takeover of state governments by white Democrats in the 1870s that signaled the end of Reconstruction. For Edmonds, "Redemption" was an environmental process as much as a political one. He concluded that the region's potential for economic growth was "far more favorable than in the West during the period of the most rapid growth of that region" and declared, "This prosperity, being free from fictitious inflation, will be permanent."[16]

Edmonds's belief that natural resources would stimulate economic growth was not just naive optimism. It was shaped by a global context where resources often did fuel development. The New South fell in the middle of what economist Edward Barbier calls the "Golden Age of Resource-Based Development," when improvements in transportation and communication facilitated "a new global era of rapid settlement, resource exploitation and economic growth." As Barbier suggests, states or firms that rely on scarce resources have to search for new resource "frontiers" to ensure sustained economic growth. Between

1870 and 1914 this process played out on a global scale as nation-states sought to secure and extract resources from "new frontiers found in the developing regions of the world."[17] Southern boosters only had to look at imperial efforts to obtain resources in places like India and Africa to see that their own natural bounty was becoming more valuable every day.

Nineteenth-century businesspeople and policy makers did not use Barbier's terminology, but they did cast the South as a new resource "frontier" of global capitalist development. As southern industrial production grew in the 1880s and 1890s, promoters concluded that economic development was drawn to areas with abundant raw materials. Edmonds predicted that "the trend of the world's economic development is toward the South." While "in the past capital could draw raw materials to it, and thus industry centered where capital was most abundant," he argued that "now raw material draws the capital and dominates the development of industrial centers."[18] New England textile magnate Edward Atkinson agreed, declaring that economic "diversity" was "not only governed by the different aptitudes and capacities of men, it is also governed by differences in soil, climate, and natural resources," which the South had in excess.[19] Because the principles of economics appeared to favor the South, boosters like Edmonds and Atkinson were confident that the region's natural bounty guaranteed financial success, even after the unprecedented destruction of the Civil War. As economic and social turmoil heightened after 1865, southern boosters embraced what they believed was the region's chief constant, its abundant natural resources.

White businesspeople and public officials also sought to take advantage of what they saw as another plentiful "regional resource": African American laborers. Development in the New South was always bound up with "the Negro question"—the term white boosters used to refer to their exploitative efforts to wring the most out of black workers. Emancipation and the failures of Reconstruction left millions of freedpeople with little land and few resources, hemmed in by the regional nature of the labor market. Despite scattered efforts to displace black workers, by the end of Reconstruction most white leaders argued that African American labor was one of their biggest assets, as long as black workers remained in low-wage industries subject to white oversight. They used this "resource" as a selling point to attract outside investment. In the 1870s and 1880s white boosters like Henry Grady even talked up racial harmony and promised to accept emancipation while working to maintain and extend white supremacy. With the collapse of Republican rule and the removal of federal authorities after 1877, Democratic governments actively rolled back the civil and political rights of African Americans to maintain the racial hierarchy and a pool of abundant and pliable labor. They tried to pigeonhole African Americans into certain jobs based on racist stereotypes and used coercion to limit the options available to black workers. White elites redrew the boundaries of political districts to lessen black voting power and devised poll taxes and other methods to disenfranchise black voters. They manipulated the criminal code to target the mobility and independence of laborers. They forced workers into exploitative labor contracts. They only allowed educational opportunities that taught industrial or mechanical skills. They fomented racial violence. They reshaped the landscape by enacting segregation laws. These measures were all intended to harden racial boundaries, keep valuable resources in the hands of white southerners, and maintain a pool of cheap and supposedly docile black laborers for economic development. In this way, human exploitation was not separate from the growing capitalist economy of the South; it was a key part of it. As historian Andrew Zimmerman contends, the "inequalities created by racist elites in the United States" could even be considered "structural features of American capitalism" in the New South era. The benefits of economic development, like so many other aspects of the New South Creed, were intended for whites only.[20]

As we will see, this exploitative vision did not resonate with African Americans, who exploded racist characterizations that they were only a "resource" and had different ideas about how to use the South's natural bounty. These plans were based on visions for resources that could not be strictly measured in dollars and cents. African Americans often saw resources as a guarantee of independence and the promises of emancipation, not just fuel for industrial production. After emancipation, freedpeople worked to achieve this vision by rebuilding and keeping families together, exerting influence over their labor, exercising political and civil rights, getting an education, and above all acquiring land. Radical Reconstruction fueled gossip that land redistribution was forthcoming, but most African Americans found that their access to land and resources—the very resources white boosters claimed were so plentiful—was deliberately curtailed. Just as they fought back against exploitative aspects of the New South vision, African Americans clashed with white boosters about who should control valuable resources, what these resources would be used for, what African Americans' daily labor would look like, and what their place in the New South economy would be.[21]

Poor whites also challenged New South promises of abundance, especially as poverty deepened and they were mired in exploitative work on farms or in mills. White farmers and industrial workers flocked to organizations like the Grange and the Knights of Labor that promised to include them in the prosperity dreams of New South boosters. These organizations made their name by calling attention to the divide between booster rhetoric and the reality of poverty, often by taking aim at claims of abundant resources. No organization posed as much of a challenge to the New South vision as the Farmers' Alliance, which gave voice to the complaints of millions of struggling farmers in the 1890s. The region might have abundant resources, but Populists called attention to the structural inequalities that kept these resources under the control of the few. No one expressed this more clearly than Georgia's fiery agrarian leader Tom Watson, who was one of the most vocal critics of New South abundance. As Watson gained state and later national political power in the 1880s and 1890s, he harped on the divide between abundance and reality for his constituents. In stump speeches in the late 1880s, Watson took aim at arch-booster Henry Grady, declaring, "Mr. Grady . . . thinks that 'Plenty rides on the springing harvests!,'" while Watson believed it actually "rides on Grady's springing imagination." Only "city fellows" could "draw ideal pictures of Farm life—pictures which are no more true to real life than a Fashion Plate is to an actual man or woman." Watson went on to describe how "in Grady's farm life there are no poor cows. They are all fat! Their bells tinkle musically in clover scented meadows & all you've got to do is hold a pan under the udder & you catch it full of golden butter." This was out of touch with reality, where "we find the poor old Brindle cow with wolves in her back & 'hollow horn' on her head & she always wants to back up where the wind won't play a tune on her ribs." Watson summed up Grady's vision as "lands all 'Rich—richer—richest.' Crops 'Good, better, best,'" but he argued that the reality was "barren wastes—Gullied slopes—ruined lowlands."[22] These were ultimately not just critiques of whether resources were abundant, they were critiques of how resources were managed and distributed that posed a significant challenge to the New South establishment.

Dissenters against the New South never gained enough traction to challenge faith in bountiful resources, however. The New South's alluring vision of resource abundance was remarkably durable—even if the disconnect between rhetoric and reality was clear—and it sometimes cut across class and racial lines.[23] Despite different and often incompatible visions for how to actually use resources, white and black southerners often shared a faith in the abundance of their natural bounty. Even one of the fiercest black critics of the New South Creed, T. Thomas Fortune, conceded major points of the arguments of white boosters in his famous 1884 volume, *Black and White: Land, Labor, and Politics in the South*. Fortune took on the exploitative class structure and racial caste system that remained in place after Reconstruction, but he also claimed that the nation, and the South, had "ample resources to meet the actual necessities of everyone." Prosperity for black workers had not been realized due to racial prejudice and ill treatment, not a paucity of resources. Fortune urged southerners to "pay less attention to politics and more attention to the development of her magnificent resources," among other things, to bring prosperity to everyone.[24] Elias Carr, the president of the North Carolina Farmers' Alliance, also acknowledged that the region had abundant natural resources, even at the height of the Populist movement. But he used this abundance to call attention to the exploitative economic structures that were hurting farmers. The region's agricultural problems, according to Carr, were even more glaring "in the face of the facts that the country is one of inexhaustible resources."[25] Belief that the South had an abundance of natural resources may have cut across class and racial lines, then, but it fueled different visions of what to do with those resources and competing definitions of the New South itself.

New South boosters were right about one thing: the region did have an abundance of certain natural resources. The South sprawled out over eight hundred thousand square miles, so how could it not? But these states were diverse. The Piedmont, Cotton Belt, Yazoo-Mississippi Delta, Appalachian Highlands, Lowcountry, and Virginia Tidewater are only a few of the separate regions that make up the American South.[26] Each has a different ecological character, and these diverse ecosystems supported enterprises ranging from sugar cultivation to the production of naval stores. Boosters never accurately described this diversity or captured the reality of conditions everywhere. But their "perceived environment" can tell us a lot about how New South boosters wanted to use their natural resources.[27] Their overblown narratives collapsed the South's diverse ecosystems into just one word—abundant—meant to justify a vision that was radically different from the agrarian Old South.

∽

Abundant natural resources provided hope for the postwar South, but they also provided a lesson about the failures of the antebellum South. For nineteenth-century Americans, an abundance of resources implied wastefulness, and New South promoters decried the fact that their forebears had ignored the region's diverse array of valuable resources by betting everything only on its rich soils. In this view, slavery and staple crop mania unnaturally prolonged a myopic plantation system and hindered industrial development that might have profited from other untapped resources. Writing for the *International Review* in 1876, one author noted, "When our country was first settled, the Southern regions excelled the Northern in soil, climate, and other natural resources" but claimed that while the northern economy boomed, "it is said by us of the South, jesting upon our own worn-out and exhausted land, that we have not done as much for the country as the Indians who dwelled here centuries ago, and left the soil as good as they found it." "The plantation system," in his estimation, "was the great barrier to Southern progress."[28] A correspondent writing for the *Manufacturers' Record* even claimed that plantation agriculture had enslaved the "Southern white man." He asked his readers, "What did it matter to him if all the earth beneath his feet was loaded with all the minerals which contribute to the wealth, convenience or enjoyment of mankind, or that the stream running by his door had waterpower enough to turn a thousand wheels?" because he "could not utilize them; he was bound hand and foot—bound to his slaves, bound to his plantation, bound to cotton, to his habits of life, to the exigencies of the situation."[29] Descriptions of abounding resources were not simply a description of the present but an indictment of the wastefulness of antebellum southerners and a key part of postbellum visions for the future.

Boosters boasted that breaking from antebellum patterns and developing these resources would bring about a far-reaching economic and environmental transformation, one that would sweep the region once all untapped resources were put to work. As early as 1870 a Texas newspaper predicted that development would result in "the wilderness blossoming as the rose."[30] John Calvin Reed lamented that in the decade after the Civil War there had been a "melancholy change" in the landscape. Reed described plantations where "the neat inclosures have fallen; the pleasant grounds and the flower-gardens, once so trim and flourishing, are a waste" and noted, "The face of the country is much altered" because "only a small part of the land, as compared with that tilled before the war, is under cultivation; the remainder becomes wild." New South development would erase these problems, and Reed claimed that the region "is in a thorough and long transition" where "her fields are to be made fertile and to smile beautifully with an infinite variety of products."[31] Perhaps no one hawked this vision as effectively as Henry Grady, the famed editor of the *Atlanta Constitution*. Grady concluded an 1888 speech at the Texas State Fair with a vivid description of the future—a "vision of surpassing beauty"—in which he claimed to "see a South the home of fifty millions of people; her cities vast hives of industry; her country-sides the treasures from which their resources are drawn; her streams vocal with whirring spindles; her valleys tranquil in their white and gold of the harvest; her mountains showering down the music of bells, as her slow-moving flocks and herds go forth from their folds."[32] These were more than pleasant images. At a time when the landscape visibly reflected the ravages of war and a century of cultivation, boosters like Grady used these descriptions to call for changes to prevailing practices, as we will see. They also made it clear that building a successful economy depended on getting the most out of their natural resources and avoiding the inefficiencies that characterized past resource use. The region could only be prosperous when all of its resources were in use and there were no more untapped minerals, fallow fields, or silent streams.

Claims that the South was a place of abundance were never an accurate description of the region everywhere. But they were not intended to be. Boosters used myth to promote a program for action. At a time when memory of the past—especially the myth of the Lost Cause—had become a useful political tool to justify the social aspects of New South development, they recast memory of the environment to make economic development a reality.[33] The myth of the Lost Cause was written in granite on monuments in courthouse squares throughout the region; the myth of abundant resources was written on the South's forests, mineral deposits, and free-flowing rivers.

☙

The break with the past embedded in the New South myth of abundance began to take concrete form immediately after the Civil War. Republican leaders of Reconstruction-era state governments throughout the former Confederacy promoted economic development to revive the flagging economy by pouring state and local capital into railroad development, distributing huge tracts of land to railroads and other businesses, easing hindrances to manufacturing, and courting outside capital for industrial enterprises.[34] Even by 1870 the term "New South" signified a program of economic development that split with the plantation South by emulating the industrial North, and it became a hallmark of the Democratic state administrations that regained power in the 1870s. According to this New South Creed, as historian Paul Gaston calls it, industrialization would free the region from its myopic dependence on staple crops, centralize jobs in urban areas, provide markets for farm goods, and hasten urban growth. New South boosters also advocated overhauling agriculture through mechanization, new labor agreements, and crop diversification.[35]

Abundant resources provided the rhetorical and material foundation on which this creed was built. Defining who were the leading promoters of the New South Creed has caused a great deal of debate, but it is clear that its most ardent advocates were a mix of "new" or "old" men, depending on the community. They included urban professionals, planters, business owners, corporate bigwigs, and public officials of all stripes.[36] Whatever their background, these groups had a direct financial and social stake in the success of development and were typically "of middle-class, industrial, capitalistic outlook."[37] Because antebellum planters had invested most of their capital in slaves, emancipation left little cash for postwar development, and these emerging groups of boosters harped on the South's natural bounty to attract capital and expertise from outside the region. This was no easy task. An unsettled banking situation, railroad policies that discriminated against the South, a lack of workers with technical expertise, and the South's poor infrastructure all worked against industrial growth. But for decades after the Civil War promoters had faith that these problems could be surmounted simply by calling attention to the region's abundant resources.[38]

Southern economic development was not just a product of slick advertising. Public officials also worked hard to open up southern resources to outsiders. Beginning with Kentucky in 1867, state governments funded immigration bureaus to attract settlers or investors from other parts of the nation or world. They provided a host of incentives to railroads, including generous land grants, to encourage construction that would open up isolated resources. State officials also sold off vast tracts of the public domain to industrialists and speculators for little more than a song, offered convict-lease labor to businesses, and granted new companies monopolistic rights to valuable resources.[39] By the twentieth century, Democratic administrations were taking even more active steps to develop resources. Generous tax breaks for industries, land deals, and direct cash payouts were all fair game in "smokestack chasing," and these strategies anticipated the efforts of powerful mid-twentieth-century state development commissions.[40] This created an atmosphere in which economic development and industrial promotion were the most compelling issues of the day for elite white southerners, and even as late as 1925 journalist George Marvin, after visiting Nashville, suggested that "the average Southerner is a born booster, and the mood is contagious."[41]

For decades, these efforts have led historians to conclude that the New South Creed was characterized by an insatiable hunger for natural resources. As we will see, southern development did create significant environmental problems, but not always for the expected reasons. Boosters were savvy enough to know that promoting development at any cost would contribute little to the region or to their own wallets. Their critique of the Old South hinged on the ways that the plantation system had prioritized agriculture over more efficient uses of resources, and boosters could not help but reflect on whether postwar development would repeat the mistakes of their antebellum predecessors. In 1872, for example, the Republican editor of the *Knoxville Daily Chronicle* lamented that Tennessee was woefully underdeveloped, with little available capital, enormous debt, few good roads, and poor schools. This was unnatural given Tennessee's abundant natural resources, and he declared, "Our coal mines, our immense beds of the best iron ore, our fertile valleys and our forests of fine timber, constitute an inexhaustible fund of wealth, the extent to which has never been fully comprehended by the most sanguine." Though it was "universally conceded" that Tennessee had "great natural resources," these resources could be used in many ways. This urban booster declared that the most pressing question of the day was "how . . . to *reap their full benefit*."[42]

This question—perhaps more than any other—shaped all New South development efforts. Scholars generally write off comments like this as fanciful rhetoric. But for decades New South boosters struggled to eke out the most from the region's natural resources. Sometimes this was an invitation to pell-mell development, but it could also channel development in more efficient directions. Abundant resources were not simply an invitation to exploitation, then, but an impetus to find new ways of squeezing the most profit out of the southern landscape for the longest possible time—a point underscored by businessmen like Robert Lowry.

☙

The New South was billed as a region of abundance, but it was born in an era of scarcity. Public officials, businesspeople, and other groups were starting to weigh the best uses of southern resources just as conservationists were starting to call for more restrained uses of Earth's resources. As southerners worked to build a lasting economy by wringing as much as possible out of their resources, their visions for the best use of natural resources were shaped by the burgeoning global conservation movement.

The rapid expansion of the nation's economy in the nineteenth century caused elite Americans to worry that resources were dwindling and unique landscapes were falling victim to development. Fears of resource depletion were made real by midcentury, when George Perkins Marsh published *Man and Nature*.[43] This alarming volume surveyed the implications of global resource depletion, and Marsh predicted a similar fate for America. In the last three decades of the nineteenth century, sportsmen, scientists, hikers, naturalists, and public officials all began to call for the conservation of the nation's resources so that they would be available for future generations. Victories protecting unique places like Yellowstone and Yosemite in the 1870s paved the way for conservation to become federal policy. While these early efforts were intended to prevent the destruction of natural wonders, they laid the groundwork for an activist federal bureaucracy that would manage resources for long-term use.

By the Progressive Era, the ethos of "monumentalism" that guided early preservation efforts had been replaced by a more nuanced vision for the management—both preservation and use—of valuable resources.[44] The idea that natural resources could, given the right kind of scientific oversight, be used in long-term ways became a hallmark of the burgeoning conservation movement as it was taken over by a professionalized bureaucracy in the first decade of the twentieth century. This was not a new idea. People had searched for long-term ways of using resources for centuries, ranging from Malthusian reactions to global population growth to nineteenth-century sustained-yield forestry in Germany.[45] In the United States, conserving resources for long-term uses was driven by the need to maintain resource stocks for economic and military purposes, especially as the United States took on an imperial role globally. This was clear in 1897, when Congress passed the Forest Management Act, opening up timber on federal forest reserves for use under the watchful eye of the Department of the Interior.[46] In his first message to Congress, President Theodore Roosevelt made it clear that conservation of forests meant managing them to guarantee "larger and more certain supplies." Forest management was "the perpetuation of forests by use," or another way to "increase and sustain the resources of our country and the industries which depend upon them," which was "an imperative business necessity."[47] Under Roosevelt's watch, efficient use was mobilized to support the nation's imperial and economic aims. These geopolitical goals, and the resource stocks required to achieve them, were necessary to ensure the "safety and continuance of the Nation" for generations to come.[48] Theodore Burton, chairman of the 1908 Conference of Governors, explained that conservation would maintain the "material resources on which the permanent prosperity of our country and the equal opportunity of all our People must depend."[49] As they justified extending American influence abroad and securing long-term supplies of resources, officials like Burton and Roosevelt made it clear that conservation meant efficient use and in this way hitched it to the permanence and prosperity of the nation.

Gifford Pinchot did more than any other federal official to popularize the idea that conserving resources could lead to environmental and economic permanence. Pinchot was the first professional forester in the United States, and he served as the architect of federal resource policy in the first two decades of the twentieth century. Pinchot's study of forestry in Europe convinced him that sustained-yield management would spawn "permanent forest industries, supported and guaranteed by a fixed and annual supply of trees."[50] After being appointed chief of the Division of Forestry, Pinchot formulated the concept of "wise use" as a strategy for efficiently using all of the nation's resources. He famously explained that "conservation means the wise use of the earth and its resources for the lasting good of men. Conservation is the foresighted utilization, preservation, and/or renewal of forests, waters, lands, and minerals, for the greatest good of the greatest number for the longest time."[51] This philosophy guided his work to conserve forests, and it became the mantra for federal efforts to manage all resources. "Wise use" also codified the idea that certain resources could be used in a permanent and renewable manner.[52]

Pinchot may have used "wise use" to promote long-term uses of timber and minerals on public lands, but the Department of Agriculture was slower to make permanent uses of soils its policy. In the late nineteenth century, Milton Whitney, head of the Bureau of Soils, rejected prevailing theories that fertility was a product of the chemical traits of soils. He contended that fertility was linked to the texture of soils, wrongly concluding that soils could be continuously cropped without losing nutrients. By the twentieth century, Whitney had made the inexhaustibility of soils official USDA policy. Whitney's view was challenged, however, even from within the USDA. Two prominent critics were Cyril Hopkins, a professor at the University of Wisconsin, and Franklin King, chief of the Division of Soil Management. Hopkins and King argued that growing crops took vital nutrients from the soil, and these nutrients had to be added back for cultivation to continue. They called their idea "permanent agriculture." Although it took decades for "permanent agriculture" to become official federal policy, debates over the long-term uses of soils contributed to a climate where it was becoming clear that some uses of resources could be considered more "permanent" than others.[53]

By the early twentieth century, then, the idea that natural resources could be used in permanent and renewable ways was a staple of federal thinking about conservation, and it informed the administration of timber, minerals, and water mostly on western public lands. In a 1918 volume, four renowned economists even concluded that "the conservation of permanent national resources" was the "foundation of national prosperity." At least until the privatizing impulse of the 1920s, bureaucrats and resource administrators believed that permanent stocks of resources had to be achieved through federal regulation. "However much may be done by private individuals and by private business organizations to husband the natural resources of the nation," economist Ralph Hess concluded that "the formulation and execution of a comprehensive conservation policy is fundamentally a government function."[54] On a national level, then, permanence was not a private impulse. It required the oversight of a cadre of federal bureaucrats trained in resource management. The concept of environmental permanence was appealing to southerners struggling to build a lasting economy, but not before it was stripped of federal vestiges and remade into a private impulse.

ல

Southerners are often characterized as having hostility to conservation written into their DNA, but this only makes sense from a recent perspective. In the late nineteenth century the South seemed like the most natural arena for conservation in the entire nation. Wholesale industrial development there had been stunted by the overriding focus on plantation agriculture and the destruction of the Civil War. Despite piecemeal efforts to cultivate industry in the antebellum era, southerners entered the industrial era later than everyone else in the United States. Conservationists argued that this unique history spared valuable resources from destruction and gave southerners a better chance to work conservation into the fabric of their developing economy. Simply put, they saw the South as a test case for making conservation a vital part of economic development nationwide. Speaking to businessmen gathered at the Southern Conservation Congress in Atlanta in 1910, Theodore Roosevelt predicted that "no portion of our country is going to show a greater rate of development . . . as the South will show in the course of the next thirty or forty years." He implored southerners to "profit by the mistakes that have been made elsewhere and to see that this marvelous development, this extraordinary growth of the new South, takes place in such fashion that it shall represent not a mere exploitation of territory, not a mere feverish growth in wealth and luxuriousness on a honeycomb foundation of morality and good judgment," but a "solid and abiding and enduring prosperity and growth which shall not only be great but permanent." This would result in a "growth in business," as well as "a growth in the use of natural resources." Although Roosevelt gave businesspeople license to "get all possible use" out of their resources, he also urged them to "handle" these resources so that "you will leave your land as a heritage to your children, increased and not impaired in permanent value."[55] Gifford Pinchot also claimed that southerners had an unprecedented opportunity to lead the nation in conservation. Pinchot was familiar with the South. He had spent three years in Asheville, North Carolina, serving as the chief forester on George Vanderbilt's one-hundred-thousand-acre Biltmore Estate. This experience showed him that the region "has an abundance of almost everything she needs," which gave southerners "a chance to save these resources for future generations." In other places "the resources are almost gone and it is almost too late for conservation to play any important part, especially in comparison to what it can do here," and Pinchot concluded that "the South needs conservation more than any other section of the country, possibly."[56] Roosevelt and Pinchot, the architects of the nation's federal conservation policy, made it clear that the South was an outlier in the conservation movement, but not in the ways we usually think. Instead of arguing that the prevalence of private property doomed conservation to failure, they predicted that the region's unique history would give it a starring role in the conservation movement and make it a test case for the success of conservation nationally. For Pinchot and Roosevelt, the New South had to usher in a new approach to nature, one in which conservation was a key part of the calculus of development.

Southern businesspeople and public officials also believed that the South was a natural place for conservation activity, and they were optimistic that stewarding resources could transform the economy. Elite southern planters had worked to conserve resources like fish and game since the late eighteenth century, but in the first decade of the twentieth century, efforts to protect sporting wildlife were subsumed by a focus on conserving industrial and agricultural resources.[57] Conservation was discussed in the pages of trade journals and newspapers, at political gatherings and barbecues, on state and private demonstration farms, in displays at agricultural and industrial fairs, and in the halls of state legislatures. Southern ideas about conservation were an extension of long-standing appeals for efficient development, and the search for permanent uses of resources became one of the key components of New South development. By 1910 hundreds of public officials and business leaders had participated in regional and national meetings devoted to conservation. These meetings familiarized southern elites with the tenets of conservation, provided them with examples from other parts of the country, and gave them an opportunity to reflect on how conserving resources could contribute to their own efforts to build a new economy. National conservation meetings also created a network of public officials and businesspeople who were invested in applying conservation principles in the South. Perhaps most importantly, these meetings gave participants an opportunity to flesh out their conception of what it meant to use natural resources in permanent ways and how to do so through private enterprise, not government initiatives.

Even before the twentieth century, groups of southern businesspeople had embraced conservation as a business necessity, but the emergence of the South as a player in the American conservation movement was evident at the Conference of Governors, called to meet at the White House in 1908 by President Theodore Roosevelt. The conference was initially intended to be a forum on managing water resources, but at the urging of William John McGee, a longtime federal bureaucrat and influential conservationist, Roosevelt expanded the agenda to consider solutions that would slow the decline of all of the nation's natural resources. The Conference of Governors brought together state leaders and representatives from national organizations in order to build a political coalition to support conservation, and southerners were prominent. More than forty representatives from the South took part, including the governors of Virginia, South Carolina, North Carolina, Mississippi, Louisiana, Kentucky, Arkansas, and Alabama. Other southern attendees included planters, a textile magnate, a cotton broker, a real estate lawyer, a judge from Mississippi, an insurance agent, state geologists, an official with the Appalachian National Forest Association, a Baptist minister, the superintendent of education in Columbus, Georgia, the president of a Kentucky coal company, a leather merchant, a corporate official with the Florida East Coast Canal, and a bevy of lawyers. The chairman of the conference, Newton Blanchard, was the governor of Louisiana, and another member of the executive committee, Martin F. Ansel, was the governor of South Carolina.[58] As lawyers by trade, Blanchard and Ansel were members of the class of urban businessmen and public officials in the South active in conservation work. One year later, almost a quarter of the delegates to the National Conservation Commission, tasked with surveying national resources and providing management suggestions, came from below the Mason-Dixon Line.[59] By 1910 southern businesspeople and public officials were a fixture at national conservation meetings. The president of the National Conservation Congress in St. Paul, Minnesota, even commented that "some of our best support and a number of the largest and most enthusiastic delegations at the conference came from Southern States" and noted that "the interest which the delegates manifested in the proceedings was intense, and they gave their hearty co-operation to all the propositions which were made."[60]

Business and political elites also organized regional meetings to deal with the particulars of conservation in the South. At the urging of Governor Jared Sanders of Louisiana—a state active in conservation work—the 1909 Southern Conservation Congress brought together governors and conservation commissioners from sixteen southern and western states, lumbermen, municipal officials, legislators, and representatives from each parish in Louisiana to discuss the ins and outs of conservation and to urge southern legislatures to pass laws "uniformly for the preservation and replanting of timber lands."[61] The motto of the conference, "Unless you preserve the timber there will be no rivers," suggests a focus on forestry, but delegates also discussed the conservation of water, minerals, and other resources.[62] The following year the congress met in Atlanta, and the five hundred delegates heard speeches from Theodore Roosevelt, recent Georgia governor Hoke Smith, Gifford Pinchot, and Henry S. Graves, the nation's new chief forester.[63] The Southern Conservation Congress was short-lived, but it created a political coalition of conservationists and businesspeople and provided a forum for them to consider the application of conservation to the peculiarities of the South.

In the second decade of the twentieth century, the ideals of the Southern Conservation Congress were taken up by other developmental organizations. Commercial and trade groups were some of the most outspoken proponents of economic development, and their embrace of conservation shows just how much conserving resources was linked to southern business interests. The inroads that conservation was making in the boardrooms of the South were most evident at meetings of the Southern Commercial Congress, an organization of businesspeople from civic and municipal organizations. Ever since it was organized in 1908, the Southern Commercial Congress had focused on publicizing resources in order to attract capitalists and immigrants from outside the South. Yet the conservation of southern resources was also an important part of the group's vision for the future, and one of their initial goals was to "show the importance of conserving rather than wasting; of using yet not abusing."[64] At their 1911 annual meeting, attendees heard from a variety of speakers about the prospects for the conservation of forests, soils, minerals, and waters. Delegates even adopted a resolution calling on "each southern state . . . to make more ample provisions for investigations looking to the most efficient development in agriculture and mining as its two great foundation industries."[65]

There were always close ties between conservation and developmental organizations in the region, as these examples suggest. The attendees at these conferences were overwhelmingly drawn from the region's middle- and upper-class urban business leaders and public officials—the same groups leading the charge for development. The participation of southern business leaders in events like the Southern Conservation Congress reflected strong support for conservation among the emerging business and professional elite. The same groups of "new men" calling for the development of southern resources, in short, were also vocal in urging their conservation.[66]

ଊ

The close link between conservation and development in the South was also on display at expositions and fairs, which were intended to promote local or regional development by showcasing the transformation of natural resources into commodities through grand displays of agricultural products, manufactured goods, and technology.[67] By the 1890s, though, expositions were starting to include conservation. Organizers, often working with federal officials, planned and constructed exhibits to highlight how to use and conserve southern resources. At the 1895 Cotton States and International Exposition in Atlanta, for instance, an entire building was filled with forestry and mineral exhibits planned by federal officials. The event also promoted private paths to permanence through displays that highlighted the use of formerly wasted raw materials in industrial processes.[68] Permanence was on display at other expositions, including Atlanta's International Cotton Exposition in 1881, the Tennessee Centennial Exposition of 1883, the 1907 Jamestown Exhibition, and Knoxville's Appalachian Expositions of 1910 and 1911, where organizers also called attention to methods of using and conserving resources.[69]

No event embraced permanence like the National Conservation Exposition, which opened to great fanfare in the fall of 1913. Instead of promoting the development of abundant natural resources, the exposition was intended to teach the "best methods" of conservation.[70] As J. L. Bowles, director of exhibits, explained, "[It] embraces a new idea in that it looks forward and not backward" by promoting "not only . . . preservation of our forests, waters and soils, but conservation of time, labor and material."[71] To this end, the exposition featured over one hundred thousand square feet of conservation exhibits. Noteworthy displays included a sixteen-thousand-square-foot bas-relief map of southern natural resources, comparisons of crops grown in fertile and unfertile soils, and an exhibit sponsored by the East Tennessee Audubon Society that provided information about the state's "desirable and undesirable" birds, as well as their most feared predator: the cat.[72] In order to demonstrate the effect of deforestation on mountain ecosystems, the Forest Service constructed models of two "miniature" mountains. One showed how deforested land was subject to flooding and erosion, while the other showed how forests absorbed water, prevented flooding, maintained soil fertility, and kept watercourses "clear and . . . pure."[73] On the outskirts of the fairgrounds, organizers erected a five-acre farm complete with a farmhouse, barn, houses for poultry and hogs, and "modern fences"—all to demonstrate the "most approved methods of scientific agriculture" for "visiting farmers." "Manufacturing displays" also provided opportunities to see conservation at work, and the *Atlanta Constitution* boasted that these exhibits demonstrated "the saving of time and labor, the prevention of waste and the utilization of by-products."[74] Conservation was even extended beyond natural resources, with displays targeted at conserving "human life" through improvements in public health, child welfare, and working conditions.[75]

Contemporaries concluded that Knoxville was the ideal location for such an event. By 1913 it was clear that the South was on the cusp of a new stage of development, and the exposition prompted visitors to reflect on how this crossroads necessitated more conservative uses of resources. J. L. Bowles argued that "having taken the initial step in civilization by developing our natural resources, we must now take the second step and so conserve those resources" so that future generations "may have the things which make for perpetual wealth and affluence."[76] Because the South had abundant resources, T. Asbury Wright, a Knoxville lawyer, suggested that "the necessity for conservation of forests and soils in this Southern Appalachian country is perhaps greater at this time than in any other section of the United States." "It was most natural," Wright concluded, to hold the exposition in the Appalachians because there "the mineral, forest and soil resources were more nearly in their native condition than in any other part of the United States and . . . the question of conserving at least the

The Bird Court, the exhibit of the East Tennessee Audubon Society at the 1913 National Conservation Exposition in Knoxville, Tennessee. This exposition provided a visible indication of the ways that conservation of natural resources could make the South's development more permanent.
CREDIT: W. M. Goodman, ed., *The First Exposition of Conservation and Its Builders* (Knoxville: Knoxville Lithographing Company, 1913), 284.

forest and soil resources of the country was of such transcendent importance."[77] Gifford Pinchot used the occasion to argue that the South was starting a stage in its history that required a new relationship with nature. He noted that the region was "just in the awakening of its development, its opportunities had largely been passed over, and it was in great part virgin," and he argued that "the South was just ripe for the application of the lessons which the costly experiences of other sections had taught so graphically." Although he had spent his career crafting conservation policy that mostly affected public lands in the West, Pinchot concluded that "it was fitting . . . that the South should hold this exposition."[78]

For all their talk about conservation, the organizers of the exposition were not trained in resource management. While occasionally aided by conservationists, the organizers were almost all prominent businessmen. Their ranks included lawyers, bankers, Chamber of Commerce boosters, owners of construction and development companies, railroad officials, coal barons, manufacturers, judges, wholesalers, and even "one of the old time carnival men of Knoxville." Several owned "vast mineral and timber properties," and one of the exposition's leading officials had reputedly "removed from the Smoky mountains more timber perhaps than any other man in the lumber business" as the owner and president of a large timber company.[79]

These businessmen saw the exposition as a fortuitous opportunity. Despite the appeals of boosters like Henry Grady, by 1913 the region's economy still lagged far behind the rest of the nation. Knoxville itself was an archetype for the economic status of the region. The city's boosters had made real progress in attracting new manufacturing establishments, and by the twentieth century it was one of the top wholesaling centers in the South. Despite this growth, city leaders struggled with lingering problems like underdeveloped municipal infrastructure, inadequate funding for public education, poverty, and social unrest—problems that hinted at deep-seated weaknesses in the New South's program of economic development. Boosters in Knoxville and the South were optimistic that these problems could be solved, however, and sought to use the exposition to advertise the region in the hopes of drawing new businesses there.[80]

For every display hailing conservation there were others sponsored by corporations or state agencies that hawked new economic development. Besides municipal displays from Baltimore, Louisville, Birmingham, Lynchburg, Knoxville, Greenville, and smaller towns, the fair buildings at Knoxville's Chilhowee Park housed displays from more than one hundred railroad, mineral, agricultural, and manufacturing companies. These exhibits were booster propaganda brought to life and sought to dazzle visiting businessmen and consumers with demonstrations of manufacturing processes, examples of industrial machinery, and samples of products and the raw materials used to make them. Corporate exhibits featured an array of products made from southern resources, including furniture, mattresses, agricultural machinery, textile goods, asphalt, gunpowder, livestock, lumber, boxes, bricks, tables, iron stoves, pipe, various crops, and even electricity generated from waterways.[81] For exhibitors, the exposition was a handy way to peddle their wares while justifying their claim to resources, and it blended conservation and advertising—though not always seamlessly. In one advertisement targeted at visitors, Knoxville's Holston National Bank proclaimed that "The Exposition Will Arouse Interest in Our Natural Resources." Tennessee marble—which had been used in the construction of Holston's new bank building—was billed as one of the most important of these resources. After extolling the beauty and quality of Tennessee marble, the bank invited visitors to "Inspect the Holston's new building and banking room where this marble can be seen to its best advantage in exterior and interior use."[82] Kentucky's Wiedemann Brewing Company used a similar strategy when it explained that conservation "means the intelligent use of the good things which Nature has provided" and advertised its beer as the best of these "good things."[83]

Organizers and visitors never saw competing displays promoting conservation and development as mutually exclusive, however, and they blended conservation and development into a vision for the future of the South. Instead of worrying that conservation would hamstring business, they insisted that it would point the way to enterprises that would be in the long-term interests of the region. As one organizer explained, the exposition would "advance the highest development and best use of all natural resources" of the South and the nation, while another claimed that it would "go beyond the promotion of mere development." Instead, it was "directed toward making the development permanent, and toward turning the natural resources of the country into perpetual sources of wealth."[84] As this suggests, the idea that there could be long-term ways of using resources played a key role in shaping the goals of the exposition, and "permanence" was the event's watchword. In opening the exposition, the governor of Tennessee claimed that the fair "holds forth so much of promise for the enlightenment and permanent advancement of the people of the South and the Nation, by providing exhibits of their resources and of means for their development and perpetuation."[85] William Goodman—a fair organizer and journalist—told the Atlanta Chamber of Commerce, "There has been some talk of building a greater nation on a greater south, but neither can become permanently greater with the present waste going on in our forests and on our farms. The south is forging to the front, but present methods of development are not what they should be." Goodman worried that "we are creating problems which posterity will find difficult of solution" and concluded that southerners needed to distinguish between "development" and "waste" in order to solve these problems.[86] Read in this light, the exposition's commercial and conservation displays did not work at cross-purposes but reinforced each other by offering a blueprint of how to maintain stocks of natural resources without having to take drastic action to rein in development. Conservation was never antithetical to the New South Creed; it was a key part of it. After visiting the National Conservation Exposition, a manufacturer from Pennsylvania declared simply, "If there is anything that typifies the spirit of the new South better than this great exposition could, I have failed to see it or to hear of it."[87] Although expositions typically functioned as promotional tools to develop the South, they could also be prophets of permanence.

୧୨

By expressing the need for conservation in the language of permanence, New South elites blended conservation and development. In the eyes of businesspeople and policy makers, it was not feasible to take up conservation if it hindered their ability to promote development, and their ideas about conservation were always subject to their understanding of the South's desperate need for economic development. This was a vision predicated on private, not state or federal, conservation initiatives. After the South Carolina General Assembly voted in 1922 not to allow Gifford Pinchot to speak, one state representative commented, "If our forests need conserving let us do it ourselves" and urged fellow Carolinians not to bet everything "on the Federal Government."[88] Southern leaders were attracted to Pinchot's vision for "wise use," but they argued that the best uses should be determined by private interests, not federal or state bureaucrats. Although conservationists often juxtaposed conservation and development, in no other region did developmental imperatives shape conservation as much as in the South.

New South boosters were never of one mind when it came to the best ways of using resources, but few believed that short-term profits should always win out over long-term solutions. It was rare for the first generation of boosters to mention conservation, though they did discuss the need to find the "highest" uses for their resources. In editorials and speeches, early boosters urged farmers, industrialists, and policy makers to promote efficient uses of resources. In 1870 a correspondent writing to a newspaper in upstate South Carolina claimed that a nation's "agricultural resources" would only result in prosperity when these resources were "fully and skillfully developed, economically and judiciously used." The author, writing in support of state agricultural education initiatives—concluded that "however rich it may be in natural resources of an agricultural character," if "people, through ignorance, indolence or any other cause, fail to develop them properly and judiciously," they "will remain poor, dependent and insignificant." These were "propositions which the people of the South are beginning to comprehend and appreciate."[89] Even arch-booster Henry Grady suggested that unchecked development was not in the best interests of the region. Grady claimed that "no people ever held larger stewardship than the people of the South. . . . It is theirs to produce and enlarge the crop of their staple that largely clothes the world," and "to conserve and develop the final and fullest supply of coal and iron, and to furnish from their enormous forests the lumber and hard woods to meet the world's demand until exhausted areas can be recovered."[90] Under Grady's editorship and after, the *Atlanta Constitution* was one of the region's leading publications disseminating information on ways to bring about conservation and resource permanence.

Public officials had also long expressed interest in economic efficiency, especially to promote regional independence before and during the Civil War. As efficiency was incorporated into a variety of national progressive crusades, it often translated into support for conserving valuable natural resources in the South.[91] In a 1902 article on the resources of the South, one writer predicted that "the greater efficiency in utilizing raw materials will enlarge the market for them as well as bring an enhanced price both to the manufacturer and the agriculturalist, the miner and the lumberman."[92] No one stressed the need to efficiently use natural resources more than Richard Edmonds. In the pages of the *Manufacturers' Record*—the premier trade journal promoting New South development—Edmonds tirelessly championed industrial development by providing statistics on regional economic growth, calling attention to new potential enterprises, and providing summations of commercial activity.[93] Despite his enthusiasm for building up the southern economy, Edmonds was also the foremost champion of the efficient uses of valuable natural resources, and this topic littered the pages of the *Manufacturers' Record* for decades. Like most boosters, Edmonds claimed that the inefficiency of the plantation system had opened the door for the South, "with its natural resources lying fallow," to learn from the "costly industrial experiments" made in other sections. Edmonds predicted that this would prove beneficial, because the region could "profit by the experience elsewhere without any great loss of time and money, or waste of energy and material." The experiences of other places made it clear that the future of the South was in industries that could use natural resources efficiently. To this end, Edmonds listed burgeoning enterprises that he believed channeled development in the right direction, such as using excess cottonseed to manufacture commercial fertilizers, more efficient methods of extracting turpentine from pine trees, and the chemical processing of "dried pine knots, stumps, and the waste of cut-over lands" for industrial raw materials. This preference for enterprises that used previously unused or discarded raw materials translated easily into a rationale for conservation. After lamenting that "the South has not been free from the wasteful methods in handling its timber that have desolated vast regions elsewhere," Edmonds argued that scientific forestry would help manage forests for long-term use. He also advocated land reclamation and the use of rivers for hydropower—all hallmarks of conservationist thinking nationally.[94] Just as Edmonds was writing, lumber companies were cutting through the region's forests; naval stores operators were killing southern pines in order to extract turpentine, pitch, and rosin from the trees' resin; mining companies were extracting iron ore and phosphates; and staple crops were sapping soils of their vitality. In this context, efficient use became an important strategy for developing southern resources in ways that could maintain economic growth and stocks of resources for long-term use. As Edmonds suggested, only the right kind of development could get the South out of its predicament and contribute to the permanent economic growth and stable natural resource stocks that boosters desperately wanted.

By the second decade of the twentieth century, the idea that there could be long-term ways of using natural resources had coalesced into a philosophy that

E. Lee Worsham. As the state entomologist for Georgia, E. Lee Worsham was one of the region's leading proponents of private conservation measures that would bring about environmental permanence. Conservation advocacy made Worsham nationally known, and in 1916 he was selected to serve as president of the National Conservation Congress, which met in Washington, D.C. CREDIT: Library of Congress, Prints & Photographs Division, LC-DIG-npcc-19549.

southern leaders were using as a benchmark to guide economic development. The math was simple: an industry was considered permanent if it managed resources rather than exploiting them to depletion. Perhaps the most outspoken advocate of permanence was a Georgian, Ernest Lee Worsham. As the state's entomologist, Worsham had participated in some of the first scientific studies of the boll weevil and had developed a strain of cotton that resisted wilt and the weevil, earning him the nickname "Crusader for Crops." Worsham was outspoken about conservation, and one newspaper noted that he had "for years been charging up and down the South, sounding in clarion tones the call to farmers and planters to arm against the weevil, the wilt, and the countless other forces of waste, decay and inefficiency." Worsham's views on conservation were never seen as opposed to the New South Creed. This newspaper even argued that he had become the "incarnate voice of the new South" by "demanding the elimination of waste, more crops, better crops, the higher uses of the land, intensive cultivation, modern scientific methods."[95]

After attending the first National Conservation Congress in 1909, Worsham used his position as state entomologist of Georgia to advocate for a far-reaching program of permanence for the South. He claimed that this was the most pressing issue of the day—indeed, "the most important issue that has arisen since the civil war." While speaking before the Southern Conservation Congress in 1910, Worsham acknowledged that "the South has had many hard struggles" but argued that "she has succeeded because of her rich gifts in natural resources," which would "aid her on the road to prosperity." Although the region's "forefathers proceeded with the idea that our vast resources were inexhaustible," Worsham argued that this path was no longer tenable. Even as reliance on natural resources increased and resources "passed into the hands of private owners," Worsham was confident that conservation would pave the way for a lasting prosperity based on long-term uses of natural resources. For Worsham, conservation was closely linked to private developmental imperatives.[96] He declared, "The resources that are still ours can be developed in such a way that will bring the greatest possible good to all the people. With all that nature has done for us this should be one of the richest spots of the earth." He concluded that "the right kind of conservation, conservation that carries with it the right kind of development, will make the south the most prosperous and the most beautiful section of all the world in which to live."[97]

As permanence became compelling to business leaders and political officials, especially in the early twentieth century, they advocated making it a cornerstone of southern economic development. At regional and national meetings on conservation, public officials and businesspeople articulated this doctrine of permanence and stressed that permanence had to come through private means. This private impulse was evident in 1910, when William Finley, president of the Southern Railway and a native of Pass Christian, Mississippi, was asked to speak on the role of railroads in conservation at the second National Conservation Congress in St. Paul, Minnesota. By 1910 representatives from the West, which had a higher proportion of federal lands than the East, had balked at having the federal government tell them how to use their resources. The meeting in St. Paul was planned by Gifford Pinchot to solidify support for his particular vision for conservation through what historian Elmo Richardson calls "sustained federal resource administration," and Pinchot stacked the deck with speakers who he knew would support a federal bureaucracy designed to supervise uses of public resources.[98] Given this context, it should not be surprising that Finley acknowledged that "the South is interested in the application of Conservation to the wise use of its soils, its minerals, its timber, and its streams" and praised ongoing federal efforts to purchase timberlands in the southern Appalachians for protection. Finley further noted, "I would define the type of 'Conservation of natural resources' that should be applied in that section [the South] as being the wise use of those resources. In some cases it may involve a measure of present self-denial," while in other cases, "conservation may mean the use of resources so as to obtain the maximum present profit."[99] On the surface, then, Finley's vision for the "wise use" of the South's natural resources seemed to be directly lifted from Gifford Pinchot.

Although he used "wise use" as his starting point, most of Finley's address to the delegates in St. Paul laid out a vision for conservation strikingly different from Pinchot's. For the majority of the speech he promoted private measures, not federal or state initiatives, to conserve resources. The only governmental responsibility that Finley even mentioned was reforming the tax system to provide incentives for conservation. Instead, he urged farmers to diversify, rotate their crops, and use fertilizer to improve their soils; he urged the owners of private forestland to selectively cut their timber; he urged private utility companies to construct dams that would generate hydroelectricity and prevent flooding; he urged landowners to keep up wooded areas that would decrease erosion. Finley even claimed that manufacturing industries were private avenues for conservation, and he declared that "manufacturing in the South has reached its present growth and is being still further developed on a basis of this kind of conservation of raw material." Like many boosters, Finley eschewed a fully extractive economy and argued that the "first step in the conservation of raw materials" was making products out of raw materials near where they were extracted. The South had already made a great deal of progress in this area, and he described a region approaching the second stage of conservation: "the use of the products of primary manufacturing as the raw materials for secondary industries."[100]

Here was a vision for conservation very different from Pinchot's. Whereas Pinchot was a professional forester and bureaucrat well schooled in the scientific principles of conservation, Finley was a lifelong businessman. He had spent more than three decades working in the railroad industry prior to being selected as the president of the Southern Railway, one of the largest railroads in the South.[101] As the president of a railroad that depended on freight traffic from the South's hinterlands, Finley could not afford to advocate policies that would inhibit development and hamstring his corporation. Yet he had vested interests in ensuring that raw materials would provide traffic for his railroad cars for years. His approach to permanence—like that of most boosters, businesspeople, and public officials—was predicated on private conservation initiatives. Only when conservation was aligned with development would the region truly prosper.

☙

Finley and Pinchot had different visions for how to bring about conservation, but each strategy shared a tendency to exclude certain groups from the process of resource management. Nature preservation in the West was dependent on imagining wilderness areas as unpeopled spaces that should be preserved for the enjoyment of white Americans. Drawing on racially motivated assumptions about who was entitled to nature, conservation leaders often blamed "new" immigrants and African Americans for the worst environmental depredations and sought to use legislation to curb the independence of these groups and circumscribe their access to nature. As the federal government imposed restrictions on landscapes that had been used for generations, it limited the ability of nearby residents to use resources in traditional ways. The creation of the Adirondack Forest Preserve outlawed traditional hunting and timber-cutting practices and redefined these subsistence activities as illegal. Establishing national parks like Yellowstone and Yosemite involved removing Native Americans from these spaces. Regulations on hunting and fishing in Pennsylvania led to fighting between game wardens and local communities that sought to continue long-standing activities.[102] In short, conservation was a wrenching social process that fell most heavily on groups with little access to governmental centers of power. As historian Carolyn Merchant concludes, the "boundaries created by natural-resource regulations restrained opportunities for people of color, while protecting white privilege and power."[103]

It was difficult for conservationists to define the South—a region with a lot of people and private property—as an untrammeled wilderness by writing locals out of the story. Conservation in the South was rarely about preserving wilderness. Yet even managing resources for long-term business uses had an important social component, and conservation in the South functioned as a way to maintain the permanence of the racial hierarchy. Early conservation measures in the 1870s were efforts not just to preserve game and fish but to cut off independent means of subsistence and access to the commons for freedpeople. As public officials placed valuable resources in corporate hands, they reduced the resources available for black southerners and cut them out of the path of private landownership, gutting the central promises of Reconstruction. Enthusiasm for conservation reached its peak in the Progressive Era just as white politicians were feverishly enacting segregation into law. Conservation of resources supported these exclusionary designs by maintaining the stability of the economy and keeping African Americans as dependent laborers mired in low-wage, exploitative jobs.[104] A 1911 editorial in the *Atlanta Constitution* openly cast efforts to limit criminal activity by "vagrants" as an extension of the conservation impulse. The editorial urged that African Americans and poor whites be forced to labor on public works projects and concluded, "This is an age of conservation. An excellent phase of that very admirable science would be one that conserved the industrial assets of Georgia and every other state by compelling members of the quasi-criminal class, now a drain upon the community, to transform themselves permanently into producers."[105]

Given that conservation was intertwined with designs for racial mastery, it should be no surprise that African American leaders expressed little enthusiasm for the forms of conservation promoted by white business and political officials. Instead, black leaders turned conservation into a doctrine that could address the particular needs of black southerners by making quality of life, not industrial longevity, central to their conceptions of permanence.[106] African American intellectuals and educational leaders were at the forefront of this redefinition of conservation. In 1896, for example, Booker T. Washington brought George Washington Carver to Tuskegee Institute to research and teach about cutting-edge methods of scientific farming that would give African American farmers in the Black Belt a modicum of independence, even under exploitative sharecropping and tenant contracts.[107] After Gifford Pinchot spoke to students and faculty at the Hampton Institute in 1909, a faculty member rounded out the evening by providing a "forceful application" of the principles of conservation "to the present needs of the South, and of the Southern Negroes in particular."[108] An article in the Hampton's *Southern Workman* expanded on what this meant, explaining how the entire nation was focused on "the conservation of the country's resources" and thanking "the men and women who are asking us to consider the future of our forests, mines, lands, and water power." The author noted, however, that "still greater than the waste of natural resources is the needless waste of human life" and called attention to the need for conservation through better public health programs.[109] In an article in the *Aurora*, the official publication of Knoxville College, R. D. Doggett provided a detailed overview of conservation and concluded, "With a nation as with a man, foresight and prudence" in the use of resources "are the foundations of successful continuance."[110] "Continuance" looked different from the permanence espoused by white businessmen, however, and was always geared toward solving the particular problems afflicting African Americans in the South.

Continuance did share one trait with permanence: an emphasis on private property as the key to maintaining environmental quality. For decades after the Civil War, black southerners fought for property ownership, claiming that it was the key to successful stewardship of the land. The failures of Reconstruction land redistribution only increased calls for land reform, and black leaders made the case that ownership would prompt more careful and efficient management of land and resources. Although business leaders also believed in private ownership as a key to conservation, the similarities ended there. White business leaders worked to put valuable resources in the hands of corporations, while black leaders worked to put resources in the hands of individuals. Even though these paths shared an emphasis on property ownership, they were incompatible. As we will see, black southerners challenged exploitative aspects of corporate permanence and defined permanence in ways that spoke to their own needs. They resisted the efforts of white elites who were trying to implement their ideas of permanence, and conflicts between these different visions of permanence shaped southern economic development in critical ways.

☙

By the second decade of the twentieth century, permanence was a key part of the region's economic development. The fate of permanence mirrors the trajectory of other Progressive initiatives in the South. By the 1920s efforts by public officials and businesspeople to foster economic growth had become intertwined with the efforts of these same groups to institute various reforms, creating the complex mix of "boosterism and reform" that George Tindall refers to as "business progressivism." As Tindall explains, "The business progressive philosophy had deep roots in both the progressive movement and the 'New South' creed of economic development." James Cobb suggests that it emerged from "the all-out devotion to the cause of growth and the unexamined faith in growth as a panacea for all that ailed the South."[111] Throughout the region, progressive politicians supported such diverse goals as good roads, tax reform, the improvement of public health, education, and the conservation of natural resources. These were not radical initiatives. Most were driven by an emphasis on maintaining economic development, regional growth, and the social status quo. Permanence also fit with the desire of Progressive Era reformers to circumscribe opportunities for African Americans through segregation.[112]

Although scholars have not seen conservation as a key part of this impulse, environmental permanence fit snugly within this tradition. It exemplified the combination of reform and boosterism that characterized business progressivism. Indeed, conservation never challenged the South's "all-out devotion to the cause of growth." It simply promised to make this economic growth more permanent by maintaining stocks of profitable natural resources that could be used indefinitely. The embrace of conservation among public officials and businesspeople was not out of a love of nature; it was simply a calculated strategy to achieve long-term economic growth in a region that desperately needed it. Permanent development was part "wise use" and part New South Creed. It was this fact that made conservation and environmental permanence so appealing to southern boosters, public officials, and businesspeople. By the 1920s, then, conservation was not only promoted by a smattering of public officials and businesspeople in the region. It was part and parcel of the South's economic development, though it was running up against far different visions for the future.

CHAPTER 2

Cultivating Permanence

IN AN ADDRESS to the Mississippi Agricultural and Mechanical Fair Association in 1872, Eugene Hilgard, professor of agricultural chemistry at the University of Mississippi and the state geologist, claimed that the South was entering a phase in its economic development that required a new relationship with the land. Hilgard argued that "in an agricultural commonwealth, the fundamental requirement of continued prosperity is . . . that *the fertility of the soil must be maintained.*" He recounted how societies ranging from ancient Greece to Moorish Spain had ignored this maxim and used up their soils through misguided methods of cultivation. Although educated in Germany, Hilgard was well acquainted with the South and had lived in Mississippi since 1855. Oxford was in the middle of one of the richest—and most intensively cultivated—parts of the South, and his experience there led him to conclude that southerners were "once more repeating history" by depleting their own soils with the "continuous cropping" of cotton and corn, by using destructive methods of farming, and by viewing land as something to cast off after only a few years of use. Although frontier conditions demanded methods that were not ideal, Hilgard declared that "*we* have long passed this stage of development, and it is high time for us to be looking forward to a state of things that can endure permanently."[1]

Permanent growth was only possible by adopting a new attitude toward the region's soils. Viewing land "as a thing to be abandoned so soon as we have succeeded in stripping it of its first flush of fertility, by a rapid process of exhaustion by injudicious cropping, without even rest or rotation," would prevent southerners from developing "those social qualities which distinguish the peaceful and civilized tiller of the soil from the nomad." The problem was not simply that poor farming led to poor soils but that poor farming had "a degree of selfishness and recklessness of consequences—a sort of 'devil take the hindmost' principle" that would "impress upon the moral and intellectual life of a community." Hilgard wanted to increase profits from the farm for the longest possible time, but his conception of what it meant to use soils in "permanent" ways also suggested that there was a moral component to treating soils as more than short-term paths to wealth. Rather than selfishly cultivating crops without adding anything back to soils, Hilgard advocated cultivating smaller tracts of land more intensively, diversifying crops, returning organic products like cottonseed to the soil, using barnyard manure and marls to increase fertility, rotating crops, subsoiling, and building infrastructure for more effective drainage. It was only when southerners learned to steward their soils in these ways, then, that they would maintain fertility for future generations and would become more than mere "nomads."[2]

Hilgard's enthusiasm for permanent methods of cultivation was part of a broader reconsideration of the best uses of soils that swept the South in the decades after the Civil War. By the end of the Civil War, these soils—in parts of the region, at least—were reeling from almost two centuries of sustained cultivation. Debates over how to build a more permanent South began on the region's farms, which had long been pushing up against their environmental limits. Few people ever conceived of permanent uses of soil as a moral issue like Hilgard, but stabilizing the agricultural economy through long-term growth was appealing. As planters, merchants, businesspeople, academics and politicians sought to remake agriculture so that it would thrive in a changed postwar environment, they urged a sharp break with the plantation past by questioning the wisdom of staple crop cultivation and calling on southerners to diversify and take up new methods of cultivation. The exploitative social and racial aspects of this creed conflicted with the vision of many small farmers—African American and white—who conceived of permanence in different terms. Clashes over the best strategies for achieving permanence on the farm shaped agriculture well into the twentieth century, and ultimately showed that permanence could be applied to enterprises off the farm as well.

❦

Permanence had been on the minds of planters long before 1865. Antebellum agricultural reformers like Edmund Ruffin urged planters who were adept at getting "the greatest *immediate* production and profit" from their soil to instead work for "the greatest *continued* products and profits" by adding marl to acidic soils, rotating crops, and generally taking more care with cultivation.[3] Promoting permanence through agricultural reform propped up the exploitative slave-based social structure and made attempts to create an independent South through secession seem less rash. Despite the efforts of antebellum reformers, however, permanence was stillborn. New economic paths were blocked by the profitability of plantation agriculture and by fears that any change might threaten slavery. Agricultural reforms simply did not seem necessary in a region where the exhaustion of eastern soils was still limited, and where there was an abundance of unused land for cultivation even if soils did give out.[4] It was not until the end of the Civil War—when national attention was focused on the South's resources—that permanence was incubated.

The end of the Civil War made southerners rethink how they used their soils in a more far-reaching way than ever before. Emancipation threw the future of the staple crop economy into doubt. Planters were left without capital, freedpeople were left without land, and war or neglect led to a marked decline in agricultural infrastructure. As production stagnated, the value of Southern farms decreased by fifty to seventy percent in the immediate aftermath of the war.[5] Although white elites sought to hang onto the antebellum social hierarchy, it was clear that the economics of plantation agriculture would have to change to meet the new circumstances of the post–Civil War world. Speaking to this uncertainty, an Alabamian remarked in 1866 that "one thing planters have got to learn: the old system is gone up, and we must begin new."[6] That same year a public official in Georgia commented, "It is evident to every thinking man that, with our changed system of labor and the impoverished condition of our lands, that a complete change of our old system of culture has become necessary before the planting interest will be very remunerative."[7] It was in this context—when planters and freedpeople were struggling over the fate of agriculture and labor—that ideas about more permanent means of using soils took hold.

These debates were made more pressing by their environmental context. By the end of the Civil War, southern farms were up against their environmental limits. Fields throughout the Southeast were reeling from two centuries of cultivation, and crop yields in states like South Carolina and Georgia were plummeting.[8] Parts of the region were in worse shape than others, but throughout the entire Plantation Belt observers described widespread erosion, declining soil fertility, and farms that seemed to be just wasting away. Shortly after the Civil War a northern reformer told John Townsend Trowbridge that when he came to Virginia he "found the land worn out, like nearly all the land in the country." Virginians growing tobacco had worked the soil "till all the strength there was left was burnt out," and he concluded that planters "have spoilt their farms" in ways that made them seem "like fools or crazy men." Traveling through Georgia and Alabama, Trowbridge remarked that "one sees many plantations ruined for some years by improper cultivation." He described farms where "the land generally washes badly, and where the hill-sides have been furrowed up and down, instead of being properly 'horizontalized,' the rains plough them into gulleys, and carry off the cream of the soil."[9] John Richard Dennett, correspondent for the *Nation*, recounted a conversation with a woman in North Carolina whose farm "was almighty poor" and "wouldn't fetch more'n a bushel o' wheat to the acre, so much of it was washed out, and all guttered."[10] When Edward King reported that "the soil of the Alabama cotton belt" was "inexhaustibly rich" in 1875, he admitted that "it has in some sections been forced, so as to be, for a time, less productive than usual."[11] Even the rich soils of northern Mississippi were feeling the effects of continuous staple crop cultivation. In 1872 a traveler on the Mississippi Central Railroad remarked that land in the state was "either . . . miserably poor, or you have abused it awfully," and added, "The whole country along that railroad looks like a turkey gobbler that has been pulled through a briar bush by the tail."[12]

These problems were most severe where soils had been cultivated the longest, especially in the southeastern Plantation Belt. In order to maximize their production of staple crops, antebellum planters invested capital in slaves and responded to declining soils with a system of "shifting cultivation," where fields were rotated to allow cultivated soils to recover. When soils were entirely exhausted, planters simply migrated west to still-fertile lands. Although shifting cultivation and migration were logical responses to the abundance of land and labor in the South, they seemed too inefficient to be permanent solutions, at least from the vantage point of 1865. Antebellum planters were easy targets for postbellum reformers hoping to find new ways to farm that would be profitable indefinitely.[13] Just after the Civil War a South Carolina newspaper claimed, "We have already urged repeatedly upon our readers the substitution of the farming or thorough tillage policy for the more slovenly staple culture—the slovenliness being due equally to the use of negro labor and the carelessness of the planter."[14] James Gray, a planter from Muscogee County, Georgia, observed in 1874 that "little improvement is noticeable about farms in this County and adjoining ones" and lamented that it was "a difficult matter for our farmers to get out of the *Ante Bellum* habits, and until this is done, we need not expect to see any improvements of a permanent character upon our farms."[15] This was a popular refrain even a decade later, when landowner John Bankston Davis told members of his local Grange in Campton, South Carolina, that forests and the "natural productiveness of the soil" had both been ruined by the plantation's "wretched system of cultivation."[16]

Perceptions that soils were declining had their basis in reality, but they also bolstered popular visions for the post–Civil War South. Industrial development was the cornerstone of the New South, but even during Reconstruction boosters were also advocating what Paul Gaston describes as a "renovated agricultural system infused with the values of business enterprise." Because the region supposedly had extraordinary soils, climate, and conditions ripe for farming—it was the nation's "garden spot"—boosters hoped that just a few tweaks to long-standing agricultural practices would allow the full use of these natural assets. To take advantage of this natural bounty, New South promoters argued for the breakup of large plantations into small farms that could be cultivated intensively under scientific management, as well as the diversification of the staple crop economy. They confidently predicted that these reforms would streamline the agricultural economy, allow farming to thrive in symbiosis with manufacturing, and make soils permanently profitable.[17]

New South visions for reforming agriculture were based on finding and implementing better uses of soils. Despite the sorry state of soils in eastern plantation areas, boosters claimed that land would heal quickly with the right kind of scientific management. Georgia's comptroller spoke to this optimism in 1866 when he noted, "We have a soil capable of being improved to almost any extent, if a proper system of cultivation and manuring be adopted," and concluded, "How this can be done, and with the greatest economy, is a question of vital interest to every citizen of Georgia."[18] South Carolina planter Alfred Huger claimed that southern soil was "more than equal to all our wants . . . whether those wants are confined to sustenance only, or whether they extend to the most luxurious fancies of civilized society, or to the highest refinement of human intellect," and predicted that they would "answer to every demand"—provided that planters "draw upon the soil, with a proper endorsement of skillful husbandry."[19]

This optimism that the South could recover from even its most drastic environmental problems was fueled by changes in the way planters valued their land after the Civil War. As economist Gavin Wright explains, emancipation suddenly forced planters to stop acting as "laborlords" and to start acting as "landlords." Henry Grady put it this way: planters were "still lords of acres, though not of slaves." This was more than a change in title. Wright contends that after the Civil War "investment strategies, entrepreneurial designs, and political schemes whose end purpose was to increase the productivity and value of *land* came to the fore," and he concludes that "the passionate Southern attachment to the soil was a post–Civil War phenomenon."[20] This corresponds to Carville Earle's observation that innovations in agricultural practices often occur during "long-wave depressions," when economic difficulties prompt people to consider new paths.[21] Southerners were dealing with each of these issues after 1865, when the changes caused by the Civil War predisposed planters to support new methods of cultivation that promised to permanently use the one resource they had left: their land.

This was never simply a question of land use and political economy. Agricultural labor was never the totality of slavery, but it was closely linked to maintaining the South's peculiar institution. Debates over the reconstruction of agriculture, then, were about who should have access to land and other agricultural resources. For freedpeople who saw landownership as a path to independence, obtaining land was an integral part of what freedom meant. They fought back against planters and reformers who sought to use agricultural permanence to maintain the South's exploitative social system.

As planters and freedpeople struggled to come to terms with the sweeping changes of the post–Civil War era, declines in soil productivity, erosion, and deforestation all made them feel as if they were running up against their environmental limits. There was no consensus about how to solve these problems. Reformers and boosters advocated strategies that ranged from halting the cultivation of staple crops to relying entirely on commercial fertilizers, touching off fierce conflicts over what permanence meant and how to achieve it in the rural South. The resolution of these conflicts helped to determine the fate not only of the South's soils but of its people and economic institutions as well.

∾

Debates over permanent uses of southern soils were under way immediately following the Civil War. Since farming was the South's dominant enterprise even after 1865, finding more permanent ways of using agricultural resources was a critical step to building a prosperous New South. Some of the first volleys in the fight for permanence related to closing off the open commons. Southern states had long protected community rights to common lands on the margins of plantations by allowing livestock to graze there and mandating that fields be fenced to prevent incursions from roaming hogs and cattle. By law and tradition the burden was placed on the farmer, not the stock owner, to build and maintain fences and to pay for any damages caused by grazing livestock. Under this arrangement livestock could forage freely on common lands—providing southerners who could not or did not want to pay for land for pasturage with a critical means of subsistence. In the 1860s and 1870s, however, traditional forage rights on the commons came under attack from the rural landed elite, who criticized the system as an inefficient holdover from the antebellum era that was ill suited for a developing New South. They sought to reverse this system by holding livestock owners, not planters, responsible for fencing their stock or damage to crops.[22]

For rural elites, closing the commons was key to building a lasting commercial agricultural economy atop the ruins of Civil War plantations, and it went hand in hand with the extension of the cotton market into the region. As Steven Hahn notes, advocates of stock and fence laws typically "represented the interests of the merchants, landlords, and the towns as well as the values of the 'free market,'" and they were aided by railroad companies that were reaching into the interior to haul cotton and other goods to urban markets.[23] These groups saw the commons as an archaic holdover from the Old South. In the pages of rural weeklies, they sought to convince leery voters to support local option legislation privatizing common lands, which would improve farms by promoting better breeds of cattle, diversifying agriculture, preventing the destruction to fields by free-roaming livestock, and allowing more farmland to be cultivated under improved methods. Rural elites also argued that fence laws would preserve timber by requiring fewer worm fences, which were notoriously lumber-intensive. A Georgia farmer spoke for rural elites region-wide when he remarked that the timber of Carroll County would be more valuable when the railroad arrived and declared, "The time to economize our timber is while we have got it."[24] Each of these measures was billed as a step to permanence for the rural South—a way to build a prosperous agricultural economy that could produce valuable goods for market while spreading out risk among a variety of enterprises.

Stock laws were also a reaction to social changes caused by emancipation, and the push to close the commons happened just as rural elites were working to limit the independence of freedpeople by enacting vagrancy laws and regulations on hunting and fishing. White proponents were keen to undercut stock raising by freedpeople, which provided African American laborers with a means of subsistence that gave them power in negotiations with landowners over labor and working conditions. Stock laws made independence more precarious, and rural elites hoped that they would make black laborers dependent on landowners who needed steady labor for commercial cultivation.[25]

Although stock and fence laws promised to put agriculture on a prosperous and commercial path by bringing humans and natural resources under control, they were bitterly opposed by people who relied on the commons for subsistence. The agricultural permanence sought by planters did not apply equally to all, and tenants and sharecroppers rejected this vision to maintain their independence. Tenants and small farmers fought to maintain their traditional rights so that their livestock could forage freely. For these groups, access to common lands was vital to guarantee their independence and security. They rightly cast attempts to reverse the commons as class-based legislation designed to hinder their mobility and ability to secure a living apart from planters who depended on their labor. Opponents held back the passage of stock laws effectively in parts of the region, though the deck was stacked against them. They were especially successful in Georgia, where the state legislature left the question up to county referendums. Although Plantation Belt counties had mostly adopted stock laws by the 1880s, opposition from poor white and black farmers stymied the introduction of stock laws in the up-country, forcing the state to move to district referendums to get laws passed. Even as late as 1890, only 37 out of 137 counties in the state had a county-wide stock law, though 41 other counties had districts that had adopted one. A similar dynamic was at work in states like Mississippi and Alabama, which generally left stock law decisions up to local referendums. The legislature of South Carolina broke with this trend and imposed a statewide stock law in the 1880s. Yet for much of the region, local opposition to stock laws hindered their implementation, and it was not until 1949 that the state of Florida closed off the commons.[26]

The clash over stock laws was about competing definitions of permanence, both social and environmental. Proponents of stock laws framed these laws as a way to expand commercial markets, which would bring market-driven efficiency and permanence to stocks of timber, to fields, and to the social hierarchy. Opponents saw them as a dangerous reversal of long-standing rights to common lands, which chipped away at their ability to survive by miring them in commercial market activity. As we will see, the passage of stock laws did not bring a new efficiency to southern rural spaces, but these conflicts do illustrate how the ideology of permanence was becoming a useful way to frame conflicts over a variety of local issues. Even during Reconstruction, the search for permanent uses of valuable resources was starting to shape the way that southerners thought about the best paths for a prosperous South, and these conflicting views established the key players in struggles that would continue for decades.

☙

Redefining the commons was just one aspect of efforts to reimagine agriculture in the years after the Civil War so that it could be more durable. These efforts were most often focused on the dominant form of agriculture: staple crop cultivation. Before the Civil War, lucrative staples like rice, sugar, cotton, and tobacco maintained the racial hierarchy and generally brought good returns. Planters—even devoted agricultural reformers—never seriously considered abandoning staples. It was not until after 1865 that southerners seriously weighed whether staple crops were in their best long-term interests.

No crop was more debated than cotton. "King Cotton" was one of the most important global commodities of the nineteenth century. It had dominated almost the entire Plantation Belt, and its future was one of the most pressing questions for southerners struggling to build a permanent economy. Cotton may not have been the "totality of southern agriculture," as Gavin Wright explains, "but for most of the region it defined the opportunities and dictated the pace of economic life."[27] In the years after the Civil War, planters, merchants in growing crossroads towns, newspaper editors, agricultural reformers, urban boosters, northern observers, businesspeople, and poor white and black farmers all clashed over whether cotton was the ideal crop for a truly "new" South. Cotton was often linked to exploitative cultivation of soils, and advocates of permanence latched onto diversification as a panacea for a range of rural problems. They urged farmers to limit their dependence on cotton, which tied farmers to the whims of national and international commodity markets, depleted soils, enriched manufacturers outside the region, and stunted industry. Diversification seemed like an easy way to solve these problems and make southern farmers more self-sufficient—a key step to making southern farmers permanently prosperous.[28]

Proposals for diversifying the staple crop economy met fierce opposition, and cotton became the subject of competing visions over the permanence of staple crops and the way that these crops treated the land. Beginning in 1865, these debates played out in the halls of agricultural societies and legislatures, in agricultural periodicals and newspapers, and on private farms. Stephen DeCanio even suggests that "overproduction" of cotton "was probably the greatest source of controversy" in the *Southern Cultivator*, the region's most popular agricultural periodical. Just in 1870, there were almost seven hundred articles in the *Cultivator* that dealt with cotton, and most considered whether it could be a long-term source of income for the developing South. These articles were simply one part of a bigger debate about whether staple crops were a permanent solution to the South's most pressing economic and environmental problems.[29]

Determinations of whether cotton cultivation could be a permanent enterprise for the New South turned on how the crop affected the region's most important resource: its soils. Postbellum reformers underlined the link between staple crops and soil degradation in their efforts to disparage the antebellum plantation system and make the case for new, more lasting types of agriculture. In 1873 a farmer from Orangeburg, South Carolina, told the members of his local agricultural society that raising staple crops "has been proved to be ruinous in the extreme" and concluded that "while the South has occupied itself with only one commercial production, the people have become impoverished; the soil worn out and the produced staple, from redundancy in the markets, so depreciated in value that a bare support, and sometimes not even that can be obtained."[30] The *Brenham Weekly Banner*—in the heart of the Texas Cotton Belt—urged local farmers to diversify their "exclusively cotton country" by claiming that "raising cotton and using the proceeds to buy bread and meat and forage for the work stock not only impoverishes the soil, but also the planter's pockets."[31] Even Henry Grady, an urban newspaper editor with little knowledge of agriculture and an inclination to downplay the problems facing farmers, admitted in 1887 that "whenever the greed for a money crop unbalances the wisdom of husbandry, the money crop is a curse." Natural resources were "the basis of the South's wealth and power," but the region's "growth shall endure" if southerners only abided by "two maxims, that reach deeper than legislative enactment." The first was that "no one crop will make a people prosperous." Southern soils were suited for growing a variety of products, not just cotton, and Grady believed that independence and economic growth could only endure through diversification. He used the *Atlanta Constitution* to promote his vision for a more diversified program of farming by sending newspaper correspondents to visit and write about farmers who had experimented with diversification. As historian Harold Davis shows, there were more than a thousand of these examples published in just six weeks in 1882, and Grady's *Atlanta Constitution* served as the most vocal proponent of agricultural reform and the folly of betting the South's future only on staples.[32]

Reformers like Grady urged planters to grow new crops to offset cotton and other staples. They understood that it did not make sense to replace cotton with a system that kept depleting the soil—no matter how profitable in the short term. Scholars have written a lot about diversification efforts but have failed to recognize how these decisions were about environmental permanence and often turned on how each new crop affected soil fertility. Deciding what to replace staples with involved a delicate calculus of profit and conservation, and reformers urged farmers to grow crops that would result in the permanent improvement of the fertility of their lands. Permanence provided a powerful promise that shifting away from cotton to an unknown future was a wise choice. Each community tried something different. In 1868 farmers from Giles County, Tennessee, organized a county-wide "wheat club" to promote the cultivation of wheat. A local newspaper urged farmers to join, claiming that because local land was "in a great measure exhausted by cotton, it is high time that our farmers were turning their attention to some crop which requires comparatively little labor in its cultivation and which does not impoverish the soil like cotton" but would still "afford some return to the farmer for his trouble."[33] After conducting experiments on his farm near Sparta in 1870, Georgia planter E. M. Pendleton concluded that "the oat crop, next to cotton, is the most valuable product of the South." Pendleton claimed oats were less labor intensive than cotton and corn, as well as "less exhaustive to the land," and he argued that the oat crop was "a great improvement to it [cotton] so far as that invaluable principle, humus, is concerned; while corn, like cotton, is a humus destroying plant."[34] Some planters and reformers advocated particular crops not as a means to supplant staples entirely but as a way to increase soil fertility enough to allow staple crop cultivation to continue. Given planters' interest in closing the commons, it is not surprising that livestock were seen as a way to diversify and maintain the soil. In 1906 farmer and stock raiser August Mayer from Shreveport, Louisiana, lamented that the cattle tick was inhibiting the raising of purebred stock, which would provide an important source of fertilization for fields besides adding to the farmer's pocket. Mayer noted that "the fertility of the soil must be increased, and this can only be done permanently by means of a healthy live-stock industry," which required getting rid of the cattle tick.[35] Cowpeas were another popular choice to restore soil fertility for cultivating staple crops. Reformers urged planters to go back to the antebellum practice of rotating cotton with cowpeas to boost the soil and provide a valuable foodstuff for livestock and people. Augusta businessman William Rowland even claimed that the cowpea had "magical properties" because it was "the best renovator known of wornout soils" and had ready markets, making it "safer than . . . producing cotton." "When the vital question comes up of how to renovate and improve our lands, or if already fertile, how to keep up their fertility," Rowland concluded that "the answer is the cowpea."[36] In 1885 humorist Bill Arp even wrote an article skewering attempts at diversification by praising cowpeas for providing soils with shade, which he considered to be the true "restoror" of both people and nature. Seeding cowpeas in each crop row would "give shade and help the corn and renew the soil."[37]

Not every crop was a success. Parts of the region did have "natural conditions" that were "favorable to the production of a wide variety of crops," as Gilbert Fite explains, but ideas about what could replace tried-and-true staples were often more ridiculous than realistic.[38] After a few unsuccessful experiments, a planter near Charleston, South Carolina, exclaimed, "Let sorghum juice, sorghum cane and sorghum mills go to—the Yankees!" He complained, "No plant I ever tried so impoverished the soil," besides requiring dangerous machinery that crushed sorghum cane to extract juice.[39] As the frustration of this planter suggests, crops that seemed like a natural fit sometimes just did not work as planned. New crops were not always better for soils, and experimental plantings frequently failed. Yet the fact that so many reformers felt the need to justify each crop by how it would affect soil fertility suggests that ideas about permanence were compelling to planters, public officials, and businesspeople and were starting to shape agricultural development in important ways.

Diversification was not just linked to white farmers and reformers. African American leaders latched onto diversification to promote their own brand of permanence for black farmers, though it was far removed from white advocates of diversification. At Tuskegee Institute, for instance, George Washington

Carver developed a program that mirrored white agricultural reformers in stressing diversification. Whereas most white reformers promoted diversification as a way to find new commercial crops, Carver promoted diversification as a way to free black farmers from a dependence on market crops. By offering black farmers a way out of the market system, Carver's model was "subversive," as Mark Hersey argues, and it posed a challenge to the prevailing vision of the New South Creed. Carver taught black farmers to practice subsistence agriculture that would make them more self-sufficient by growing crops like sweet potatoes, cowpeas, and eventually peanuts. He also called attention to "wasted" products of nature, which offered black farmers a new source of foodstuffs and farm aid. From 1897 into the second decade of the twentieth century, Carver experimented with these and other crops on the Tuskegee Experiment Station to see what had the most promise. He held Farmers' Institutes for Black Belt cultivators, traveled throughout Alabama promoting his methods of cultivation, organized Negro Farmers' Conferences to provide cutting-edge advice to black farmers, used the Tuskegee Experiment Station as a model for the local community, and even got the USDA to provide seeds for food crops.[40] While diversification was a goal of reformers region-wide, black agriculturalists like Carver used it to help black southerners by pulling them away from the capitalist system, rather than substituting cotton for yet another market crop.

Despite their efforts to link staple crops with soil depletion, reformers and boosters were stymied by merchants, landlords, and urban businesspeople who claimed that staples were the region's best long-term option. These groups argued that staple crops like cotton were more profitable than any other crop, could stand in for credit, and were hardier than potential replacements. They also argued that staples were a longer-term solution to the South's environmental needs. Even advocates of cotton acknowledged that it was never acceptable to just run down soil fertility and made the case that cotton was a more realistic way to achieve environmental and economic permanence than pie-in-the-sky visions of diversification. Despite efforts by scientists, agricultural reformers, journalists, and academics to convince planters to abandon cotton because it exhausted the soil, vocal planters and merchants claimed the mantle of environmental permanence by suggesting that cotton was no more exhaustive than any other crop. "The much abused 'cotton crop,'" as one farmer wrote in the *Southern Planter* in 1885, "if properly managed, was a great renovator of the soil—possibly the best renovating crop in the world." Because only the lint had commercial value, the nutrients contained in the seed, stalks, and leaves were all "returned to the soil."[41] A merchant from Georgia also claimed that cotton "does not take anything away from" the soil, while W. F. Massey, an author and a farmer from North Carolina, believed that "tobacco and cotton have not been the cause of the unproductive condition of our lands" because "other money crops treated in the same way would have exhausted the surface soil just as effectively as tobacco or cotton—in fact, more rapidly than cotton."[42] These arguments have a grain of truth. Cotton is not a particularly exhaustive crop.[43] But the fact that even advocates of cotton felt compelled to justify the continuance of the staple in terms of its environmental footprint sheds light on the powerful ideology of permanence and its role in shaping agricultural possibilities in the South.

☙

The merchants, planters, and landlords who opposed diversification also used the ideology of permanence to secure tractable labor for their farms. Ever since the end of the Civil War, conservative white planters had worked to hinder the mobility of African Americans in the rural South to maintain steady agricultural labor and the racial status quo—an effort that was clearest in the passage of a series of "Black Codes" in 1865. By holding black farmers up to the yardstick of environmental permanence, white planters and merchants also justified legislation that ensured a steady supply of labor for their fields and deftly elided blame about rural economic problems while seemingly supporting long-term growth and soil conservation.

Merchants and planters supported staple crops because of their role as land and credit lords in emerging systems of labor, especially sharecropping and tenant farming. Sharecropping and tenant farming were initially a logical response to the lack of a defined labor system, and they quickly came to dominate the Cotton and Tobacco Belts. Because cash was scarce and freedpeople did not want to work as gang laborers under conditions resembling slavery, planters and freedpeople negotiated labor contracts dependent on crop lien laws, in which a landlord would provide tenants or croppers with a house, seed, and all necessary implements for farming in return for a portion of the crop.[44] This represented a "balance" between the interests of freedpeople and landlords, but these labor systems quickly became exploitative when Redeemer governments changed credit laws to mire croppers in debt.[45] Cotton itself was a way to maintain a steady supply of black agricultural laborers. The authors of a 1907 USDA bulletin explained that while a "dishonest tenant can dispose of eggs, butter, grain, pork, or truck without the knowledge of the creditor . . . a cotton bale is too large to escape undetected."[46] Because crops like cotton and tobacco commanded cash and did not provide subsistence, merchants and landlords typically mandated that their tenants plant these staples, no matter the environmental cost.

Black laborers resisted abusive contract terms and escaped indebtedness through mobility. Migration gave them an opportunity to escape poor conditions, negotiate with new landlords, and exert some control over their labor and the terms of their contracts. Mobility posed a direct challenge to the power of rural merchants and planters who claimed that it prevented black tenants from adequately caring for their land. Because croppers did not own the land, these groups claimed they had no incentive to look out for its long-term interests by taking measures to prevent erosion and keep up soil fertility. In a study of Alabama's cotton production, Eugene Allen Smith, a geologist at the University of Alabama, claimed that tenants "do not own the land, have no interest in it beyond getting a crop from a portion of it . . . and are not interested in keeping up the fertility, at least not to the extent of being led to make any attempt at the permanent improvement of the same." Most landlords were "interested in the improvement of [their] land" but were stymied by their labor contracts, which caused landlords to be "further removed from personal care of the land."[47] A farmer from Georgia implicated landlords for soil degradation, arguing that "the tenant system, as a whole, has a tendency to reduce the average production per acre of most of the crops, because a great deal is left to the management of the ignorant negro farm hand, the landlord being interested only to the extent of his rent." Tenants "go in and get what they can out of the land at the least possible expense, and pay no attention to building up the land or saving it," and this farmer castigated "native Georgians" for allowing this to happen. He concluded that "public opinion is against the tenant system in Georgia for the reason that the crops and the land are neglected."[48]

Given the prevalence of African Americans as sharecroppers and tenant farmers, it should not be surprising that race played the most significant role in delineating who was using soils in permanent ways and who was not, at least in the eyes of the white plantation elite and their urban counterparts. Throughout the New South era, middle- and upper-class white southerners used treatment of the land as a way to stigmatize black southerners. Claims that African American farmers did not understand how to use the region's soils properly were intended to justify greater control over workers or to promote the complete displacement of black labor with white immigrants. In fact, labor was a perennial concern of Reconstruction and New South public officials, planters, and businesspeople. Since the end of the Civil War there had been a strong push to encourage immigration to the South in order to bring unsettled lands into cultivation. Private immigration societies, state immigration bureaus, and railroad companies advertised opportunities to potential immigrants, employed hundreds of immigration agents, and sold hundreds of thousands of acres of land to settlers. Although their efforts never had much payoff, advocates of immigration wanted to bring unused lands into cultivation and displace the region's wholesale reliance on black labor by attracting white immigrants from Europe or the North.[49] This was evident in 1872 at a meeting of the Memphis Chamber of Commerce, where speakers decried the tenant system for "impoverishing the soil" and imperiling the commercial prospects of Memphis. One member declared that black tenants were a "thorn in the commercial kidney of the valley," while another claimed that "impoverishment of the land" was due to "the eating up nature of the negro cultivation of soil." He concluded that "the labor that will make this country great must be accumulative labor," noting that black labor "is not that sort of labor that was calculated to build up the South." Only "white labor was accumulative." As a result, chamber officials concluded that "it becomes our imperative duty to look after our roads out West" in order to provide a path for potential immigrants.[50]

Improved methods of farming were also used to stigmatize the efforts of black tenants to ensure a greater measure of social control over them. Perhaps the most honest assessment of how agricultural reforms would help ensure a ready supply of black laborers came from Jonathan Miller, a South Carolina planter who argued that diversification would maintain white supremacy. He complained in 1875 that planters "are not adopting such measures as are calculated to make us independent." He suggested that planters, despite their overreliance on cotton, could become more independent if they "raise [their] own grain and forage, stock, milk and butter, mutton and bacon, make more manure, and buy less of the fertilizers, make [their] lands better, homes more comfortable, farm more and plant less." Black labor was a key part of Miller's vision, and he concluded, "More farming and less cotton culture will make the negro more dependent upon us and more tractable."[51] Even three decades later, planters were using permanence as a yardstick to make laborers more "dependent." While explaining how to farm in a more businesslike manner, W. B. Mercier, a planter from Centreville, Mississippi, claimed that labor problems "can be partially met, and perhaps successfully so, by substituting crops that can be grown and harvested by the use of improved machinery, and turning out more of our thin lands to pastures for growing more stock." He linked this strategy to labor control by arguing that "the peaceable and successful employment of the negro as our only farm help will soon be a thing of the past unless some more stringent laws for his management and control can be devised."[52] For decades, arguments like these supported strengthening crop lien laws, justified withholding necessary supplies for cultivation from tenants, and allowed planters to avoid blame for rural poverty and agricultural stagnation by placing blame on their tenants—not on the destructive system of staple crop cultivation. Value judgments about the inability of black farmers to farm correctly were not simply a way to stigmatize African Americans, then. They instead served a deeper racial and developmental purpose, maintaining the racial hierarchy and ensuring a steady supply of docile and cheap laborers.[53]

⁂

Reformers and boosters talked a big game when it came to diversification, but they faced an entrenched opposition from landlords and merchants. It was clear early on that cotton was not going away quickly. Even before the war ended, army officers, speculators, Treasury officials, white southerners, and northern investors had stymied efforts to distribute land to freedpeople in the South Carolina Sea Islands and—in a pattern that was repeated throughout the region—bought up plantations to continue the commercial cultivation of staple crops, especially cotton. With the failure of land distribution, the Freedmen's Bureau turned to overseeing labor contracts between freedpeople and planters for plantation labor, prioritizing commercial uses of agricultural lands and hastening the postbellum growth of the staple crop economy.[54]

Diversification did make headway in pockets of the region, but even by the late nineteenth century it was clear that cotton was too engrained to be quickly changed. Few planters had the capital to make an abrupt change in their method of farming, and there was a steep learning curve to growing unfamiliar crops. Diversification was made more risky by the credit system in the South, where cotton and other staples stood in for cash and merchants would not advance credit needed to purchase essential goods on any other basis. Crossroads merchants and planters dictated what tenants could grow, almost always choosing staples like cotton and tobacco, which limited their options even if diversification was compelling. Even the boll weevil, which scoured cotton fields in the twentieth century—an insect that planters incorrectly claimed had forced them to diversify—could not shake reliance on King Cotton.[55] In the late 1920s the South was producing almost fourteen and a half million bales of cotton, an increase of more than ten million bales from 1870.[56] The expansion of railroads and commercial fertilizers, the system of credit, and the financial interests of public officials, businesspeople, and merchants more firmly cemented the staple's place in the region's economy.[57] Complaints about cotton's monopoly continued into the twentieth century and were intensified by consistently declining prices for cotton and recurring hopes for agricultural permanence. George Tindall even calls the "diversification campaign" a "perennial Southern growth," while Gilbert Fite claims that by the twentieth century diversification "had become little short of a religion."[58] But by the twentieth century the repeated failures of four decades of advocacy made it clear that environmental permanence would have to come another way.

༺༻

The expansion of cotton cultivation did not signal that southerners had abandoned efforts to find long-term ways of farming, just that they were turning to less dramatic methods of achieving permanence. In 1880 the Census Bureau commissioned Eugene Hilgard to prepare a comprehensive report on cotton cultivation in the United States. Despite the failure of most diversification campaigns, Hilgard surprisingly noted that North and South Carolina "have been the first to place cotton culture upon a permanent foundation by adopting a system of regular returns to the soil." This remarkable change was due not to growing less cotton but to artificial means of fertilizing fields. Hilgard chalked up the permanence of cotton to "the use of fertilizers, and, with it, better methods of culture." He suggested that the better production per acre seen in the Carolinas compared to more western states proved that fertilizer could lead to permanence on even the most degraded lands.[59] As Hilgard's comments suggest, the failures of diversification changed the terms of debate about long-term uses of soils, cementing a shift from radical solutions that could have entirely changed the direction of the region's economy to solutions that required less sacrifice. By the late nineteenth century, diversification had mostly been eclipsed by other methods of promoting improved soils within the bounds of staple crop cultivation, which signaled that other options were becoming popular as southerners considered the best route to permanence.

As the South entered the twentieth century, then, debates over permanence were increasingly manifested in conflicts over how to soften the effects of staple crop agriculture while still growing staple crops. Agricultural reformers preached the gospel of diversification at the same time that they promoted other reforms that ensured that staple crops would continue to play an important role. Reformers like David Dickson and Farish Furman conducted experiments on fertilization on their farms, and newspapers publicized their results. Agricultural societies gave planters a forum to discuss agricultural improvements, methods of fertilization, and agricultural techniques. Farm journals published articles from practical farmers and scientists at new agricultural schools. In the 1870s and 1880s, states organized experiment and demonstration farms, which studied the best methods of farming and provided concrete examples for farmers to emulate. Even corporations got into the mix. Railroad companies hoping to increase their freight were active in promoting agricultural reform, and larger companies hired agricultural experts and established corporate demonstration and experiment farms.⁶⁰ By 1900 groups of planters, agricultural writers, railroad agents, scientists, public officials, and businesspeople were all debating new methods to stem the loss of soil fertility and erosion while maintaining staple crop culture.

The most divergent visions revolved around restoring soil fertility, especially with commercial fertilizers. In the 1850s planters in the Southeast had used Peruvian guano or chemical fertilizers like superphosphate to maintain fertility on their plantations. Fertilizers were too expensive to ever be universal, however, and southern planters relied on the system of "shifting cultivation," which maintained fertility through land rotation.⁶¹ Fertilizer use spiked in the aftermath of the Civil War as planters and croppers desperately tried to increase crop yields in a worsening market.⁶² This was largely due to a southward shift in the manufacture of fertilizers as new phosphate deposits were discovered in coastal South Carolina and Florida in the late 1860s and railroad expansion connected farmers with markets for fertilizer and crops. Phosphates provided the raw materials for fertilizer manufacturing within the South, and the prevailing systems of credit from crossroads merchants provided farmers with the means to buy fertilizers even if they did not have ready cash.⁶³ It seemed like the South had all it needed to make its farms prosperous once again.

After the Civil War, planters turned to these readily available commercial fertilizers to restore soil fertility. For many planters, it seemed foolish not to use commercial fertilizers. Roger Ransom and Richard Sutch note that fertilizer use was logical because "to the sharecropper, expenditures on fertilizer brought immediate returns commensurate with the costs," while landlords found that "fertilizer not only increased the current output, but had the additional advantage of forestalling the depreciation of the farm." By 1891 planters in the Cotton Belt alone were using more than half a million tons annually—an eleven-fold increase since 1875. This made southerners the biggest consumers of commercial fertilizers in the nation, and planters spent almost five times as much per acre on commercial fertilizers as the rest of the country.⁶⁴

Commercial fertilizers were popular because they promised to make long-term cultivation of staple crops possible without painful crop reductions or radical changes to established modes of farming. The phosphate-based fertilizers popular in the Southeast provided soils with depleted or scarce nutrients that dramatically boosted crop yields—usually between 25 and 60 percent—and made it seem like fertilizers would make permanent uses of the South's soils possible.⁶⁵ After French chemist Georges Ville popularized the idea in 1870 that there could be a "complete fertilizer"—one that contained enough of the ammonia, phosphorus, and potash that crops removed from the soil to prevent soils from ever declining—southerners experimented with a range of chemical compounds.⁶⁶ The very notion that there could be a "complete fertilizer" implied that continuous cultivation was possible with just the right chemical mix, and state officials, university scientists, planters, and extension agents scrambled for a formula that would allow soils to be in permanent use.

Fertilizer manufacturers themselves argued that their products were the secret to perpetual cultivation. Atlanta's Swift Fertilizer Works sent a circular to planters on letterhead that simply promised, "Swift's Fertilizers are soil builders."⁶⁷ The New York–based German Kali Works posted an advertisement in North Carolina's *Progressive Farmer* in 1896 telling readers to buy its products because "more potash in the fertilizers applied on the farm means larger and better yields of crops, permanent improvement of the soil and More Money in the farmer's pocket."⁶⁸ Powell Fertilizer and Chemical Company of Baltimore advertised a fertilizer made by combining its "prepared chemicals" with farm wastes like "Ashes, Hen Droppings, Wood's Earth." This would produce a compound "rich in Ammonia, Potash and Phosphoric Acid, which will be quick acting, producing large crops and at the same time permanently improve the soil"—all for only twelve dollars per ton.⁶⁹ The Florida-based Lakeland Phosphate Company advertised a phosphate-based fertilizer that it called NATURSOWN by telling planters that "its use with the right crops and proper cultural methods, not only increases yields, but adds to the permanent soil fertility," and concluded that it was "the kind of soil medicine that a good doctor gives his patients as a tonic."⁷⁰

A volume published during World War I by Richmond's Virginia-Carolina Chemical Company made the most complete link between fertilizers and permanence. Entitled *Making Soil and Crops Pay More*, the volume was an advertisement for the company's products in the guise of a farming manual. The overriding theme was that permanent soil fertility was possible through the chemical adulteration of soils, which could provide "unlimited wealth" if used properly. The book quoted a western soil scientist to explain, "The problem of the past was production; our problem today is *productiveness with permanency*," while the authors themselves noted that keeping soils supplied with nutrients was the key to ensuring "permanent fertility." Permanence was more than just a buzzword, however, and they even used it to define the ideal type of agriculture. As the authors explained, "A system by which the available plant-food is indefinitely maintained is the permanent system of Agriculture."⁷¹

Permanent agriculture was dependent upon commercial fertilizers, and the company made the case that fertilizers did not harm the land and would add to long-term soil fertility. Because manure did not contain enough of the "mineral substances which all plants demand" to make it effective on its own, the authors argued that it should be combined with a system of chemical fertilization. They included detailed descriptions of the chemical composition of different soils, the biological processes affecting plant growth, testimonies from farmers and businesspeople on the benefits of chemical fertilization, excerpts from extension bulletins, and detailed descriptions of how to apply fertilizers. The goal, however, was to make the case that commercial fertilizers could lead to soil permanence. As Dr. Bradford Knapp, son of famed extension agent Seaman Knapp and the head of USDA extension work in the South, explained, "The wise and judicious use" of commercial fertilizers was necessary for "profitable farming." Echoing Gifford Pinchot, Knapp predicted that farmers would eventually find ways of using fertilizers that would "bring the best results in the long run," and he concluded that "a complete cropping system which aids in building up the soil fertility, coupled with the wisest and best use of Commercial Fertilizers will, in the end, be the system of Agriculture which will last longer and be the most permanently profitable."[72]

Southern promoters of fertilizers were far ahead of the federal government, which did not officially acknowledge that soils were exhaustible until the twentieth century. As we have already seen, Milton Whitney, head of the Bureau of Soils, rejected the findings of chemist Justus von Liebig, who in the 1840s concluded that cultivation of crops removed chemical nutrients, although he believed these nutrients could be replaced with man-made compounds. Whitney concluded that fertility was a product of the texture of soils rather than of their chemical composition, leading him to argue that Americans did not have to worry about the "danger of permanent loss of fertility of our soils through loss of mineral plant-food constituents" from farming.[73] Whitney's views were controversial even at the time, and southern farmers especially rejected them—even if those farmers did not know they were doing so—when they embraced commercial fertilizers that promised to chemically augment soils to make continuous cultivation possible.

Commercial fertilizers were never the magic solution to soil depletion that promoters claimed, but it was difficult for farmers to see all this slick advertising and not start to believe that fertilizers could lead to permanence. The evidence, in fact, was all around them. In the first two decades after the Civil War, farmers were often warranted in using commercial fertilizers to keep up soil fertility. Fertilizers increased yields—even on worn-out fields in the Southeast—and brought new land into cultivation without requiring the cotton, corn, and cowpea rotation that antebellum planters had adopted in the 1840s and 1850s. Commercial fertilizers also allowed fields that were otherwise worthless for farming to be brought into cultivation, proving that expansion was possible despite declining soils. No one was more confident than Henry Grady, who claimed that fertilizers were enabling the growth of the cotton kingdom. In 1881 he noted that increases in the cotton crop were due to fertilizers and described "millions of acres of land, formerly thought to be beyond the possible limit of the cotton belt," that "have been made the best of cotton lands by being artificially enriched."[74] Grady was right: commercial fertilizers did expand the boundaries of staple crops. In the wiregrass region of Georgia, the mania for commercial fertilizers in the 1870s and 1880s extended cotton cultivation even into the sandy soil of the piney woods, shifting the economic focus from subsistence to market activity.[75] Commercial cotton production also pushed into upstate North and South Carolina. These regions had been dominated by yeomen growing crops for subsistence before the Civil War, but they were connected to markets and fertilizer after the war by rail, extending cotton cultivation "to the very foot of the Blue Ridge."[76] Commercial fertilizers also allowed farmers to boost fertility on sandy or poor soils in coastal Florida, Georgia, and the Carolinas enough to grow truck crops like watermelons, strawberries, and tomatoes that could be profitably shipped to northern markets on express trains.[77] Commercial fertilizers were a way for farmers to simply purchase permanence, and they surpassed environmental limits in ways that made them seem ideal for a developing region. By the turn of the twentieth century, fertilizer was an accepted means of achieving environmental permanence in much of the rural South, and its success muted diversification and other potential paths.

Landlords also found that they could wield commercial fertilizers to exercise power over tenants and sharecroppers. White planters were hesitant to put fertilizers in the hands of their tenants both because they thought tenants would use fertilizers incorrectly and because they feared that tenants might be able to use fertilizers to produce a good crop and pay off all their debts.[78] Ned Cobb, a black tenant farmer in Alabama, explained in the early 1900s that his landlords would typically "furnish me the amount of fertilize [sic] they wanted regardless to what I wanted." After producing just two bales of cotton for an entire season's effort in 1907, Cobb described how his white landlords framed commercial fertilizer as a question of risk, rather than social control, by explaining, "Can't take too much risk." On another occasion, a white landowner even convinced local fertilizer dealers not to sell to Cobb in order to force him into signing a labor contract.[79]

While Cobb chafed at white oversight and the difficulty of obtaining supplies, he—like many sharecroppers and tenant farmers—shared a faith in commercial fertilizers as a path to permanence. In 1907 Cobb explained to his landlord that the 2,200 pounds of fertilizer he supplied were only half as much as Cobb needed for a profitable crop. He commented, "I knowed I oughta use more fertilize to make a better crop—if you puts nothing in you gets nothing, all the way through." Cobb explained, "If you don't put down the fertilize that crop aint goin to prosper." The difficulty for tenant farmers like Cobb was that labor contracts gave them little say over how their soils were worked, even if they wanted to do more. Cobb rejected the idea that soil depletion was caused by the carelessness of tenants, noting that he "had to do what the white man said, living here in this country. And if you make enough to pay him, that was all he cared for. . . . That crop out there goin to prosper enough for him to get his and get what I owe him; he's making a profit but he aint goin to let me rise." "If he'd treat me right and treat my crop right," Cobb concluded, "I'd make more and he'd get more—and a heap of times he'd get it all!" Cobb summed up his experience, noting that "sorry land" and "scarce fertilize" guaranteed a poor crop.[80] Commercial fertilizers may have been a path to permanence for white planters, but, as Cobb suggests, they allowed planters to exercise greater control over tenants and keep them from this same permanence and prosperity.

☙

Despite the initial success of fertilizers, over time it became clear to some farmers that commercial fertilizers were not an ideal path to permanently fertile soils. Commercial fertilizers may have increased yields for a time, but they did not return nitrogen to the soil. Declining yields led farmers to apply larger quantities of fertilizer to keep producing staple crops, which spawned debt and financial instability.[81] By the 1880s these problems were already becoming evident, and many farmers worried that commercial fertilizers were mortgaging the region's independence for only a temporary boost in soil fertility. These groups sought to limit the use of commercial fertilizers and advocated other ways to farm perpetually.

Clashes over commercial fertilizers nearly always revolved around the extent to which they offered a permanent improvement of land. Even as early as 1870 the North Carolina–based journal the *Reconstructed Farmer* expressed misgivings about commercial fertilizer use and urged local agricultural societies to commission an essay contest on the best methods "to render our lands independent of commercial fertilizers, and at the same time to keep up (or what is better to increase) their productiveness." The paper's editor experimented with planting rye and peas among the rows of ripe cotton just before harvesttime to see what might "renovate land" both "speedily" and "effectively."[82]

Opposition to fertilizers mostly came after their heyday in the 1880s, when it was becoming evident that they were not an ideal long-term solution to declining soil fertility. In fact, early calls for ending the region's reliance on commercial fertilizers were linked to the Populist revolt of the 1890s. As Farmers' Alliance groups multiplied throughout the South, Populist leaders urged their members not to purchase commercial fertilizers—or at least to limit their dependence on them. For Populists, commercial fertilizer manufacturers were simply another corporation hurting American farmers, and they worried about the economic and environmental effects of an overreliance on chemical additives. Leonidas Polk's *Progressive Farmer*—the mouthpiece of the North Carolina Farmers' Alliance—took the state's governor to task in 1887 after he explained that North Carolina's soils that had been depleted by "slave labor *demanded strong and stimulating fertilizers*," an argument he used to justify spending money on a new experiment station. The *Progressive Farmer* explained that his solution had been "exploded by the most practical and successful agriculturalists" and lamented that this "delusive idea" had already led "thousands of our farmers . . . to their ruin." To show the folly of fertilizers, the paper compared poor soils to a tired and hungry man and asked, "Should we give him plenty of good nourishing food or should he have a stimulating drink of whiskey?" The author concluded, "As well might we expect to satiate his hunger and restore his strength with the whiskey as to give strength and vigor to exhausted soils by the use of 'strong and stimulating fertilizers.'"[83] Other Alliance groups also expressed concerns about the financial and environmental effects of commercial fertilizers and sought to use the organizational machinery of the Alliance to fix these problems. In 1892 members of the local chapter of the Farmers' Alliance in Washington County, Georgia, resolved: "[We will] bind ourselves in the most sacred manner that we will not plant one acre of cotton until we have made ample provision for all necessary feed crops, and that even then we will not buy commercial fertilizer to make cotton with, unless we can do so with a cotton option at a fair price."[84] Efforts to reduce the acreage of cotton in South Carolina were defeated, but representatives to a statewide meeting of Alliancemen also resolved to "use as little commercial fertilizer as possible," and one newspaper reported that "several speeches were made favoring its total disuse."[85]

Alliance leaders opposed chemical fertilizers because they distrusted fertilizer manufacturers, and their efforts to distance farmers from fertilizer manufacturers was always part of their general distrust of large corporations. Yet there is evidence that they were also influenced by arguments about how cotton monoculture and fertilizer use would affect soils. The Farmers' Alliance and popular rural cooperatives like the Agricultural Wheel and the Grange that had preceded it all promoted "scientific" methods of farming as a key part of their vision for how to reform exploitative agricultural and economic structures.[86] In fact, many of the most outspoken agricultural leaders—notably, North Carolina's Leonidas L. Polk and Alabama's Reuben Kolb—came from the ranks of agricultural reformers and had experimented with different ways to increase the fertility of their own farms. Their knowledge of improved methods of cultivation played a key role in raising their profile among their fellow farmers and positioning them to take the reins of organizations like the Grange and the Farmers' Alliance.[87]

There was opposition from Alliance leaders who worked to limit members' dependence on commercial fertilizers, but Alliance members could also be of a more divided mind. In some cases, Alliancemen provided strong support for fertilizer use, as long as it was on their terms. In 1890 and 1891 the Alabama Farmers' Alliance partnered with the experiment station of the Agricultural and Mechanical College at Auburn to sponsor tests of fertilizer efficiency on the farms of thirty Alliancemen in order to "learn what fertilizer the ordinary cultivated lands of the section need." They provided each farmer with free samples for fifteen tests, as well as all instructions.[88] In North Carolina, members could buy commercial fertilizers directly from an Alliance official who obtained large quantities from manufacturers at a reduced cost, saving farmers between 10 and 50 percent per ton.[89] At a July 1891 meeting of the South Carolina Farmers' Alliance, representatives from each county voted on an acceptable formula for an "Alliance fertilizer" that would be manufactured and sold to members. The fertilizer's composition—"four per cent. of ammonia, nine per cent. of phosphoric acid and two per cent. of potash"—mimicked common commercial products.[90] Like members of the South Carolina Alliance, other Alliancemen supported the continued use of commercial fertilizers by testing the best-suited fertilizers for their areas, distributing fertilizers to their members, and even developing Alliance-owned fertilizer manufactories that freed small farmers from the tyranny of manufacturers, but not the tyranny of fertilizers.[91]

The Alliance was not always convinced of the problematic effects of fertilizers, but for decades prominent agricultural writers criticized the South's dependence on commercial fertilizers in agricultural manuals and guides and argued that fertilizers were bad for the long-term health of soils. An 1890 volume billed as the first agricultural book written from a "Southern standpoint" declared, "The experience of farmers with artificial fertilizers since the war ought to be sufficient to open their eyes to the folly of such a system of farming" and "the necessity of adopting a different one." The authors compared planters to merchants, who needed to increase "capital . . . in proportion with [their] annual amount of sales." Obtaining higher yields was important, but farmers needed to make investments in land, "the capital of the farmer," to bring about "evident improvement, or increase, in the productiveness of land each succeeding year." The authors urged farmers to adopt a system that "will obviate the outlay of so large an amount of money, and will, while it yields a good return in crops, give 'permanent' improvement to the land."[92] Textile magnate Daniel A.

Tompkins made his fortune spinning cotton grown by fertilizers into thread, but even he worried that commercial fertilizers were not ideal. In a 1901 volume on the cotton industries, he claimed that "under a proper system of agriculture it should not be necessary to rely to such a great extent upon the mines and chemical works for restoring fertility to the soils, in return for the drafts made upon it by humanity."[93] In another popular volume on cotton cultivation published in 1906, authors Charles Burkett and Clarence Poe declared that "there is no such thing as worn-out cotton soils." Worn-out soils were simply poorly managed. Burkett and Poe concluded that adding "nitrogen, phosphorous and potassium in chemical forms is only a temporary arrangement to make better crops for the time being." "No permanent improvement of the soil" could occur "unless tillage and an abundant amount of humus become the basis of such improvement," and they concluded that commercial fertilizers should only be used as "supplementary helps."[94] Despite these statements, by the first decade of the twentieth century it was difficult to find many other people who were not enamored with fertilizer. South Carolina's commissioner of agriculture lamented in 1913 that "soils are being treated today as if conditions of soil exist as they did when the use of commercial fertilizers was first introduced," even though "continual use has rendered them acid to a high degree." It was necessary to "take some decisive action towards stopping this great expenditure and financial drain upon the farm and inevitable ultimate exhaustion of the soil."[95] Although there was still widespread enthusiasm for fertilizers, by the twentieth century vocal groups of reformers, planters, and agricultural experts were arguing that commercial fertilizers were not ideal because they prolonged an exploitative staple crop economy, increased fertility only temporarily while undermining the long-term value of the soil, and made farmers dependent on fertilizer manufacturers.

By the twentieth century, George Washington Carver had also toned down his enthusiasm for commercial fertilizers. The experiment station at Tuskegee—like most others in the South—was funded in part by a tax on fertilizer sales, but Carver had realized that chemical fertilizers designed to increase yields of staple crops offered little for Alabama's black farmers. The financial consequences of a fertilizer addiction could be ruinous for farmers with little capital. Although he initially tested fertilizers and provided farmers with guidance about how fertilizers should be used, after 1900 he focused his experiments on organic methods of maintaining fertility, including crop rotation, growing legumes, manuring, and new methods of plowing. In a bulletin from the Tuskegee Experiment Station in 1908, one of Carver's colleagues counseled farmers not to take "the lazy way of improving, not the fertility of their land, but the yield of the current season's crop, by the application of inferior ready mixed commercial fertilizers."⁹⁶ In another bulletin, Carver advised farmers in Macon County, Alabama, to "never lose sight of the fact that nothing will build up soil as quickly and permanently as barnyard manure" and urged them to "save as much as possible."⁹⁷ By 1903 Carver had settled on compost as the most practical way for black farmers to maintain soil fertility without being indebted to merchants, landlords, and fertilizer agents. Unlike barnyard manure, which required livestock, composts that could be found in nature were within the reach of even the most indebted sharecroppers. Composting required near-constant labor, but Carver urged black farmers to find decaying materials that could be used to enrich the humus of their soils. In 1911 he wrote that Tuskegee needed to do more to utilize wasted materials that were at hand instead of relying on chemical fertilizers and concluded, "We should look to the permanent building up of our soils." "We know that commercial fertilizers will stimulate and for a while produce good results," but he predicted that "by and by a collapse will come."⁹⁸ For a while Carver's program dictated the research and extension work at Tuskegee. Within a few years, however, it was replaced by what Mark Hersey calls a "more conventional" program of agricultural reform under extension agent Thomas Campbell—a program that made commercial fertilizer again into a silver bullet for permanence.⁹⁹

Like Carver, the concerns of agricultural reformers went deeper than simply the environmental effects of commercial fertilizers. There was a sense that chemical adulteration of soils fostered a dangerously short-sighted way of viewing the region's lands. Reformers cast the choice to use fertilizers in moral terms. In many cases, this reflected the social and racial anxieties of white southern planters as they worked to secure a stable labor supply. Testifying before a congressional committee in 1900, Harry Hammond of South Carolina claimed that "the use of fertilizers tends to make the farmer more shiftless and less careful in saving, and in the cultivation of his land," while an article appearing in the *Southern Planter* that same year announced that "there is no method of so using land, even though supplemented with heavy fertilization, which will not in the long run ruin the land for crop production and make of its owner a poor man." This was "contrary to all the laws of nature and science."¹⁰⁰ Tom Watson's *Jeffersonian* urged southern farmers to stop land robbing and start land building. Planters were losing millions of dollars annually in their use of commercial fertilizers, chiefly from planters' "failure to apply [fertilizers] to the right crops and the right soils and in the right proportions." The paper did not advocate buying less fertilizer but claimed that commercial fertilizers would only be effective in combination with homemade manures and legumes and concluded that "without these to give life and body to our soils, commercial fertilizers are a mere expedient and makeshift, merely postponing the certain day of gullied waste and exhaustion."¹⁰¹ Using commercial fertilizers, then, was not simply a practice that degraded land over time. Reformers argued that fertilizers symbolized a general lack of care about land use and cultivation, which undermined farmers' ability to permanently use their soils.

☙

To counter the sway of commercial fertilizers, reformers promoted other methods of scientific cultivation, though there was no consensus about how to achieve permanence without fertilizers. The merits of terracing, crop rotation, the use of organic manures and marls, and a number of other techniques for improving fertility and preventing erosion were endlessly evaluated in the pages of agricultural periodicals and newspapers, at the meetings of agricultural societies, and on experiment farms. As planters, public officials, reformers, merchants, and others clashed over the best ways to make the rural South permanently prosperous, new groups also became players in southern agriculture. Perhaps most significant was the federal government, which paved the way for agricultural colleges in the region after 1862 and funded a series of university-affiliated agricultural experiment stations after 1887. In 1902 the U.S. Department of Agriculture appointed Seaman Knapp as a demonstration agent for the southern states. Knapp's successful demonstration work in Louisiana's rice fields in the 1880s showed federal officials that he was effective at teaching new techniques of agriculture to farmers. As a demonstration agent, Knapp established a regional network of private demonstration farms, where a few local farmers in each community were taught improved methods of cultivation. In just a decade Knapp recruited one hundred thousand farmers to demonstrate new methods on their own farms, providing farmers throughout the region with concrete examples of agricultural reforms.¹⁰² Officials from the Department of Agriculture also published a flurry of bulletins directed at southern farmers on topics ranging from how to head off the boll weevil to "common errors in cotton production."¹⁰³ In one 1913 bulletin on "intensive farming in the Cotton Belt," a USDA agent used the techniques of an African American farmer as evidence that giving soils "more organic matter" was "fundamental to permanent agriculture everywhere."¹⁰⁴ The efforts of federal reformers culminated in the passage of the Smith-Lever Act in 1914, which provided congressional funding for state agricultural extension programs. It should be no surprise that the authors of this bill, Hoke Smith and A. F. Lever, were native southerners. Their support for agricultural extension reflected their awareness of the continued challenges facing southern farms and the persistent struggle for agricultural improvement and permanence in the rural South.¹⁰⁵

Even as federal officials became more involved in promoting permanence, they worked with reformers and businesspeople in the region to reimagine new ways of achieving long-term uses of soils. Bradford Knapp, the head of all federal extension work in the South, advocated a system that he termed "safe farming" in 1915. Knapp decried the prevailing one-crop system because it was always subject to market fluctuations, did not promote raising livestock or using "waste lands," made inefficient use of labor, only paid off one time each year, kept people impoverished with an uncertain future, and did "not provide for the maintenance of soil fertility." "Safe farming," a concept initially developed by Texas cottonseed supplier R. L. Bennett, addressed these issues by taking farmers back to a system akin to the safety-first agriculture that had dominated yeoman areas before the Civil War. Knapp and Bennett advocated primarily producing products that were needed to support life on the farm by keeping up a garden and raising livestock, especially by growing "winter and summer legumes, which not only produce hay but also enrich the soil." Only after cultivating products for subsistence should farmers grow staples like cotton, tobacco, or rice. Knapp realized that this would be a difficult program to put in place and urged bankers and merchants to weigh how closely farmers and tenants were following this path before extending any credit.[106]

In the 1920s the Central of Georgia Railway promoted its own path, which it called "redintegration," and it was more successful than "safe farming." Redintegration was the brainchild of Jesse Frisbie Jackson, an outspoken New South booster who had served as agricultural agent for the railroad for more than a decade. The railway ran through major agricultural districts in Georgia, and the company had long tried to "help the farmer get off the all-cotton plan" in order to provide a more regular freight. To this end, the company established test farms to experiment with new methods of farming, organized children's crop and livestock clubs, connected farmers to purebred livestock dealers, established test pastures for demonstrating the profitability of livestock, and held contests promoting scientific stock raising and cultivation.[107] By the 1920s the company had put significant resources into redintegration, which simply meant growing legumes like beans and peas in winter and plowing them under in spring to provide nitrogen and other nutrients to soils. Jackson explained that this "will enable us to make such deposits as will not only restore, but even increase the amount of our original soil fertility balance." He concluded that "soil conservation, preservation, restoration, rejuvenation, improvement, and rebuilding" all together could not "so fully describe the process we are talking about, as if you had said Redintegration." Decades later he even wrote to conservationist Russell Lord, suggesting the word "redintegration" as the ideal substitute for conservation—one that satisfied Lord's search for a word "more active and hopeful than 'conservation' when we speak of regenerating soil, water sources, forests, livestock, wildlife, people and all the renewing sources of life."[108]

Jackson and other agents toured the company's lines in Alabama and Georgia, met with farmers, conducted redintegration demonstrations, and even showed movies illustrating redintegration. The company also partnered with agricultural colleges to underwrite half the cost of redintegration plots to find the ideal winter legumes for each county that the railroad ran through. The Central of Georgia made a lot of headway promoting redintegration, at least until the Great Depression, and between 1924 and 1928 the amount of seed purchased for winter legumes in the areas serviced by the railroad increased from 10,000 pounds to 1.6 million pounds.[109]

Even with the success of redintegration, perhaps no solution to limiting commercial fertilizers was as popular, or contested, as cottonseed. Cottonseed contains nitrogen, potash, phosphoric acid, and other nutrients found in soil, and for decades antebellum planters would feed it to livestock or spread it on fallow fields to restore soil fertility.[110] Just after the Civil War a newspaper in Georgia commented that "there are few manures surpassing that which we formerly had in some abundance, viz: cotton-seed," and a merchant later explained that cottonseed was "one of the best fertilizers we have."[111] By the 1880s, however, this use of cottonseed as fertilizer was threatened by demand from manufacturers who were using it to make a low-grade oil. The seeds of short-staple cotton contain trace amounts of oil, and the rising price of compound lard and vegetable shortening in the 1870s and 1880s made cottonseed, which could be used to manufacture these products as well as cooking oil, more valuable. Because of the high cost of transportation, the South's poor railroad facilities, and the tendency of cottonseed to deteriorate, mills had to be built close to cotton fields or railroad depots, where manufacturers could secure seed from farmers, ginners, or seed agents.[112]

The cottonseed oil industry turned previously "wasted" raw materials into valuable products, and boosters lauded it as a quintessential example of permanence through efficient use.[113] In 1882, for example, the *Atlanta Constitution* argued that "it is clearly a waste to bury this vast treasure in the earth or in the bellies of cattle when it does no good in either place," while another observer claimed that the industry illustrated the maxim that the "chief profit of Northern industries consists in saving the waste, and this must ultimately be the profit of Southern industry likewise."[114] Cottonseed oil manufacturing offered other benefits. Luther Ransom, one of its most ardent proponents, claimed that farmers had "no outlet for seed that gives them such value as the

Cottonseed being unloaded at a Mississippi railroad station sometime in the 1880s. As the cottonseed oil manufacturing industry expanded in the South in the 1870s and 1880s, selling cottonseed to manufacturers provided southern farmers with a new way to earn cash. But it required abandoning a time-honored method for maintaining soil fertility without using commercial fertilizers, touching off debates about the best ways to maintain the fertility of southern soils for continuous cultivation.
CREDIT: William Henry Jackson. Library of Congress, Prints & Photographs Division, Detroit Publishing Company Collection, LC-DIG-det-4a27011.

oil mills."[115] Boosters like Ransom sought to quell fears about industrialization by using this "home industry" to prove that manufacturing was symbiotic with agriculture. Because oil manufacturing gave value to wasted resources and provided ready cash to struggling farmers, promoters believed that farmers would be just as enthusiastic.

As the industry expanded in the 1870s and 1880s, however, farmers loudly protested selling their cottonseed to oil mills. They argued that their long-term interests were better served by using cottonseed for fertilizer. Even as early as 1863, one Charlestonian claimed that the slow development of the industry was due in part to "the great value of the seed as a manure," which caused most planters to be "indifferent" to selling seed to oil mills. By the 1870s "indifference" had become outright hostility throughout much of the Cotton Belt.[116] An 1872 article in *Southern Farm and Home* claimed that "we have long deprecated the exportation of cotton seed from the South, as a ruinous waste of the essence of the fertility of our lands," and argued that this was "selling [the soil's] productive power, and getting nothing, or next to nothing for it."[117] Eugene Hilgard similarly argued that "the soil ingredients are our capital, and it is this we sell, at a mere nominal value, in selling our cotton-seed," and he urged the South's farmers to "return their cotton-seed religiously to the soil on which it grew."[118] One South Carolinian took aim at industry advocates, claiming that "our cotton oil mills and chemists tell us that the oil in seed is of no value as a fertilizer, and that it is a loss to put it on land, but it is cheaper for the farmer to lose the oil at home than it is to haul it off to the mills and give it away."[119]

Profit potential was always important in deciding whether or not to participate in cottonseed oil production, but opponents of the industry altered profit-and-loss calculations to include soil fertility. In 1900 G. H. Turner, a farmer from Lafayette County, Mississippi, estimated the value of cottonseed to the average cotton farmer using a calculus far different from the one used by industry boosters. Rather than focusing on the direct profits realized from selling seed to mills, he calculated the dollar value of nutrients that were lost when cottonseed was sold away. The annual crop of cottonseed contained nitrogen, phosphoric acid, and potash worth around $48,356,000 "for enriching the soil," and Turner concluded that "when restitution instead of spoliation shall be the order of the day" the South would achieve great gains.[120] This was a radical redefinition of profit from industry boosters, but Turner was only suggesting that cottonseed was important as a way to maintain soil fertility even beyond cottonseed's cash value. It was difficult for any southern farmer to turn down cash, and Turner's environmental calculus suggests something remarkable: southern planters did not always favor immediate payouts over long-term solutions that had the potential to maintain the productive power of soils.

In the 1890s the opposition to selling cottonseed to oil mills was given momentum by the Farmers' Alliance. Alliance distrust of the practice varied by locale and was at least partially based on the perception that the cottonseed industry was controlled by powerful trusts. Yet evidence suggests that it was also intertwined with the concerns of farmers about declining soil fertility. At a national meeting of the Farmers' Alliance and Agricultural Wheel in Birmingham in 1889, delegates adopted a resolution calling for farmers not to sell their cottonseed unless they could get prices that were above cottonseed's "real agricultural value as fertilizer."[121] Just four years later the Alabama Alliance started a campaign to "stop the sale of cottonseed" to oil mills. One newspaper reported that this campaign was "based on the idea that the removal of the seed impoverishes the soil and will ultimately render the land sterile and valueless." Some farmers "refused to abide by the agreement," but similar attempts were made by local Farmers' Alliance groups throughout the Cotton Belt.[122] The struggle of the Farmers' Alliance provides a good illustration of the divided mind about the cottonseed oil industry, however. Despite concern about the loss of this organic fertilizer, some Alliance groups actually constructed their own oil mills, suggesting that they had few qualms about cottonseed oil production as long as it occurred on their terms.[123] In 1890 southern Alliancemen even provided staunch opposition to congressional attempts to regulate oleomargarine, believing that it would stunt the southern cottonseed oil industry by favoring northern dairy interests.[124]

As concerns about cottonseed oil mills spread, a substantial number of farmers decided that it was not in their best interests to sell their seed to the mills. Planters and tenants often continued using seed as they traditionally had, either through direct application to the soil or for livestock feed. Even as late as 1889 only a quarter of all cottonseed produced was sold to mills. The rest was used on the farm or thrown away.[125] Sales of cottonseed to mills were especially low in the Southeast, where soils had been depleted by more than two centuries of staple crop cultivation.[126] In an 1890 Department of Agriculture report, county agents in the Cotton Belt reported that farmers were not selling cottonseed to oil manufacturers. A report from Georgia noted that farmers "are slow to sell cotton-seed, the majority using it to compost with barn-yard manure and acid phosphate, the best known fertilizer for cotton."[127] Even industry boosters had to admit that farmers were reluctant to sell their seed, and as late as 1904 one promoter observed that the "seed[s] are used directly by farmers for fertilizer in no small quantity." By the turn of the century, sales of cottonseed in the Southeast made up only around 30 percent of all cottonseed produced.[128] Because the industry was reliant on obtaining raw materials from farmers, this threatened the future of cottonseed oil production, and manufacturers increasingly had to turn to cotton ginners and seed agents to obtain raw materials.[129]

Conflicts over cottonseed continued into the twentieth century, but the terms of debate gradually shifted. By the late nineteenth century, scientists were starting to see that nutrients needed for fertilization were still available in cottonseed meal, a by-product of oil production.[130] Oil mills developed a system in which farmers could exchange cottonseed for meal, getting cash for their seed without stripping it of its fertilizing properties. This prevented farmers from having to make a stark choice between selling their seed or returning it to the soil. Cheaper fertilizers also made it more cost-effective to use chemical products, and by 1900 cottonseed was no longer the cheapest option for restoring soil fertility.[131] Cottonseed producers were able to address the concerns of growers enough to allow the industry to expand greatly, and by 1910 the oil industry bought up nearly 80 percent of all cottonseed produced in the country. At its peak in 1915 there were over eight hundred cottonseed oil mills throughout the South processing around four million pounds of cottonseed annually, and cottonseed oil production had become a quintessential New South enterprise.[132]

Cotton had long been used by white merchants to maintain a grip on poor white and black tenant farmers or sharecroppers, but the cottonseed oil industry gave black farmers an important means of independence. Selling cottonseed to oil mills undercut the ability of farmers to maintain soil fertility, but it did provide black farmers with cash. By the 1920s and 1930s sharecropping contracts typically allocated at least part of the cottonseed to croppers, and Oscar Johnson, president of Mississippi's sprawling Delta and Pine Land Company, noted that seed was "the only unmortgaged asset" of sharecroppers and tenant farmers.[133] In the decade after 1923, for instance, sharecroppers were able to sell their cottonseed and make around twenty-five dollars each year, depending on the price of cotton. Despite the ability to leverage cotton into cash, it was generally never enough to offset the debts incurred in sharecropping. Croppers were hamstrung by their lack of access to all the supplies necessary for farming, their inability to effectively maintain soil fertility, and low crop yields and prices. In this way, cottonseed mirrored the central New South dilemma: obtaining short-term cash payouts or selling out land. Some groups could afford to maintain soil fertility by turning down cash, but tenants, who were hemmed in by structural inequalities in the South's social and economic system, rarely had this luxury.[134]

Cottonseed may have reflected the New South preference for waste industries that brought increased efficiency to fields, but it facilitated the production of commercial fertilizers and cotton monoculture, wreaking havoc on soils. Still, debates over cottonseed suggest that even within cotton monoculture, which scholars credit with some of the worst environmental problems of the New South era, attempts were made to implement more permanent methods of using soils for farming. The future of the industry hinged on decisions about whether using cottonseed on the farm or in the mill would be in the long-term interests of the South—choices that were anything but clear. These visions were no doubt myopic, but they show that neither cotton farmers nor oil processors were always willing to have industrial expansion at the price of soil fertility.

ꙮ

Ultimately, redintegration, cottonseed, safe farming, and other proposals for making agriculture more permanent by limiting planters' dependence on commercially available fertilizers lost out to arguments that chemical fertilizers themselves were a permanent solution to the South's rural woes. In 1929 the region consumed more than five and a half million tons of commercial fertilizer—more than 70 percent of all the fertilizer purchased in the nation. The biggest addicts were in the longest-cultivated parts of the Southeast, but by 1929 even states farther west were turning to fertilizer to halt soil decline. In the decade after 1919, for instance, the amount of fertilizers purchased in Texas increased by more than 300 percent.[135] By the second decade of the twentieth century, the rich soils of Mississippi and Louisiana were starting to require regular additions of chemical fertilizers for continuous cultivation—even on business plantations in the Mississippi Delta that centralized production.[136] This boom in fertilizer was due to the unique credit structure of the South, the failure of efforts to reform the systems of tenant farming and sharecropping, and the expansion of railroad lines. Fertilizers also offered a social permanence that gave planters a method to critique the use of the soil by African Americans and justify oversight of their tenants and sharecroppers. What most scholars have missed, however, is that fertilizers provided the easiest path to environmental permanence. Continuous cultivation was possible, at least in theory, simply by applying more fertilizer to the land. Commercial fertilizers required cash or credit and a knowledge of soil fertility, but they did not require reinventing the entire way that southern farmers cultivated the land.

By 1930 it was clear that permanence had succeeded, but not in the way that many reformers had hoped. Southern public officials and planters never let their dream of diversification die, and into the 1930s they struggled to solve the region's problems of staple crop overproduction, even making headway in some parts of the region. Yet farmers' understanding of the best ways to continuously farm their soils was wedded to their use of commercial fertilizers. After decades of struggling over the meaning of permanence and the best ways to achieve it, merchants and fertilizer manufacturers were able to effectively hawk commercial fertilizers as a form of purchased permanence and overcome strategies to limit the use of fertilizer promoted by academics, planters, and reformers. Commercial fertilizers may have promised permanence and the ability to continuously cultivate soils, but they actually kept farmers from making drastic changes to the way that they farmed and inhibited the shift away from a one-crop system. In this sense, Eugene Hilgard was right. By maintaining staple crop monoculture, commercial fertilizers fostered short-sighted methods of cultivation that only looked to boosting the next yield. Permanence through commercial fertilizers proved illusory for chemical reasons as well. Because commercial fertilizers do not return nitrogen to the soil, they undermined the ability of farmers to work their fields continuously and made it more difficult to achieve permanent economic growth.[137]

Although southern farms never became models of permanence, debates about how to bring permanence to southern soils to promote continuous cultivation first made it clear that natural resources were not as inexhaustible as boosters had thought. These debates also put the region well ahead of the rest of the nation. Long before the idea of "permanent agriculture" became popular among federal officials, soil scientists, and conservationists, permanence played a key role in debates over the best forms of economic development for the rural South.[138] Ultimately, the pursuit of environmental permanence on the farm through continuous cultivation contributed to enthusiasm for finding more permanent ways of using other natural resources.

CHAPTER 3

Utilizing Southern Wastes

IN 1926 Robert Griffith, president of the Champion Fibre Company in Canton, North Carolina, penned an article for an Asheville newspaper defending the environmental record of his company's pulp and paper operations. Champion was not a newcomer to the area. It had been an integral part of the economy of western North Carolina since 1905, when the company was organized by industrialist Peter Thompson to supply his Ohio paper mill with the rich timber of the Appalachian region. After acquiring three hundred thousand acres near Asheville, Thompson broke ground on a fiber mill in Canton that would convert Appalachian hardwoods into wood pulp.[1] The company boomed. By 1911 North Carolina's state forester reported that it was "the largest mill of its kind in the South" and had single-handedly established pulp and paper as an important industry in the state.[2]

The expansion of Champion's logging operations brought the company into conflict with other forest stakeholders, and by 1926 Griffith was one of the key players in a clash between industrialists and a coalition of businesspeople, tourist promoters, preservationists, and federal officials over whether the federal government should create a national park in the southern Appalachians.[3] Much of the company's timber fell within the proposed boundaries of the park. Champion depended on these forests for profit—what a guidebook described as "grinding the beauty of the mountains into pulp for paper to print comic Sunday supplements."[4] Griffith's article was an attempt to convince the public that this image of corporate irresponsibility was overblown. As he explained, Champion opposed the park because it would remove valuable natural resources from use and "inevitably handicap" the "future development" of western North Carolina. He lobbied for a national forest, a strategy that would "conserve" Appalachian "attractions for the tourist and industrialist."[5]

It is all too easy to write Griffith off as a stereotypical industrialist with little interest in the natural environment and to write off his defense of paper manufacturing as a thinly veiled plea for keeping forests open to industrial exploitation. Ever since C. Vann Woodward characterized the economy as "colonial," historians have made extractive industries like lumbering, pulp and paper, mining, and naval stores—enterprises that were closely linked to the exploitation of natural resources—emblematic of the New South.[6] Yet Griffith envisioned a different role for extractive industries. He argued that environmental permanence set Champion apart in the southern Appalachians, where logging companies that lived by a "cut and get out" motto were the norm. Griffith contrasted Champion's "efficient" operations with loggers who had no plans for "conducting a permanent industry."[7] Although national park supporters liked to claim that only federal bureaucrats could keep rapacious corporations like Champion in check, Griffith suggested that not all corporations were created equal. He believed that his company would be just as good a steward of North Carolina's resources as federal foresters and urged the public not to judge Champion without understanding the company's long-term vision.

Although Champion relied on forests for raw materials, Griffith outlined how his firm used these resources in more long-term ways than other forest products industries. For one, pulp and paper mills brought efficiency to forests by providing markets for wood that could not be used as timber and had previously gone to waste due to quality or size. The massive investment required to build a pulp mill also meant that companies could not afford to cut out timber and move on. Pulp and paper mills were financially required to treat timber as a renewable resource. As one of the pioneers of industrial forestry in the United States, Champion had poured money into efforts to secure a perpetual supply of timber by hiring foresters and reforesting more than one hundred thousand acres owned by the company. These programs were based on "sound forestry principles" and were, according to Griffith, "evidence of the company's faith in the practice of sound conservation of forest resources." Providing new markets for useless raw materials and reforesting their timberlands were part of the same impulse, and Griffith touted that both demonstrated the company's "expectation of conducting a permanent industry in this location . . . with the purpose of obtaining a continuous supply of raw material."[8]

For Griffith, environmental and economic permanence made pulp and paper—and other similar waste industries—ideal for the entire South. The region's economy was too dependent on lumbering and naval stores, which extracted raw materials and transported them to factories outside the South to be manufactured into finished goods. This provided northern capitalists with profits while diminishing stocks of southern natural resources. Instead of taking the path of extraction—a short-term solution—Griffith suggested that the region's economy could be reimagined to prioritize enterprises like Champion that promoted efficient and renewable uses of natural resources in the South. He urged southerners to pursue industries like pulp and paper that could use wasted or overlooked resources as their raw materials. This would re-

Champion Fibre Company's Mill in Canton, North Carolina, 1910. For southern boosters, pulp and paper mills like Champion Fibre Company exemplified permanence. Because they required large amounts of capital, these firms could not afford the "cut and get out" strategies used by lumber companies, and they invested in forestry to maintain a steady supply of pulpwood. Pulp mills also had the ability to use timber that had previously gone to waste, showing how permanence was linked to the drive for efficiency through the use of wasted materials.
CREDIT: Herbert W. Pelton. Library of Congress, Prints & Photographs Division, LC-USZ62-71827, LC-USZ62-71828.

duce pressure on declining resources, make renewable resources the foundation for growth, provide markets for raw materials that had little value, and attract finished goods manufacturing to the region. Even better, these industries did not require reining in the use of valuable natural resources to keep up stocks of raw material. In short, waste industries promised to maintain economic growth even as communities ran up against their environmental limits. The South may have been past the stage of its development where resource extraction was ideal, but Griffith was hopeful that forest industries would still thrive. He concluded that enterprises like pulp and paper were the best hope for a prosperous South because they created "sound values . . . where none had existed."[9]

For more than six decades, industrialists like Griffith—who pointed to opportunities that did not depend on the short-term extraction of resources—have not fit into the literature on the New South. Yet as public officials looked for solutions to declining natural resources and corporate officials modified business strategies to prolong their stocks of raw materials, they were guided by the ideals of environmental permanence. Their efforts ultimately shaped both corporate strategy and the structure of the South's developing economy into the twentieth century.

One of the earliest and most significant battles over the meaning of permanence played out just after the Civil War, when policy makers in Washington clashed over the fate of forty-seven million acres of federal land in Alabama, Arkansas, Florida, Louisiana, and Mississippi. Providing land for freedpeople was an outgrowth of Republican "free soil" ideology, and radical Republicans in Congress and freedpeople themselves believed that reserving these public lands for homesteads would promote landownership and economic independence. With the sponsorship of Republican congressmen George Julian of Indiana and John Rice of Maine, in June 1866 the Southern Homestead Act opened up public lands in these five states for settlement by homesteaders in parcels of eighty acres, contingent upon swearing a loyalty oath to the United States. Their measure was intended to address the failure of land redistribution efforts, and radical Republicans hoped it would also punish the South for the war, prevent speculation in and hoarding of public lands, allow freedpeople to set up independent homesteads, and demonstrate the viability of free labor in the South. Freedpeople, who had long held out hope for land, hailed the Homestead Act as a guarantee that the federal government would follow through with its wartime promises, and they enthusiastically wrote to federal officials about how to get land.¹⁰

This legislation ran up against white public officials in the South, however, who banked on industrial development as the key to transforming the region. Opposition to the Southern Homestead Act was spearheaded by public officials from the five states involved, and they worked to strike it down as the power of radical Republicans waned in the late 1870s. Their opposition was based on a social calculus as much as an economic one. White public officials opposed the distribution of land to freedpeople because it had the potential to upend the exploitative racial hierarchy. During congressional debate, Hernando DeSoto Money, a former Confederate, postwar planter, and Democratic congressman from Louisiana, made this clear when he argued that the Homestead Act was simply intended to punish "the leading rebels, as they called them," and asked why land "should ... not be secured to the people of all the United States without respect to color." Ignoring the near impossibility of navigating the bureaucratic morass to actually acquire land and the expense of clearing virgin territory, Money argued that the small number of freedpeople who had settled on lands opened by the Homestead Act since 1866 proved that they preferred to stay on plantations. He concluded with a thinly veiled plea for white supremacy and keeping freedpeople as plantation-style laborers, declaring, "We are competent to regulate our own affairs, to speak for our own people, to say what they need."[11] Led by Powell Clayton, a Republican senator from Arkansas, opponents of land distribution rejected the social engineering and outside meddling that they believed were at the heart of the Homestead Act and articulated a vision for public lands based on extraction and industrial development. As one scholar notes, their arguments against the Southern Homestead Act mirrored visions of "the preachers of the New South gospel" and had little room for African American freedpeople—except as low-wage industrial laborers.[12]

These white public officials were staunch proponents of the New South Creed, but they did not believe that this was incompatible with the wise use of natural resources. In congressional debate, opponents of the Homestead Act made the case that industrial development would actually be a more efficient use of natural resources on public lands than subsistence agriculture. For years public officials and even federal agents had complained about the prevalence of illegal timber cutting on these lands.[13] Senator James Alcorn, a Republican from Mississippi, claimed that timber thieves were constantly stealing from public lands, which resulted in "hundreds of acres perhaps ... being denuded each year."[14] As governor of Mississippi, Alcorn had struggled to crack down on thieves who were unabashed in cutting on public lands, and he argued that only private companies had the resources and impetus to protect timber.[15] Repealing the Homestead Act would allow public lands to be sold for their timber and would provide the federal government with cash, "whereas if the present law remains the timber will be taken, the land will be stripped, and will be valueless upon the hands of the Government."[16] Powell Clayton also claimed that selling public lands to corporations would help "prevent the destruction of the timber by fire and otherwise."[17] Clayton did not want to see the South's timber destroyed without purpose, an outcome that clearing land for agriculture would bring on. This timber was "valuable," and "if men purchase these lands they will be interested in protecting the timber" and would take efforts to protect it from forest fires. Repealing the Southern Homestead Act was not intended "to perpetuate or to increase the destruction of timber," in short, but would "give the people of these five States an opportunity to use a limited portion of that timber for useful purposes, and to take care of the rest of it."[18] These arguments were no doubt attempts to deflect criticism that throwing public lands open to industry would hasten the destruction of timber and minerals. Yet they were also a product of frustration at how timber thieves were able to operate with impunity on public lands despite governmental attempts to crack down on this illicit trade. The point that Clayton, Alcorn, and other congressmen were making was not just that industrial uses of public lands were preferable to subsistence agriculture but that corporations were better able to protect natural resources than farmers or government agents because they had substantial financial interests at stake. In effect, these congressmen advocated a kind of corporate permanence that would allow firms to use the resources of public lands while keeping stocks of timber available for the future.

What this stance ignored, however, was that the timber being illegally taken from these public lands was often done at the urging of nearby mills. There were more than sixty-seven thousand official entries for public lands under the Southern Homestead Act, but historian Christie Farnham Pope has found that only 41 percent of the claimed acres were under titled ownership by 1883, suggesting that significant portions of the remaining lands were used only for resource extraction by companies with little need for an official title.[19] Policy makers talked a big game about corporate responsibility, but their visions of industrial permanence were disconnected from established corporate practice in the 1880s. The end of the Southern Homestead Act was not the lesson in efficient use that the bill's opponents claimed. As the nation's commitment to Reconstruction waned in 1876, white public officials from the South stymied the redistribution efforts of radical Republicans and repealed the Homestead Act, throwing public lands of the South onto the market and keeping them out of the hands of freedpeople. Immediately, lumber and mining companies and speculators snapped up huge tracts of timber and mineral lands. In just a decade more than 5.5 million acres of public land were sold off for corporate use, paving the way for what Woodward calls the "irresponsible exploitation of southern timber."[20]

This process was repeated throughout the region in the 1880s and 1890s as boosters worked to open up all industrial resources, not just those on public lands, leading historian Albert Cowdrey to characterize this as an era of "exploitation unlimited."[21] As the forests of the Great Lakes region were depleted, northern lumber companies bought up vast tracts of cheap virgin timberland in the region from state officials and private landowners. By 1870, even, thousands of sawmills were cutting over a billion board feet of timber each year—approximately 11 percent of all timber cut in the United States—and by 1909 the region topped out at twenty billion board feet of lumber produced in just one year. The expansion of railroad infrastructure, the construction of high-capacity sawmills, and new techniques for drying timber all fueled the growth of the lumber industry in forested parts of the South, especially the southern Appalachians.[22] As North Carolina's longleaf forests declined, naval stores operators moved into Georgia, Florida, Alabama, and Texas in search of profitable stands of longleaf.[23] In the Appalachians, coal outstripped timber as the most important market resource, and the coal boom reshaped the physical landscape of Kentucky, Tennessee, North Carolina, and Virginia. The discovery of oil in Texas in 1901 started a scramble between Standard Oil, the Gulf Company, and the Texas Company to build oil wells there. By 1910 more than 60 percent of all workers in the South labored in some kind of extractive industry, and industrial cities like Louisville, Chattanooga, Knoxville, and Roanoke had emerged as hubs for shipping raw materials to outside manufacturers. By the late nineteenth century, as Woodward explains, the region was mired in a "raw-material economy" that left few communities untouched.[24]

The corporate efficiency promoted by supporters of repealing the Homestead Act did not mirror the reality of business strategy at the end of the nineteenth century. Timber and mining industries had little interest in using resources in restrained ways even if they did have money at stake, and the cheap price of land only exacerbated this neglect. As the environmental effects of these industries became noticeable, businesspeople and community leaders desperately called attention to the reckless destruction of timber and mineral resources and questioned whether these industries were in their best interests. Even as the frenzy of extraction was happening, some boosters turned the common thinking that resources were "inexhaustible" on its head. As early as 1869 the General Assembly of Georgia prohibited cutting chestnut trees in response to scarcity, though it took no more action on forests until the twentieth century.[25] Farther west, the *Memphis Daily Appeal* worried that "even if the destruction of the forests in the United States had not produced any apparent evils, the experience of the countries of Europe would be sufficient to warn us of the danger of denuding our country of timber."[26] In the 1890s a Kentucky lumber dealer lamented "the slaughter of timber" near the Tennessee and Cumberland Rivers and even declared that "the supply of everything is exhaustable [sic]."[27] By 1889 concerns about the depletion of valuable resources like timber had reached the point where a senator from Mississippi even introduced a bill to reinstate the Southern Homestead Act, which was passed by Congress without debate.[28]

Making public lands off-limits to private entry again did little to stem the destruction of forests and mineral lands. By the beginning of the twentieth century state officials, conservationists, and business leaders predicted that valuable resources would soon be gone. The region's environmental limits seemed near. Robert Fullerton, president of a lumber company with mills throughout the South, noted that demand for yellow pine was growing and worried that "unless we make an effort to husband our timber supply, we will find ourselves within a very few years regretting our imprudence in foolishly making haste to grow rich by manufacturing into lumber pine trees which, if allowed to stand, would repay us threefold."[29] On the twenty-fifth anniversary of the founding of the *Southern Lumberman*, the premier trade journal for the region's lumber industry, the editorial board worried that increases in lumber prices were due to "the small and rapidly diminishing supply of timber" and concluded that "practical lumbermen . . . do not themselves realize how fast the supply is diminishing, or how immensely consumption exceeds the natural increase of forest growth."[30] The editor of the *Panama City Pilot* predicted in 1908 that "unless the forests of Florida can be preserved from the destruction which threatens them a few years will see the state [an] arid waste and the great naval stores industry a thing of the past."[31] That year Governor Braxton Bragg Comer of Alabama kicked off a statewide forestry campaign by explaining that "the people had ruthlessly destroyed the timber of this country without thought of the economic value of the trees they were cutting down."[32] And naturalist Enos Mills partnered with the Alabama Forestry Commission and Alabama Federation of Women's Clubs to travel throughout the state, calling attention to the need to save "the timber of the South . . . from destruction."[33]

Viewed from a national perspective, the depletion of southern resources was even more troubling because the South seemed to be one of the few places with resources left. Within decades of George Perkins Marsh's 1864 warning, evidence of resource depletion nationwide was mounting. By the 1880s the rich timber of the Pacific Northwest and Great Lakes region was cut out, and timber barons had moved south. Bison populations in the Great Plains, which stood at approximately twenty-seven million in the early nineteenth century, were reduced to just a few hundred by 1900, a process that mirrored the fate of plumed birds, which were hunted nearly to extinction to provide feathers for fashionable women's hats. Placer mining, river mining, and hydraulic mining had depleted deposits of gold by midcentury and caused flooding and sedimentation on western rivers. The gold rush also prompted a population migration that resulted in millions of acres being cleared for agriculture and settlement.

By 1902 the scarcity of water in the West even led Congress to pass the Reclamation Act, which earmarked money for building irrigation infrastructure and signaled that resource depletion was a growing concern among policy makers. Perhaps most troubling was the exhaustion of coal, a resource that fueled the global industrial revolution and was required for economic and geopolitical purposes. In the 1860s British economist Stanley Jevons predicted that England's supply of coal would last only a century before becoming too expensive to extract from the deep recesses of the earth, and in the early 1900s American mining engineers predicted the same fate for coal in the United States. These troubling developments underscored the need to conserve resources before the region followed other parts of the nation and the world.

⁓

For southerners, the decline in timber and mineral resources was a crisis of permanence of both resources and industries. Extractive industries were migratory, which was just another word for impermanent. The depletion of timber and minerals exposed the sandy foundations of a reliance on migratory industries for long-term growth. Public officials and business elites had little concern about the resources themselves, but they worried about what would happen when the region's biggest employers suddenly ran out of raw materials. Extractive industries like mining and lumbering depended on a low-wage, unskilled labor market that was strictly regional in nature. Because of the migratory nature of extractive industries, bosses did not feel compelled to provide the social services that more long-term industries, like textile manufacturers, did for white millhands. Extractive industries also helped to naturalize Jim Crow by confirming for white elites the specious idea that black workers were not able to succeed in high-skill jobs.[34] The end of extractive industries was not just a challenge to the economic order; it threatened to shift the labor market and undermine the ideas about race that shaped the social hierarchy. In an area still struggling to rebuild decades after the Civil War, the economic and social results of the end of extractive industries seemed dire.

In the 1900s and 1910s these fears were starting to play out as sawmills picked up and moved on after cutting through local timber supplies. Reports of resource exhaustion and industrial migration provided a disconcerting counterpoint to the statistical tabulations intended to show off growth in publications like the *Manufacturers' Record*. For instance, the Southern States Lumber Company in Millview, Florida, was forced to end operations in 1907 "due to the lack of timber in that section." The mill had operated for almost three decades, but a local newspaper described how "nothing but small timber now stands on the land controlled or owned by the 'Southern States.'" Besides laying off most of its 250 employees, the company sold its railroad line, pulled up the track, and shipped it to Alabama, and the *Pensacola Journal* concluded that "the loss of the plant will prove a heavy one to Millview" because the mill "afforded employment to a large number of the residents."[35] As big lumber companies moved or went out of business, portable sawmills, derogatively called "peckerwood mills," moved in to cut whatever timber remained, regardless of size or quality, hastening the destruction of forests.[36] Between 1909 and 1919 almost seven hundred sawmills in Georgia alone went out of business or left the state, and the state forestry board described "dismantled mill plants and deserted communities throughout the lumber regions" that served as "forbidding reminders of the migration of an industry, which, under wise and proper management of our forestlands, should be a permanent and leading industry in the state."[37] The migratory nature of forest products industries was evident from just looking at the landscape. By 1909 the region had 156 million acres of land, mostly in the Maritime Pine Belt, deforested by forest industries. This was half the cutover in the nation, and these lands were visible manifestations of the impermanent nature of forest products industries.[38]

All of these problems forced southerners to think deeply about the consequences of resource extraction and to consider whether other industries would be in their long-term interests. These questions did not occupy the time only of foresters. They also concerned public officials who wanted to make their states prosperous, urban boosters who wanted their cities to grow permanently, and businesspeople who relied on exhaustible resources for raw materials. Indeed, F. R. Pierce, president of the Louis Werner Saw Mill Company, a firm with sawmills throughout the Ouachita Valley of Arkansas and Louisiana, shed light on this dilemma in 1908 while reflecting on the future of yellow pine. Pierce acknowledged that his industry was in trouble because the forests would not survive another half of a generation at the rate they were being cut. He raised troubling questions for industry leaders: "Is our conduct of affairs reasonable and sensible from a commercial standpoint? From an ethical standpoint, are we just to those who will come after us? Is there any way by which we can perpetuate our forests, or at least greatly retard their disappearance? Must we read the future of the yellow pine business in the story of the seal and the buffalo?" At heart, Pierce wanted to know if yellow pine could be made into a permanent industry in the South. He concluded with a question that echoed Atlanta's Robert Lowry: "Is the yellow pine man to be ever destructive, and never constructive?"[39] As the problems of resource depletion became clear in the early twentieth century, southern businessmen, public officials, and boosters all looked for more "constructive" paths of development that would allow for continued economic expansion while easing pressure on the most-used resources. Although there was no consensus, faith that there could be permanent solutions to these issues shaped the paths that business elites believed were ideal as they sought to come to terms with their reliance on resource extraction.

☙

In the early twentieth century, industrial boosters adopted what might be termed a conservation boosterism. Certain commercial trees like loblolly and slash pine grow quickly in the region, and boosters crowed that climate made the South uniquely suited for permanent industrial growth by promoting the rapid regeneration of renewable resources. Conservation-minded businesspeople made it seem like forests would reappear almost as soon as they were cut. The secretary of the North Carolina Pine Association, John Walker, wrote that the Pine Belt was growing just as fast as it was being cut down and estimated that with the right kind of management South Atlantic forests "may be depended upon almost to the end of time for a comparatively large lumber yield."[40] Gifford Pinchot disputed Walker's claims of inexhaustibility, but even he admitted that perpetuating forests was "easier" in the South than "where trees grow slowly or not at all unless planted and cared for during many years."[41] This view was especially prominent among industry officials hoping to make their business appear more stable, and a 1923 advertisement from the Southern Pine Association argued that claims that "Southern Pine forests are near depletion" were "erroneous." The SPA predicted that "it appears entirely reasonable to expect a permanent supply of Southern Pine" as virgin forests fell and were replaced with new growth.[42] In short, public officials, businesspeople, and conservationists believed that the characteristics that made the region so appealing to timber barons also suited it for conservation.

Permanent forests were never assured only by ecology, however. Conservationists lamented that the tax system nationwide assessed standing timber and cutover lands at a high rate that encouraged clear-cutting. Forest fires, which were especially prevalent in the South, also threatened the bottom line of lumber companies and made them less likely to engage in reforestation. Reforestation was time consuming, and most companies could not afford to see if their investment paid off decades later. Finally, in the twentieth century nearly half of the region's timber was cut by small operators who did not have the financial wherewithal to even think about renewable uses of timberlands.

There was little action on forest fires, which were endemic to the South, but as outcries over deforestation grew in the 1920s state governments passed piecemeal legislation promoting reforestation. Louisiana passed legislation promoting forestry in 1904, but it was not until 1910 that the state provided money and an apparatus for enforcement. The Timber Conservation Contract

Act allowed the state to sign contracts with landowners that would provide favorable tax assessments for forty years on lands that were reforested. Henry Hardtner, president of the Urania Lumber Company and an avowed conservationist, was the first business owner to take advantage of this legislation and one of the few to do so in the 1920s.[43] In 1923 the General Assembly of Alabama passed legislation allowing the governor to designate land as an "Auxiliary State Forest" by signing an agreement with the landowner exempting the timber from taxation for five years. This was subject to one critical requirement: the landowner had to reforest the land and protect it against fire under rules established by the State Forestry Commission.[44] The onus was on private forest owners to maintain timber, though they did reap financial benefits. Other states followed, though not as enthusiastically as Alabama and Louisiana. In 1925 the Georgia General Assembly recognized that the "declared policy of this State" was "to encourage reforestation of cut-over lands, and timber culture generally, on all lands not better suited for farming or other purposes," though the legislature provided little to ensure that this happened for a decade.[45] Even the federal government initially worked with private forest industries. In the early twentieth century the U.S. Bureau of Forestry under Gifford Pinchot devised management plans for a handful of southern corporations that had requested help managing their timberlands on a permanent basis.[46] The "cooperative" impulse of the Forest Service was magnified in 1920 when Pinchot was replaced by William Greeley, who drew praise from industry for his emphasis on federal assistance to private enterprises instead of regulation to maintain timber resources.[47]

Despite the realization that lumber and mining industries were exploiting resources to depletion, even in the twentieth century there was little state support for action to stem the destruction of timber at the hands of "cut and get out" loggers. These halting steps to curb the most exploitative uses of timber resources never amounted to much. When state agencies tasked with conserving timber and mineral resources were organized in the late nineteenth and early twentieth centuries, they were notoriously underfunded and had little to offer except weak suggestions about how to manage resources. This was largely because in a region desperate for industry and short of capital, few people could ever conceive of completely halting industries engaged in lumbering, mining, or extracting turpentine—even if their unsavory environmental record was clear. Public officials and businesspeople worried that state conservation would cordon off natural resources and stunt business. Instead, the South's business elite developed strategies for achieving permanence on their own terms, allowing them to continue industrial activity while maintaining stocks of natural resources. Permanence was a private, not a state, imperative.

In the early twentieth century, industry representatives emerged as the key players in the search for environmental permanence. Select businessmen took steps to extend their supplies of resources either by modifying corporate practice or by working with federal officials to develop resource management plans. In the forest products industries, trade unions started as a way to regulate competition between firms as lumber became difficult to obtain—often by establishing consistent grading standards and prices—and it was natural that these groups would also be interested in finding solutions to declining resources.[48] One of the earliest indications of trade association support for conservation was in 1907, when yellow pine manufacturers formed a trust to address declining prices for lumber. In an era characterized by trust busting, this trust was viewed with suspicion by regulators, and manufacturers promised to implement industry-wide forestry policies so that Gifford Pinchot would convince federal officials to let the trust stand. This agreement had less to do with conservation than with preventing the destruction of the trust, and the Yellow Pine Manufacturers' Association eventually turned down Pinchot's proposal that they should pay federal officials to manage their timber.[49] By the 1920s, however, trade unions were more serious about the need to conserve timber, and groups like the Southern Pine Association established conservation committees tasked with lobbying for state forestry laws, developing more favorable tax codes, studying uses for lower grades of lumber, developing sustained-yield strategies, and keeping detailed statistics on available timber. In the 1920s industry trade unions even lobbied for the Clarke-McNary Act, which gave the Forest Service new power in extending federal protection to forestland and supported joint federal and state efforts to encourage reforestation, promote private timber growth, prevent forest fires, revise state tax policies, and manage waterways.[50]

Industry groups also spearheaded the first attempts to deal with cutover lands, though their conceptions of permanence for the cutover sometimes undermined their other initiatives. Before World War I, only a few forest landowners or firms—like Louisiana's Urania Lumber Company—had experimented with reforestation and crop plantings to determine what the cutover was best suited for. When the Southern Pine Association organized a cutover land committee to study the issue, they promoted conflicting approaches. This was evident in 1917, when the SPA brought hundreds of businesspeople, conservationists, and public officials together for the first regional conference on cutover lands. Delegates expressed little interest in reforestation and mostly promoted converting cutover lands into pasture or farms.[51] The solution seemed easy enough, as a state official from Grant County, Louisiana, explained when he urged local residents and corporations to "let something else be planted" once "the timber is cut off."⁵² A newspaper editor even suggested that Louisiana should exempt cutover lands from taxes to promote cutting, which he claimed would clear land for farming that would be worth more than it had been as forest.⁵³ For these boosters, clear-cutting itself could lead to permanence by hastening agricultural development—even though this worked against competing proposals for reforestation, waste industries, or selective cutting. Permanence, it seemed, could be attained even as the size of the cutover grew. Otto Wernicke, an official with the Pensacola Tar and Turpentine Company, cast cutover lands themselves as a permanent solution to southern economic problems. Although the "saving of various by-products from its mills and its forests are proven necessities and accomplished facts," Wernicke concluded that "the one great by-product permanent in character and indestructible in its nature is the cut-over land."⁵⁴

Wernicke and other business leaders did not believe that African Americans had much agency in the forest, but black southerners used cutover lands and employment in forest products industries as a way to ameliorate the dramatic social changes sweeping through the rural South. At a time when sharecropping and tenant farming were increasingly grim, many black workers turned to forest products industries for seasonal employment that allowed them to maintain independent farms, at least until prices for crops plummeted in the second decade of the twentieth century and African Americans began migrating out of the region en masse. Seasonal black workers who could return to farming also staunchly supported unionization efforts in the forest products industries into the 1920s.⁵⁵

After World War I, the out-migration of African Americans from the rural South forced lumber companies to pay more attention to attracting and retaining laborers, and industry representatives often proposed agricultural uses of the cutover that were intended to be tools of labor stability and corporate paternalism. Wernicke, for instance, claimed that unless cutover lands were used "in a more logical manner," the exodus from the countryside would continue, and he urged companies to create more agricultural opportunities for African American laborers. Wernicke concluded that this would provide for "the raising of more and better negroes in the South," which "is as much to be desired as the raising of good animals."⁵⁶ Other industrialists marketed the cutover for white immigrants, who, they hoped, would fill in the labor void created by black migration, though this was typically short-lived. In the 1920s and 1930s these efforts were subsumed when large companies turned to providing a range of paternalistic social services to attract and retain full-time workers. Like these new social programs, white businesspeople never intended that their proposals for finding permanent agricultural uses of the cutover would alter the racial hierarchy. Instead, these proposals were designed to keep African Americans as low-wage workers.[57] For white business leaders, social permanence was a desirable by-product of environmental permanence, though black southerners still found ways to carve out a measure of independence.

Using cutover for pasture or agriculture was harder than it seemed. Businesspeople were stymied in converting cutover lands to pasture or farmland by cattle ticks and thousands of pine stumps that made farming difficult.[58] These roadblocks gradually shifted plans for the cutover. In the 1920s reforestation became a more accepted option, and a few large firms experimented with programs for regrowing trees on cutover lands. Although they had varying amounts of success, by 1925 there were more than four and a half million acres of cutover in the region being reforested by private owners. In 1929 the National Lumber Manufacturers' Association even issued a policy on forest use that advocated "forest-growing" to achieve "well-managed 'sustained yield' forests"—a strategy that would provide lumber manufacturers with cash, maintain valuable stocks of raw materials, allow cutover lands to be sold for more money, and head off Progressive reformers in the federal government who were targeting the industry with regulation.[59] This strategy also promised a more stable black labor supply by giving employers the ability to offer paternalistic social services that could keep workers in the region.[60] In short, industry officials argued about their visions for the cutover to justify different paths to permanence. Yet these shifting goals suggest a key reason permanence was so hard for businesspeople to achieve: it could in theory be achieved with many strategies, and the least difficult paths were typically the most popular.

˜

As corporations and trade unions struggled to find solutions to declining raw materials and cutover lands, their interest in conservation stemmed from a conservative impulse, one that did not always fit neatly with the policies proposed by federal resource managers. Over time, trade unions shifted from promoting permanence through reforestation and regeneration to less radical measures. By the mid-1920s major trade unions were funding research to find more efficient means of production in order to prevent established industries from crashing due to declines in resources.[61] The Forest Service established the Southern Forest Experiment Station in 1921 in Louisiana and the Appalachian Experiment Station in the mountains of North Carolina, and their research frequently had an industrial bent.[62] After 1925 the Pine Institute of America initiated laboratory research geared toward finding new ways of using naval stores.[63] In the 1920s the Southern Railway even purchased ten thousand acres in South Carolina for experimenting to see if sandy lands in the coastal plain could "be made to yield satisfactory profits if devoted to growing successive crops of pine trees."[64] After the passage of the McSweeney-McNary Forest Research Act in 1928 these efforts were expanded through a nationwide forest research agenda that was backed by the Southern Pine Association and other trade groups.[65] These efforts signaled that by the 1920s industry representatives were turning to technological fixes that allowed businesspeople to retool existing industries so that they did not deplete resources as quickly.

A clear example of how industrial research supported permanence happened in the naval stores industry. Longleaf forests had been tapped for resin to manufacture tar, pitch, and turpentine long before the Civil War. Even in the twentieth century, naval stores operators relied on the same methods that they had for two centuries. Workers cut a V-shaped "box" in each trunk and a hole at the base of the tree that served as a catch basin for resin. This severely damaged the pines, which usually died within five to seven years. The industry brought good returns for a brief time, but it was the quintessential migratory industry. As longleaf pine was depleted in North Carolina in the mid-nineteenth century, turpentine operators moved into Georgia, Florida, and Alabama, looking for new stands of pine.[66]

By the twentieth century it was not clear how much longer the industry could continue to move around in search of new stands of longleaf. A newspaper correspondent in south Georgia urged the state legislature to regulate the cutting of boxes to prolong the industry but admitted that if nothing was done, then naval stores operators would continue "killing the goose that lays the golden egg" until Georgia's pine forests were all "scrub barrens."[67] Industry representatives were not oblivious to the environmental consequences of turpentine extraction, which were exacerbated by low prices for turpentine in the early twentieth century. The industry's future looked so bleak in 1901 that company representatives in the Wilmington area voted to cut back production to raise prices and "prolong the life of the industry."[68] Several years later, members of the Turpentine Owners' Association—the industry's trade union—voted unanimously to "cut no new boxes" for two years. This was largely due to low prices, but the association admitted that "the supply of timber is limited and is constantly decreasing."[69]

As longleaf forests disappeared, industry representatives hoped that technological innovation could prolong their operations, though they devoted few resources to research until the early twentieth century. Entrepreneurs and industry operators had already developed new methods for harvesting turpentine in the nineteenth century—J. C. Shuler's cup system based on French methods, for instance—but operators rarely had enough capital or expertise to try something new.[70] By the turn of the twentieth century, however, the depletion of longleaf forests led naval stores operators to devote significant resources to applied research and lobbying. The *Times Picayune* reported that "factors and producers desire to invent a better method . . . by which the owner may derive a permanent, in place of a temporary, revenue." One of the key supporters was the Savannah-based National Tank and Export Company, which was trying to "introduce better processes of manufacture" and "enlist the co-operation of the government in the preservation of the yellow pine forests of the south." The industry also tried to convince public officials to act, but one newspaper reported that it was "impossible" to get legislation for conserving timber passed.[71] In 1902 industry leaders organized the Turpentine Operators' Association largely to deal with the rapid destruction of pine forests and the temporary nature of the industry. The trade association was formed at the prodding of W. W. Timmons, a naval stores operator from Tifton, Georgia, who reportedly "pointed out to the turpentine operators of the south the reckless destruction of the pine forests and urged the organization of the turpentine men to put a stop to this."[72]

The most successful innovation that resulted from the support of the Turpentine Operators' Association was the cup-and-gutter system, developed by Georgia native and Johns Hopkins–trained chemist Charles Holmes Herty. In 1901 Herty left his job at the University of Georgia to research improved methods of naval stores production. Through applied chemical research, he hoped to develop a new way to extract turpentine that would leave pine trees in better shape for future generations.[73] Herty was a die-hard New South industrial booster, and he believed that science could show the most lasting paths for development. In his view, laboratories and manufacturers were interdependent, and "pure research" was a key aspect of promoting industrial development.[74] Herty later explained that he wanted to show "industrial leaders" that chemistry should play a role in "all their thoughts of future development" because "it is along chemical lines that the clear road leads to the highest industrial development." Applied chemical research had the potential to discover new uses of valuable resources, more efficient methods of producing products like cottonseed oil and steel, and profitable uses for formerly wasted products. To this end, Herty urged policy makers and businesspeople to "consult the chemist as readily as the lawyer, the engineer or the geologist" so that the region could reach its industrial potential.[75]

After learning about improved methods of naval stores production in France and Germany, Herty lamented that southern producers were "not only killing the goose that laid the golden eggs" but "failing to pick up all of the wealth during the dying process."[76] When he returned to the United States in 1899, he set out to find long-term ways of tapping pines. Working with the Central

Charles Holmes Herty. A Georgia native and Johns Hopkins University–trained chemist, Charles Holmes Herty believed that chemical research could help to make southern economic development more efficient. In 1901 Herty left his position at the University of Georgia to research a more efficient way to harvest resin for naval stores, one that would stave off the industry's destruction of pine forests. This resulted in the development of his unique cup system for extracting resin, which prolonged the life of this extractive industry. CREDIT: Library of Congress, Prints & Photographs Division, LC-DIG-ggbain-32461.

of Georgia Railway Company, Herty secured a test site on a private piece of timberland outside of Statesboro where he could test different methods of extracting turpentine, with all expenses initially paid by the state's naval stores factors.[77] After a series of experiments, Herty developed a new system where iron gutters were placed into the bark and directed resin into a pottery cup hanging from the tree. This provided an inexpensive alternative to boxing trees and maintained the integrity of the trees longer. As Herty explained, this invention would prevent "the waste of the later years" and cause naval stores operators to "think more and more of the possibilities of these later years, in the end reap a much greater profit, and at the same time do less injury to the forests of Longleaf Pine, upon whose preservation depends the existence of the naval-stores industry."[78] After honing his discovery in 1902 on the Ocilla holdings of Powell, Bullard and Company, Herty reported his findings to the Turpentine Operators' Association. He urged members to use his system by claiming that it would pay for itself and perpetuate the industry. Herty even convinced John Powell, a Savannah banker and owner of a considerable naval stores operation, to loan him money to invest in the Chattanooga Pottery Company for manufacturing clay pots. By 1904 Powell and other members of the Consolidated Naval Stores Company had purchased enough shares in the Chattanooga Pottery Company to give naval stores operators a majority share, and they shifted the company's operations to manufacturing clay pots that could perpetuate the naval stores industry.[79] Herty's discovery was hailed as a more efficient way to harvest resin and prevent the destruction of pine forests, and the system was endorsed by an array of influential trade and conservation groups, including the editorial staff of the *Manufacturers' Record*, the Forest Service, and the American Forestry Association.[80] By 1904 the Jacksonville Board of Trade—in the heart of Florida's Turpentine Belt—noted that naval stores operators were starting to use Herty's process, which "will prolong the life of the trees indefinitely, and transform a transient into a permanent business in Florida."[81] John Powell, Herty's business partner, predicted that the system would "revolutionize the turpentine industry in the South" and explained that "people in my section have realized that Doctor Herty has the solution of the question of the preservation of the trees and the preventive for the waste that has been general all of these years."[82] Industry officials even touted their reforms and the industry's new permanence in order to head off federal regulation. In an exchange between J. Allen Taylor, president of Wilmington's Chamber of Commerce, and Democratic senator James Taliaferro at a 1909 hearing, Taylor argued that regulation was unnecessary because the industry had a positive impact on the state. He explained that North Carolinians were making progress in "improving our country" through reforestation, hoping to draw naval stores operators back. These efforts were "creating an estate for the future" and "providing for our children" by "adding to the resources of the entire country, because by reason of this reforestation we are contributing to the maintaining of our water courses." He urged Congress not to "interpose its hand and pass an enactment which will tend to disable those things."[83] As the Chattanooga Pottery Company churned out clay pots for Herty's system, naval stores operators steadily bought them and implemented the system throughout the Pine Belt. Historian Robert Outland shows that between 1909 and 1914 the use of Herty's system by industry increased by almost 400 percent, and by 1919 80 percent of operators had adopted it.[84]

The Herty system did prolong the life of the industry, but it did not make naval stores a permanent industry. Even in 1909 a Forest Service official lamented that Herty's cup-and-gutter system could never "bring about the perpetuation of the forest" because it could not solve problems like the high risk of fire.[85] Although Herty's system was never enough to make the industry completely permanent, it did allow it to survive longer than most observers believed was possible, and even into the 1940s naval stores operators were still tapping southern pines.

Florida pine trees tapped using the Herty system, 1936. In 1901 Charles Holmes Herty began experimenting with methods to prolong the life of the naval stores industry. Herty developed a system that used cups and gutters to extract and hold resin, which lessened the damage to the tree.
CREDIT: Dorothea Lange. Library of Congress, Prints & Photographs Division, FSA/OWI Collection, LC-USF34-009462-E.

There is a dark epilogue to this successful industrial reform, however. By prolonging the life of the industry, Herty's reforms kept naval stores workers, who were overwhelmingly black, mired in some of the most exploitative working conditions imaginable at remote turpentine camps. Workers received low wages, labored in difficult conditions far from any legal oversight, and were forced to live in unhealthful conditions that bosses justified by the short life of each camp. Because labor was scarce, producers pulled out all the stops to recruit and hold on to their workers. In the early twentieth century the Georgia-Florida Sawmill Association convinced several state governments to pass strict vagrancy laws, and employers used them to limit the mobility of laborers. By paying employees with company credit, employers forced workers into debts that they could not pay off. A number of bosses even turned to violence or intimidation, snaring workers in peonage that was little different from slavery. Indeed, some of the most shocking peonage cases in the early twentieth-century United States occurred in turpentine camps in Florida, Georgia, and Alabama.[86]

In 1901, for instance, Samuel Clyatt, a Georgia naval stores operator, tracked several of his former employees to a turpentine camp in Florida that was owned by James R. Dean. Claiming that these workers were still indebted to him, Clyatt traveled to Dean's camp with an armed posse. There he refused Dean's offer to pay down their debts and had local law enforcement arrest two of the workers, Mose Ridley and Will Gordon. Ridley and Gordon were chained at gunpoint so that they could be returned by rail to Clyatt's camp, where he intended to "make an example of them." When details of the incident came to light, the Department of Justice put Clyatt on trial for violating federal antipeonage statutes, though he was never convicted, and Ridley and Gordon disappeared. Even without a conviction, the case did uphold the constitutionality of laws against debt peonage that were used to prosecute forced labor for the next several decades.[87] Despite federal oversight, it was difficult to prove that workers were being held against their will, and the isolated nature of turpentine work facilitated the exploitation of workers. In 1925, for instance, Sallie Tolbert asked a local attorney to help find her husband, Richard, who had been lured to a naval stores camp near Holopaw, Florida, by the promise of a job. After arriving there Tolbert evidently found that he could not leave until he paid off the cost of his transportation, and he complained in a letter that his employers "treat these colored people like they was dogs." It was even rumored that Tolbert's son-in-law had been gunned down while trying to escape from this same camp. Although little was done to help Tolbert, Fred Cubberly, U.S. attorney for the Northern District of Florida, admitted that the camp was located in a "very thinly settled country in which the timber has recently become available"—a location far from any oversight where there had been numerous complaints of peonage.[88]

Despite the efforts of officials in the Department of Justice, peonage in turpentine camps persisted even into the 1940s. Although work in forest products industries sometimes provided black southerners with a way out of exploitative agricultural employment, remote turpentine landscapes also facilitated racial violence and intimidation that persisted out of the public eye. Incredibly, producers justified these measures as the price of doing business and had little concern for the exploitative nature of the industry, since workers were black. Maintaining the racial hierarchy did not play the only role in fueling efforts to maintain stocks of raw materials, then, but it was always close to the surface.

☙

Renewable resources like timber fueled visions of permanence, but there was little hope minerals could ever be the basis of permanent economic growth. Nevertheless, public officials and businesspeople sought out more efficient ways of using minerals in order to reap profits for as long as possible. In the nineteenth century, for instance, South Carolina's public officials clashed with businesspeople over how to manage phosphate mining from coastal lands and waters. In the 1830s scientists had discovered mineral accretions of phosphorous scattered along seventy miles of the Carolina coast, and the spike in fertilizer use after 1865 encouraged the growth of a mining industry that provided desperate Carolinians with a source of private and state profit.[89] The largest deposits were on riverbeds, and in 1870 the probusiness Republican govern-

Phosphate dredge, crusher, and washer used by the Central Mining Company to mine for riverine phosphates in the Coosaw River, near Beaufort, South Carolina. In the 1880s and 1890s, mining companies and public officials clashed over the best ways to manage the state's phosphate resources for long-term profits.
CREDIT: Courtesy of the South Caroliniana Library, University of South Carolina, Columbia, S.C.

ment granted mining rights to eight companies for two decades, provided that companies pay the state one dollar for each ton mined.[90] By the end of the year, thirteen corporations were working the state's phosphate beds, and South Carolina was emerging as a major player in the global phosphate market.[91] Governor Franklin Moses even noted that "phosphate deposits lying in the beds of our navigable streams and waters form the only source of revenue to the state of any importance exclusive of taxation," and by 1887 over $200,000 a year were pouring into the treasury from phosphates alone.[92] Public officials never considered not using their phosphates, but deciding how to reap the largest return became a political issue in the 1880s and 1890s. After a lengthy investigation of the industry, the state's attorney general put it this way: "The main question of interest to the State is under which system the largest and most continuous revenue can be obtained."[93]

Figuring out how to receive "continuous revenue" from phosphates revolved around how much latitude to give mining companies. In 1878 the state legislature granted phosphate companies the exclusive right to mine a set territory.[94] Within a decade, however, politicians and industry representatives were at odds over whether exclusive corporate control truly was the most efficient use of phosphate resources. In a series of hearings, officials from large phosphate companies defended exclusive rights on the grounds that giving one company a monopoly over these resources would prevent wasteful mining practices and slow resource depletion. Samuel Lord, director of the Charleston Mining Company, contended that general rights were "ruinous to the State" because they worked "as if you rented out your ground to a man and allowed him to cultivate only the good parts, having no interest in the soil." Lord concluded that corporate monopoly would promote wise use and bring the biggest royalty, arguing that "where a miner has exclusive rights and a long term of years, the longer the better, the property becomes practically his property, and he works it thoroughly and economically," with the result being that "the State gets out of it the most it can, because his interests and those of the State are one." With only a general right, each operator "takes the best and leaves the worst for those who come after him." Moses Lopez, the superintendent of the Coosaw Mining Company, also argued that general rights made "miners . . . very apt to exhaust the best deposits and pass over the bad," which would "make the territory undesirable to others."[95] Operators like Lord and Lopez did not claim that their corporations would ensure the permanence of phosphate resources—no one could reasonably make that claim—but they argued that exclusive corporate control was more efficient and lucrative than any other system.

Corporate officials were thwarted by a political sea change that undermined the system of exclusive rights. In the 1880s Benjamin Ryan Tillman, a small farmer and politician from Edgefield, South Carolina, rode a wave of agrarian unrest and white supremacy to political power. As Tillman became a Democratic power broker in the 1880s, he called for doubling the phosphate royalty and using assertive state power to regulate the industry.[96] His attacks on phosphate interests were motivated by his desire to swell the treasury, his plan to decrease taxes on farmers, his populist appeal to small farmers who wanted cheap fertilizer, and his vehement hatred of Lowcountry aristocracy and political power. Tillman also argued that phosphate resources were limited and should be used wisely. Because the "value" and "quantity" of phosphate resources was "unknown," he wondered if the state was "wasting an inheritance placed here by the Almighty, by selling at a price below its real value, in our greed to get money into the Treasury." Tillman concluded, "We are in a manner killing the goose that lays the golden egg, and we may be wasting fertilizing materials that may be absolutely essential to the future prosperity of South Carolina."[97] After being elected governor in 1890, Tillman created a strong Board of Phosphate Examiners empowered with the "exclusive control and protection" of riverine phosphates and the task of surveying these resources. Tillman authorized the board to raise royalties on any company, provided that they not exceed two dollars per ton—double the going rate.[98]

Tillman also decided to make an example out of large mining companies and singled out the Coosaw Mining Company, one of the largest operations in the state. The company had been granted the exclusive right to mine some of the richest territory on the Coosaw River in 1876.[99] In March 1891 Tillman had the board confiscate the company's territory and redistribute it to other companies.[100] This touched off a struggle over the best ways to line the state's coffers and promote efficient uses of phosphate. The *Greenville News* worried that he was not going to make the industry more efficient and compared his actions to the tenant farming system. Even though a tenant farmer "might be getting rich on the land," the paper argued that it was not in a landlord's interest to subdivide the land and replace the single tenant with several tenants "who would work the land to death in two years—whose plain interests required that that piece of land should be made unproductive and valueless."[101] Although the company stalled Tillman with an injunction, the state received its own court order to halt the company's mining.[102]

The state's injunction was reviewed by the U.S. Supreme Court in March 1892. Although it was decided on technicalities, the case raised questions about the most efficient ways of using declining phosphate resources. Each argument was about who was best suited to protect dwindling phosphates: a powerful corporation or an activist state government. Justice John Marshall Harlan framed the suit as a nuisance case and ruled that the state could act preemptively to protect the public's phosphate resources from harm. Because phosphate beds were common property, interference would result in a public nuisance. In this case, Harlan suggested that the public good was jeopardized not by state regulation of the industry but by the Coosaw Mining Company's monopoly on public resources. The Court unanimously upheld the injunction against the company, cementing the destruction of Coosaw's monopoly and placing the right to manage phosphate resources in the hands of public officials.[103]

The destruction of the Coosaw monopoly opened the company's deposits up to new companies, and by November 1892 the legislature had granted six companies the right to mine there while again doubling the royalties they owed.[104] Yet the halt in production during the state's legal battles allowed newly discovered Florida phosphates to overtake South Carolina in national and international markets. Higher royalties and declining prices undercut Carolina companies, and the industry's infrastructure was destroyed by a catastrophic hurricane in 1898. By the turn of the century, the state's phosphate industry was in a shambles and was never rebuilt, illustrating the fears of businesspeople and public officials that state regulation would hurt their business. Tillman's regulation of the industry did not work as expected, but it does shed light on how even in the mineral economy—where there was no illusion that minerals could ever be permanent—business leaders and public officials still debated the most efficient ways to use these valuable resources. Historians Tom Shick and Don Doyle claim that the phosphate industry shows the "stillbirth of the New South," but debates over how to manage the phosphate industry actually show strategies for avoiding resource depletion that were an integral part of the New South Creed.[105]

By the twentieth century, efforts to get the most out of minerals had extended to coal, oil, and gas, largely due to the influence of the national conservation movement. Conservationists worried that Americans were overusing their minerals, which were critical to fueling American economic expansion and maintaining national security. American conservationists and public officials argued that the rapid use of valuable fossil fuels threatened to hasten the decline of the nation—an alarming prospect as the United States was expanding its foreign policy and military infrastructure to maintain imperial gains in the early twentieth century. Throughout the first decades of the twentieth century, mining engineers and federal scientists worked feverishly to survey and call attention to the need to conserve fossil fuels that would benefit the nation. Federal politicians started to remove certain oil lands from public entry in 1907 and created reserves for naval forces in 1912. Businesspeople also worked to conserve mineral resources in the extraction of coal, oil, and natural gas so that these supplies would be prolonged.[106]

The South had vast quantities of coal, oil, and natural gas, and public officials sought to eliminate waste material in mining operations to get the most revenue out of these resources. In Meade County, Kentucky, the state indicted two men in 1903 for boring natural gas wells to manufacture lampblack and allowing gas to escape "with the unlawful purpose to waste the gas and destroy the gas territory." The indictment came under an 1899 law that prohibited "wasting" petroleum, natural gas, or saltwater "as a protection of the natural resources of the State." The defendants argued that this should have no bearing on their situation, because surely lawmakers did not intend to make it "criminal" for a property owner to use his property, "even though that use brought him no pecuniary profit or was unwise." On appeal, the judge concluded that the state could "protect from waste the natural resources of the state" because they were the "common heritage of all." Private owners had no right to use their property in ways that would infringe on the rights of others, and he concluded that permitting the "storehouse of nature to be exhausted by the waste of the gas" would "deprive the state and its citizens of the many advantages incident to its use."[107] The implications were clear: the state had the power to dictate what constituted waste and what constituted a legitimate use of resources, and public officials used this to maintain resource stocks for as long as possible.

Kentucky's law was part of a crackdown on wastes of natural gas and minerals where these resources were prevalent. By the twentieth century, four legislatures had taken action to halt the waste of mineral or gaseous resources in order to wring as much money as possible out of them. To prevent the "premature exhaustion, extinction, or destruction of the common supply or common reservoir," the legislature of Louisiana made it a misdemeanor to waste or "unduly use" natural gas in 1918. People or corporations could only take as much natural gas as could be "marketed without waste" under penalty of law.[108] A year later the General Assembly of Texas lamented the "great waste of gas ... in the oil fields of Texas" and suspended the regular rules of order to pass emergency conservation legislation—largely because state officials wanted to collect a tax on all gas produced. They adopted a broad definition of waste that included burning gas lights during the day, covering potentially productive wells with water, allowing wells to burn "wastefully," or even allowing gas to escape from the earth without being taken.[109] Besides its 1899 law, Kentucky also mandated in 1922 that all petroleum, natural gas, and salt wells be capped when not in use to prevent these resources from going to waste. The law even gave adjacent landowners the right to cap a well on someone else's land without permission and to bring a suit for the cost expended. A similar law in Arkansas placed the power of preventing the waste of oil and gas in the hands of the railroad commission, a regulatory agency with more teeth than its predecessors.[110]

These measures sometimes changed business practices, but they also shaped boosters' preferences for the ideal types of development. In 1920, for instance, Maj. George Butte, the chief of the Texas Railroad Commission, asked that a proposal to build a carbon black plant in the Potter County gas field near Amarillo be denied because "the conservation law of Texas was intended to prevent such waste as a carbon plant would lead to." Carbon black, a soot-like carbon-based material used in a variety of industrial products, was manufactured by burning natural gas in an enclosed space. The industry was a model of wastefulness because it took huge amounts of natural gas to produce just a little carbon black, and the state geologist of Kentucky estimated that the amount of soot produced was less than 5 percent of the total volume of gas required to make it.[111] Butte was a former law professor and progressive reformer who believed deeply in a symbiotic relationship between business and regulators, and he cast the conflict between carbon black manufacturers and the public in terms of permanence. "The heart of the natural gas conservation problem," he explained, was "the conflict between the present and the future." Gas companies only wanted "immediate present personal returns," but the general public "is interested in conserving the supply and bringing about a slow, wise and economical exhaustion so as to insure continuity of service for the future." Butte argued that the Railroad Commission needed to act in the interest of the public by preventing industrial users from getting access to valuable natural gases. Although the "history of the natural gas industry... is an appalling condition of incredible waste," he argued that the public was starting to call for "the careful husbanding and wise utilization of this precious resource." "True conservation is not hoarding, but is the wise use of natural resources," Butte concluded, which "implies not merely the preserving in unimpaired efficiency but also a wise and equitable exhaustion with a maximum efficiency and a minimum of waste."[112]

Butte's argument won the day, at least for a little while. In 1920 and 1921 the Railroad Commission held a series of hearings on the carbon black industry. At the end of these hearings the commission approved Rule 41, which prohibited the production of carbon black by burning natural gas "where there is any reasonable expectation... of the utilization of the gas for domestic or manufacturing purposes." Constructing carbon black plants was prohibited unless approved by the Railroad Commission. Blackballing an entire industry was a dramatic step, but only a fleeting one. Two years later the commission voted to amend Rule 41 to allow carbon black manufacturing, provided that plants use only "residue" gas from other industrial operations as raw materials.[113] After this rule change, carbon black plants started appearing on the Texas landscape, first in Stephens County in 1923. By the mid-1930s there were more than thirty carbon black plants scattered throughout the gas fields of north-central and northwest Texas, and the state was still struggling to deal with wastes from the carbon black and natural gas industries, not to mention the air pollution generated by this form of manufacturing.[114] Other states also regulated the industry. Arkansas killed the carbon black industry off entirely by fixing substantial fines—ranging from $1,000 to $10,000—for anyone who used natural gas to manufacture carbon black or even tried to sell the product. In Louisiana the state set up a regulatory apparatus that mandated that carbon black manufacturers apply for permits to operate and use gas "economically and efficiently"—all overseen by an elaborate system of reporting and inspection.[115] These efforts to regulate the carbon black industry suggest that public officials were often enthusiastic about finding efficient ways of using nonrenewable resources so that they could be used for the longest possible time. They also shed light on the difficulties of using regulation, which was always dependent on the dynamics of state politics and a favorable regulatory environment, to bring about permanence.

☙

Struggles over the carbon black industry suggest some of the difficulties that southerners faced in achieving permanent stocks of natural resources through state regulation, which was unpopular with business and often difficult to enact. Instead of mandating that businesses change their exploitative ways, by the 1910s and 1920s boosters put their energy into efforts to attract industries that would be better stewards of their natural resources. As resources became scarce, officials latched onto nearly any enterprise that could use discarded by-products from existing industrial processes, resources that had been idle, or raw materials that never had much commercial value—a trend that Richard Edmonds called the "utilization of Southern wastes."[116] These waste enterprises attempted to wring as much money as possible out of the earth and assured the South's leaders that perpetual growth was possible even in a region up against its environmental limits. Waste industries promised conservation through development. As Missouri lumberman and conservationist J. B. White explained, "Unless some profit will accrue from saving," there would be "no inducement to save" or conserve resources, and he urged businessmen to look to the wastes in "forest and mill" as a way to make their operations more long-lasting.[117] This appealed to businesspeople and public officials who did not want to make difficult decisions about which resources to use and which to conserve and were leery of state and federal efforts to regulate their use of resources. Although Samuel Hays shows that the "gospel of efficiency" was a key component of the conservation ideal throughout the nation, southern interest in efficiency through waste industries linked conservation to development in more far-reaching ways than in other parts of the United States.[118] Local boosters, corporate officials, and even some state governments put money into efforts to discover new ways of using resources that had gone to waste, supported research on private industrial and demonstration farms, and sometimes even provided direct incentives like tax exemptions and subsidies to enterprises that promised to transform wasted resources into lasting economic growth.

Waste industries were always linked with permanence, and industrial boosters and public officials worked to attract these industries to the region. In 1903 the *Manufacturers' Record* reported that throughout the South was "an ever-increasing interest in plans for the economic utilization of what has long been regarded as the waste of the lumber trade."[119] Georgia's governor, Hoke Smith, told the National Conservation Congress that, "assisted by the study of our resources, we will find substitutes for many things now used less expensive than

HIS INSPIRATION.

His Inspiration, a cartoon published alongside an article in the *St. Louis Lumberman* in March 1913 discussing the waste wood plants of the Forest Products Company at Slidell, Louisiana. The cartoon suggests that using wasted raw materials in production processes was a goal of lumbermen who were concerned that supplies of timber were declining.
CREDIT: *His Inspiration, St. Louis Lumberman*, March 15, 1913, 63.

those now used" and will "learn how to use in the best possible way what we have." Smith concluded, "Knowing what we have all over the land, conservation will come, not from a lessening of activity, but from a quickening of those forces in the best possible way, with the best results, due to the knowledge of what we have, and how to use what we have." This strategy was exemplified by a number of burgeoning enterprises, including the manufacture of portland cement from Georgia slate and lime, "which must . . . largely relieve the pressure upon our iron-ore beds."[120] A cartoon published in the *St. Louis Lumberman* in 1913 even showed a lumberman dreaming of adding a pulp and fiber factory and a stump distilling plant to his operations, with a cartoon duck explaining that "the things other people throw away are what the wisenheimers make fortunes from these days."[121]

The fullest explanation of the benefits of waste industries came from H. S. Sackett, vice president of the New Orleans–based Forest Products Company. In 1913 Sackett spoke at the annual convention of the National Lumber Manufacturers' Association, where he laid out his vision of a South dependent on waste industries. Since lumber had been plentiful, the industry had not been forced to streamline its operations. The growing scarcity of timber, however, was changing the wasteful methods of industry, and Sackett urged corporate officials to act before other entrepreneurs "come in and take a vast wealth that rightfully belongs to the lumbermen." The waste industry revolution, in fact, was already under way. Sackett pointed to advances in distillation of wood alcohol, the production of goods from sawmill waste, and pulp and paper manufacturing to show that entrepreneurs were changing the complexion of development through waste industries. He concluded that "it is no longer necessary for any lumberman to apologetically view his waste pile" and urged lumbermen to investigate all "opportunities to profitably utilize" wood wastes, rightly predicting that these enterprises would soon rival cutting timber itself.[122] Sackett echoed what southern boosters had been promoting for more than a decade, but his role at the helm of one of these waste industries made him an authority. His talk made waves, with one trade journal even calling his address an "era-making paper."[123]

Making extractive industries more efficient by minimizing waste was not just a southern concern. Finding technological methods of conserving declining resources appealed to all businesspeople, conservationists, and public officials with probusiness leanings. As President Calvin Coolidge explained at the National Conference on Utilization of Forest Products in 1924, "We must husband our supplies," because "it would be poor business to go to the expense of growing timber if we should persist in losing a large part of the crop by unsatisfactory ways of manufacturing and using it." Coolidge concluded, "A tree saved is a tree grown."[124] This was also reflected in the formation of the U.S. Forest Products Laboratory in Madison, Wisconsin, in 1910. Originally a collaboration between the Forest Service and the University of Wisconsin, the FPL was designed to address concerns from the report of the National Conservation Commission about wastes in the lumber industry. To this end, FPL scientists studied better ways of preserving wood, forest diseases, uses of varied types of timber, processes for paper manufacturing, and techniques of distilling valuable chemicals from wood that otherwise had little value. The lab was supported by the forest products industries, and the southern-dominated National

Lumber Manufacturers' Association even issued a statement encouraging the lab's efforts in "develop[ing] methods whereby material now wasted may be put to use, or for prolonging the life of forest products," and argued that "the elimination of waste is as truly a conservation as the growing of trees."[125]

The Forest Products Laboratory had a national focus, but much of the lab's research was intended to perpetuate southern industries. As Carlile Winslow, director of the laboratory, explained, the future of southern forest products merited national attention because "what is good or bad for the Southern States is also good or bad for the United States," and he admitted that the key issue facing the region was how to make reforestation a paying investment. To this end, the lab devoted a great deal of time to finding new ways of determining which trees to cut, ways to use waste products from sawmill operation, and improvements in the grading of lumber that could take advantage of many different species of wood. The pulp and paper industry received early technical assistance from the FPL, and Winslow even noted improvements in resin harvesting and turpentine production, which were "welcomed by the industry." Winslow concluded that the lab's research would eventually allow for "the full development of the present and potential values inherent in southern woods," the "enlargement of merchantable yields per acre per year," an "improvement in the quality of the raw product," and ultimately "closer and better utilization including the development of new uses for and from wood."[126] Winslow's vision was a far cry from the extractive economy that still dominated the region, but his ideas about waste and efficiency mimicked the faith in permanence that had been promoted in the South for decades.

With the help of industrial and academic research, industrial boosters and businesspeople looked for any industry that would use formerly wasted products to help make the southern economy more permanent. Even as early as 1902 the *Savannah News* reported that it was "remarkable how many formerly waste products are now being utilized" and compared industrialists with meat-packing barons in Chicago who used "all of a hog . . . save the grunt."[127] Newspapers breathlessly reprinted any success and urged local boosters to set their sights on waste industries. In 1916 the *Manufacturers' Record*, for instance, printed a special issue entirely dedicated to promoting the chemical industries of the South, which were always bound up with using wasted products and finding new uses for old resources.[128]

In forest products enterprises, these new industries offered ways of using timber that had previously been wasted, though there were competing proposals for what would be best. In 1907, for instance, an official from the Howard Vulcanizing Company traveled to Charleston, South Carolina, to encourage lumber firms to use the company's unique vulcanization process. This system, which was developed in 1894 by Charles Howard, made it possible to season timber that had a high concentration of water, such as swamp gum and punky pine. Although the system had been around for more than a decade, boosters claimed that the scarcity of lumber was making vulcanization more important as a solution to timber depletion. Company officials and boosters concluded that this process would revolutionize the forest products industries by allowing these trees, which had no commercial use, to be sold on the market. The company's attempt to break into the Charleston market was part of a broader interest in vulcanization for the South. For several years the National Wood Vulcanizing Company, located in Brooklyn, had worked with the Hilton-Dodge Lumber Company of Savannah to test the applicability of the process on "old field" pine and tupelo gum from forests just outside Savannah. Company officials discovered that tupelo gum, which mostly grew on watery lands, dried quickly and evenly with this process, and boosters hailed this discovery for its potential to bring "millions in dollars for those who own the swamp lands of the South." No one was more enthusiastic than Daniel Purse, a member of the Savannah Board of Trade and one of the city's most active industrial promoters. Purse noted, "Progressive, conservation business men in the South are a unit in the campaign to develop the resources of our section and to bring wealth from all latent heritages Nature has so lavishly bestowed upon us," but he lamented that so far "we are not getting from the land even a modest percentage of its value." He claimed that vulcanizing wood would allow the South to "become at once what Nature designed her to be, not only the garden spot of the nation, but its financial backbone." Purse likened vulcanization to conservation, and after a year of experimentation he concluded that it would encourage the use of "now worthless and inferior grades" of wood and allow for the "perpetuation by reproduction" of loblolly pine. More than anything, this appealed to Purse's keen business instincts, and he was "convinced that its utilization will extract millions for the South from now non-profit-bearing lands of that section." Purse could "see no reason why this process should not revolutionize the sawmill and lumber business and the wood-manufacturing trade, and help to preserve our forests, and on certain lines perpetuate them, an end which we are all united to achieve."[129] Vulcanization companies did make limited progress in the South. The *Southern Lumberman* reported that vulcanization was being considered by industrialists in Georgia, Florida, and Virginia and that businessmen were working to develop mills in Savannah, Brunswick, Atlanta, Jacksonville, Tampa, Pensacola, Norfolk, Mobile, and New Orleans. Another lumber trade journal reported that the North Land and Lumber Company was building a vulcanization mill near Norfolk, where its business prospects were being investigated by the Baltimore and Ohio Railroad and a local piano manufacturer.[130] By the second decade of the twentieth century, however, the nation's leading railroad companies had conducted tests showing that vulcanized wood was not nearly as hardy as wood that had been treated with creosote, and the industry lost momentum.[131]

Although vulcanization only gained a little traction in the South, there were countless other solutions to determining how to make extractive industries more permanent through waste products. Wood wastes promised to make development more efficient without affecting the lumber industry. As one Detroit businessman explained, "The installation of a chemical plant will not interfere with saw mills as now operated."[132] In 1905 a Virginia newspaper reported that a New York industrialist had purchased a farm, hotel, stave mill, and mail route from a local business in the Shenandoah Mountains of Virginia. The businessman planned also to construct a mill that would manufacture wood alcohol "on a considerable scale, having acquired large bodies of forest land." The paper noted that "it is not his purpose to denude the forests" but that "he has been an intelligent student of forestry, and it is his purpose to cull his timber very carefully, all the time improving the character of the forest."[133] In 1917 a group of chemical engineers from the West traveled to New Orleans to find sites where they could profitably manufacture potash from the wastes of pine sawmills.[134] In 1928 the Southern Railway reported that businesspeople and scientists were experimenting with sweet potatoes to see if they could serve as a raw material for new industries, primarily by making "a heat-resistant paint, a resinous rubber substitute, and several shades of dyes," as well as various food products.[135] There was so much talk about making waste products out of "pine knots" that the editor of the *Quitman Free Press* was reminded of "another great South Georgia resource which is going to waste" and joked, "Why not evolve a new breakfast food out of wiregrass?"[136]

Waste industries were occasionally the stuff of utopian-like ideas about how to achieve permanent economic growth with a limited resource base, but some did take hold. Southerners eagerly took up the production of Masonite fiberboard from "sawmill waste," which was molded into boards by steam and pressure. The pioneer in this enterprise, the Mason Fibre Company, was located close to the Wausau Lumber Company in Laurel, Mississippi, and the two companies thrived in symbiosis until the late 1930s, when the supply of waste material from the sawmill was no longer enough to supply the burgeoning demand for the Mason Fibre Company's fiberboard.[137]

The furniture industry also emerged as a way to maintain permanent stocks of timber. After 1888 furniture manufacturing developed into a vibrant industry in Tennessee, Virginia, Georgia, and especially North Carolina, where it was located close to abundant supplies of high-grade hardwood.[138] Not only did furniture manufacturing offer high prices for finished goods, but by the twentieth century it offered a more permanent way of using forest resources. As stocks of abundant high-grade wood declined, the industry was forced to adopt new types of wood like gum, to use veneers and plywood, and to maintain a "closer utilization of by-products" in order to continue to operate profitably.[139] In 1901 George T. Winston, president of the North Carolina Agricultural and Mechanical College, predicted that the industry's record of conservation would "reserve enough trees to renew the forests forever."[140] After an in-depth investigation, a silviculturist working for North Carolina's Department of Conservation and Development concluded that the future of furniture production "depends primarily upon a sustained and self-contained timber supply" but optimistically noted that "all indications . . . point to a steady expansion and a permanent place for the furniture industry in the South."[141]

In the late nineteenth and early twentieth centuries, declining longleaf pine forests on the Gulf Coast forced some timber owners to replace longleaf pines with tung trees, which were native to Asia and could be used to manufacture oil used in a variety of industrial processes. Throughout the 1920s timber owners began planting tung trees throughout the Gulf Coast region, and their efforts were given direction by USDA officials hoping to offset imports from China. By 1930 there were eight thousand acres of tung tree orchards, mostly in Florida, Louisiana, and Mississippi. The Goodyear family alone planted more than twelve thousand acres in tung trees and established Bogalusa Tung Oil in 1935.[142] No one was as enthusiastic as Lamont Rowlands, a Mississippi timber baron who became the biggest "apostle of tung." Besides planting tung trees on nine thousand of his own acres in 1925, he traveled throughout the region calling attention to the benefits of tung growing. Tung tree plantations quickly spread throughout the Gulf Coast, and by 1927 there were around three hundred thousand trees planted on twelve hundred acres near Gainesville, Florida.[143] Even state officials were enthusiastic about the possibilities of tung trees as a way to restore profit to cutover lands. In 1934 the Mississippi state legislature authorized Harrison County to plant tung trees on county land using convict labor, with all profit from the trees going into the county's school fund. Two years later Louisiana promoted the tung oil industry by giving land for growing tung trees and property used for manufacturing tung oil a tax valuation of only 10 percent of the prevailing rate.[144]

Certain corporations even combined multiple processes to make themselves over into total industries that could utilize every product they had formerly wasted. A good example happened in Elizabeth, Louisiana, a company town that only appeared on the map after the Industrial Lumber Company built a substantial sawmill there in 1906. The company initially planned only to cut timber but gradually adopted reforestation and added other enterprises that promoted the "utilization of previously considered waste materials," according to one observer. These included a turpentine company that produced nearly two hundred thousand gallons of turpentine and ten thousand barrels of rosin a year in 1923; a company that made turpentine, pine oil, tar, and charcoal from pine knots using a "destructive distillation process"; and a company that chemically processed stumps from cutover lands to produce wood pulp, resin, or turpentine. Company officials also established regulations for cutting standard stump heights, because the stump "must pay for its own elimination." By 1926 the Calcasieu Paper Manufacturing Company—another subsidiary of Industrial Lumber—had a paper mill up and running that extracted resin and turpentine from stumps and manufactured kraft paper out of the rest.[145] The *American Lumberman* chalked up these plans to the long-term vision of company executives, who hoped to make Elizabeth "one of the model little towns of the country" in the form of a "continual growing community." The journal characterized the company's president, R. M. Hallowell, as a "practical idealist" who wanted to "see something left and growing after the trees are gone and the buzz of the great saws is heard no more," and it lamented that the South's pine forests were "far too spotted with the dying and dead communities which depended solely on the sawmill and which ceased to live when the mill shut down." The company's strategies ensured that "when the sawmill is gone the community will be left, continuing its growth" and providing revenue for the state and county, freight for railroads, and stable homes for residents. These strategies did allow the town to survive, but they also maintained poor working conditions in the company's mills, which culminated in violent clashes between management and labor in the mid-twentieth century after the company worked to crush unionization efforts in its mills.[146]

Although states were hesitant to promote industrial development directly until the mid-twentieth century, public officials did provide liberal incentives for waste industries to lure them into the region. In Mississippi the General Assembly amended the tax code in 1918 to exempt all "permanent factories or plants" that were involved in manufacturing wood alcohol, acetate of lime, acetone, "and other by products from wood waste" from taxation for five years.[147] Eight years later the state extended this exemption to "all manufacturing plants for carbonizing hard wood and hardwood waste for the manufacture and distillation of wood alcohol and other by-products."[148] The General Assembly of Louisiana declared that all "plants engaged exclusively in utilizing waste materials, such as pine stumps, roots, limbs, and other waste resinous dead pine wood in the manufacture of rosin, turpentine, pine oils, pitch, and other naval stores, allied products, wood pulp and paper" would only be assessed at 10 percent of their value for ten years, which was later lengthened to twelve years.[149] In 1926 Louisiana's governor approved a tax exemption for "plants engaged exclusively in the utilization of waste materials such as water hyacinths, rice hulls, rice straw, cotton stalks or other waste materials from either rice or cotton in the manufacture of cellulose or cellulose derivatives and the products and by-products thereof."[150] By 1940 the state had expanded this list to include "resinous dead pine wood, sugar cane stalks, bagasse, cane reed, swamp grass, waste rags, rag clippings, waste paper, used newspaper and oyster shells" for making naval stores, cellulose material, wood pulp and paper, insulation, or wall board.[151] Alabama totally exempted waste industries from taxes for ten years, including rayon manufacturers, cotton mills, pulp mills, bag manufacturers, and ceramic factories.[152] The North Carolina legislature deemed several small streams in Macon County, in western North Carolina, "floatable" as a way to promote the "acid wood" industry there.[153] In 1918 the governor of Georgia ordered that state offices use "waste wood and superfluous trees and limbs on the capitol grounds for fuel."[154] Although officials there were leery about the possibilities of manufacturing alcohol for consumption, in 1925 even Georgia passed a law encouraging the manufacture of ethyl alcohol from wood wastes.[155] Public officials in almost every state expressed strong support for a variety of waste industries, which were given some of the first industrial subsidies from newly empowered state development interests in the twentieth century.

❧

The quintessential waste industry was always pulp and paper manufacturing. In the 1890s entrepreneurs developed a method for manufacturing low-grade paper used for packaging—known as kraft paper—out of yellow pine, which opened up the piney woods to paper manufacturers. For the next several decades, chemists worked on ways to manufacture higher-quality paper from resinous pine, but in the 1910s and 1920s paper manufacturers opened their doors in the South. By 1930 the region's kraft mills even led the nation in the production of low-grade paper products.[156] As paper manufacturing expanded, boosters declared that it was the ideal industry for the South. Because paper mills only needed wood chips to fuel their operations, they provided markets for pieces of wood that had never had much commercial use. Building a paper mill also required a massive outlay of capital, and corporations could not afford to pursue the cut-and-get-out strategies used by other forest industries. Reforestation was not optional for these firms. They relied on fast-growing slash pine, which quickly replenished stocks of raw materials. Paper companies even ensured that they would receive a steady stream of pulpwood by employing the region's first corporate foresters.[157] All these qualities added up to permanence for boosters, who lauded the industry for using in more long-term ways forest resources that other industries had wasted. In 1921 Hugh Baker, secretary of the American Pulp and Paper Industry Association, boasted that "the paper industry is a permanent industry, and not nomadic in character as is the lumber industry." He also claimed that "the paper manufacturer has been the first of the large users of products taken directly from the forests to see the need of proper forest use—a use that means perpetuation of the forests in such a way as to take care of industry in the future."[158] Baker was echoed by an official from North Carolina's Department of Conservation and Development who praised the pulp and paper industry for its "omnivorous appetite" in utilizing "formerly neglected woods" and because it promoted "more permanent means of reforestation." These factors made pulp and paper enterprises ideal for the South because of their "permanent nature."[159] Unlike naval stores operators and loggers, then, pulp and paper manufacturers seemed to be moving south to stay.

Businesspeople and public officials were optimistic that the paper industry could be permanent because paper could theoretically be made from a range of raw materials. Even in the early 1870s an Atlantan, Henry Banks, was reportedly manufacturing paper from palmetto leaves and wiregrass, "which proved a greater success than his most sanguine hopes had anticipated." In 1872 Banks sent eight thousand pounds of this product to paper manufacturers in Philadelphia, and one observer reported that "palmetto paper is superior to that made of wood, straw, or rags, both in texture and cost of production." In 1901 a trade journal even commented that palmetto would replace hemlock bark for papermaking, which "has been almost exhausted by the tanneries." This idea even persisted into the late 1920s, when a realtor wrote to Charles Herty asking for information on using the fiber of the scrub palmetto.[160] In 1909 the Southern Cotton Stalk, Pulp and Paper Company started construction on a mill in Cordele, Georgia, that would convert cotton stalks into pulp and then paper—one of several similar enterprises built in the region.[161] Palmetto or cotton paper never gained much traction, but the idea that pine could be made into newsprint did. In the early 1930s Charles Herty started a laboratory in Savannah—funded by industry and state money—where he set to work trying to determine a process for making newsprint out of pine, spurring the expansion of the industry into the South.[162]

Southern boosters faced an uphill battle before pulp and paper could become permanently profitable, and finding raw materials was only part of the problem. As William Boyd notes, by the twentieth century lumber and naval stores operators had already cut through a huge swath of the region's forests. Tax codes penalized timber owners for keeping standing timber, and the structure of industry financing mandated that loggers get as much money as possible out of their trees to keep operating. Compounding these problems were a lack of experienced foresters in the South; the region's frequent fires, which made it risky to keep timber standing; and an abundance of privately held land not easily subjected to industrial forestry.[163]

Despite these problems, boosters worked to bring pulp and paper enterprises to the South. In the twentieth century, states and municipalities began exempting enterprises that manufactured paper from taxation or providing them with bounties and other subsidies to lure them into the region. Although this can be explained by the South's general mania for industrial development, evidence also suggests that conservation played a role. For instance, in 1922 the Mississippi General Assembly passed a law that exempted "all factories for making paper or paper products out of wood pulp, cotton stalks or other material" from having to pay taxes for five years in the hopes of encouraging pulp and paper manufacturing. When the meaning of the law was challenged a few years later by a corporation that did not process wood pulp but still hoped to take advantage of the tax break, the Mississippi Supreme Court ruled that "it was the manifest purpose of the legislature to encourage the conservation of such raw materials as were going to waste, such as wood from which wood pulp is manufactured and cotton stalks from which paper may be produced."[164]

From the 1920s onward, municipal and state enticements were commonly provided to pulp and paper manufacturers as part of a far-reaching campaign to "sell the South."[165] The General Assembly of Mississippi exempted all factories manufacturing wood pulp or paper that had capital of at least $20,000 from taxes for five years and authorized municipal officials to provide the same incentive for up to ten years.[166] A similar initiative was enacted by Alabama legislators in 1927 to lure manufacturers of wood pulp into the state.[167] Louisiana reduced the tax assessment on all waste industries, including pulp and paper, to 10 percent of the total value of the property for ten years in order to provide incentives for the industry.[168] By 1930 Florida had even exempted pulp manufacturers from taxation for up to fifteen years.[169] Industrial recruitment was not just a state initiative, however. In 1930 Georgia Power advertised its services to pulp and paper manufacturers, noting that Georgia was ideal because "trees grow twice as fast" there and because it offered a supply of pine that was "close at hand, economical, and *permanent*."[170] The next year municipal officials in Savannah hired Charles Herty to develop a process to make white paper out of pine, and he opened the Savannah Pulp and Paper Laboratory, which served as a research station for all things pulp and paper.[171] The city of Charleston successfully convinced the Piedmont Pulp and Paper Company, a subsidiary of the West Virginia Paper Company, to build a plant in the city in 1937 by leasing the company land for only one dollar each year.¹⁷² These recruitment efforts were wildly successful, and by 1950 the region was producing more than half of the nation's wood pulp.¹⁷³

The largest paper corporations were typically operated by outsiders with little interest in the health of forests, but corporate officials had to manage raw materials in long-term ways to keep their mills continuously supplied with pulpwood. Perhaps the best example was Louisiana's Great Southern Lumber Company, which added a pulp mill to its operations in the second decade of the twentieth century as a way to head off a potential timber famine. The firm had been located in Bogalusa, thirty miles north of Lake Pontchartrain, ever since 1908, when it constructed the largest sawmill in the world there. Although the company owned more than four hundred thousand acres of yellow pine in Louisiana and Missouri by 1914, officials still worried that its days of cutting timber were numbered.¹⁷⁴ These fears came to a head when the Great Southern failed to find a new source of timber in South America, and plans to resettle its cutover lands in the South did not work as well as expected. After touring pulp and paper facilities in Sweden, the firm's president, A. C. Goodyear, lauded the "wonderful system" that "assured" that country of a "perpetual undiminished forest." He proposed paper manufacturing as a solution to the company's declining southern forests, and in 1916 Great Southern officials financed the construction of a pulp mill in Bogalusa that ran off the waste generated by its sawmill.¹⁷⁵ When the pulp mill began operating in 1919, the company converted the five hundred cords of "slabs, edgings, branches and trees too small for saw logs" that had been burned each day into raw material for its operations.¹⁷⁶ Company officials even memorialized the "death" of the mill's refuse burner by inscribing its steel surface with a note explaining, "The complete utilization of the sawmill refuse in the manufacture of paper has my fire forever extinguished."¹⁷⁷

Efficient use of waste was only one aspect of permanence. The new pulp and paper mill also pushed Great Southern officials to develop a reforestation program that would maintain a steady supply of pulpwood by hiring corporate foresters, establishing nurseries, developing methods for fire control, and replanting pines on cutover lands. Company lobbyists pressed the General Assembly of Louisiana to make parish tax codes more favorable to reforestation, and foresters educated local farmers about how "the poor rugged and waste acres can be profitably used in growing fast loblolly pine trees for pulp."¹⁷⁸ This strategy entailed enormous costs, but the firm's president explained that pulp production and reforestation were "not the product of impractical idealism" but "the healthy offspring of business necessity." Goodyear admitted that this strategy might be considered an "adopted child," but he argued that it was

Refuse burner, Great Southern Lumber Company in Bogalusa, Louisiana. In 1919 the Great Southern Lumber Company finished building a pulp mill that ran off the waste generated by its sawmill, converting five hundred cords of wasted wood that could not be used for timber into valuable raw materials. Company officials memorialized the "death" of their refuse burner by inscribing its steel surface with a note explaining, "The complete utilization of the sawmill refuse in the manufacture of paper has my fire forever extinguished."
CREDIT: Slide #10, from the Center for Southeast Louisiana Studies and Archives, Bogalusa, La.—Bankston Collection. Courtesy of Southeastern Louisiana University, Center for Southeast Louisiana Studies.

"adopted because it pays" and would provide the company with a means of operating indefinitely.[179]

Obtaining a perpetual supply of raw materials also gave company officials a unique way to ensure the stability and availability of labor. As African American workers migrated out of the region in search of better opportunities and conditions after World War I, many of the largest firms used their plans for permanent operations to develop corporate welfare work for employees.[180] Municipal and corporate officials incorporated permanence into their paternalistic management of Bogalusa and championed the city as an example for other communities that depended on resource extraction for their daily bread. No one was more enthusiastic about the civic possibilities of pulp and paper than William Sullivan, the company's general manager and Bogalusa's mayor. While Sullivan acknowledged that "no sawmill town has ever been considered permanent," he claimed that Bogalusa was bucking this trend. Sullivan's vision for Bogalusa was intended for "our children and our children's children," and he outlined a program that involved the construction of an expensive new high school, pay raises for teachers, an ambitious program of residential construction, and "building regulations that give no possible chance for congestion if the present population of 15,000 grows to 100,000." Coming just two years after company officials hired an armed group to violently prevent unionization, resulting in the murder of three union activists and the destruction of the union, Sullivan likely hoped to bring stability to an unsettled city and promote a positive image that would attract new residents and workers. These ambitious plans depended upon the success of the Great Southern's paper-making experiment. As Sullivan explained, "The minute it became clear that we could put our finger down on a point in the calendar and say: 'Here's where the lumber gives out,' why, that minute we began to work on plans to make Bogalusa permanent," and he concluded, "It's on paper that we're depending to make Bogalusa permanent." There were, no doubt, "profits . . . in paper," but Sullivan was attracted to permanence for more than just profit.[181] Social and civic visions for the New South were always intertwined with decisions about how to use natural resources, and Sullivan's vision for a permanent Bogalusa suggests just how much issues like civic growth and labor stability could depend upon the wise use of resources.

The Great Southern Lumber Company was one of only a few firms that drastically modified their business strategies to promote permanence in the 1920s, but its reforms became more popular in the next few decades. Great Southern officials did more than perhaps any other group to publicly link permanent uses of resources with the pulp and paper industry, and people throughout the nation took notice. After visiting the town, the president of a northern paper manufacturing company claimed that "while Bogalusa, the lumber town, would come to an end soon, Bogalusa, the paper city, is built for all time."[182] In January 1921 Richard Edmonds commissioned a series of articles on the company's efforts. Although the "destruction of . . . forests" was one of the most pressing problems facing southerners, Edmonds noted that the company's work "gives assurance of the feasibility of reforestation and also of the profitable operation on a large commercial scale of paper mills using the waste products of pine sawmills and other pine timber." The subtitle of the articles proclaimed what Edmonds saw as the main lesson provided by Bogalusa: the "Perpetual Timber Supply through Reforestation" was the "Basis for [the] Industrial Permanency of Bogalusa."[183] The Great Southern might not have touched off a complete revolution in private forest management, but the company firmly established the connection between waste industries and permanent uses of natural resources—at least until it folded in 1938—and suggested that other firms could profit by securing permanent supplies of raw materials.

The pulp and paper industry provides a window on the different ways that permanence shaped southern economic development in the decades after the Civil War. For these firms, permanence was always an aspirational goal—one that was contested by stakeholders with different visions of how to achieve it and who should benefit from it. In a context in which enterprises were constantly vying with one another for access to resources, permanence sometimes seemed like little more than a buzzword used by corporations to distinguish themselves. Indeed, the wide variety of enterprises that boosters could consider permanent—including those that used formerly unused raw materials, those that used wastes from industrial production, those that lengthened the amount of time that products could be used, or those that lessened the strain on intensively used resources—made it difficult to stake out a coherent path to permanence. Yet the experiences of the Great Southern Lumber Company and Champion Fibre Company suggest that corporate officials were keen to improve aspects of their environmental performance and sometimes modified their business strategies to prolong their supply of raw materials.

෴

On the eve of the Great Depression, boosters were crowing about their successes in offsetting resource extraction in the New South with a variety of waste industries that promised permanence through efficient development. A report from the Southern Pine Association claimed that the forest products industries had wholeheartedly embraced waste industries. Although there was still waste in the South's forests, the SPA declared, "There is a constant effort in our industry to more adequately utilize raw material that is usually wasted," which "has given rise to the development of a number of new manufacturing practices and policies during recent years."[184] The *Blue Book of Southern Progress*, an annual publication from the *Manufacturers' Record* that provided statistics on southern development, reported in 1930 that "on every hand new methods, entirely new materials . . . are competing with products that were once considered indispensable." The authors concluded that the "competition of new materials and substitutes has wrought a real industrial evolution." This industrial "evolution" diversified southern industry, contributed to real economic growth, and maintained profitable resources.[185] By 1930 southern states had indeed made great strides in converting from resource extraction to a waste economy. Pulp and paper manufacturing, furniture manufacturing, the utilization of wood wastes, the manufacture of chemical products like rayon, portland cement production, and attempts to streamline the use of valuable minerals all reflected the desire to bring permanence to the South's extractive economy. As boosters and public officials worked to deal with declines in profitable raw materials, then, they turned to waste industries as a way to promote permanent growth and industrial development. Waste industries were perhaps the ultimate example of conservation through development, and this private impulse gave conservation in the South a cast that was different from that in the rest of the United States.

Still, the South was far from having imposed an environmental permanence on its forest or mineral resources or from securing permanent economic growth. Even into the 1930s boosters lamented that resources were still being wasted. Despite the rapid regrowth of slash and loblolly pine, enterprises that relied on hardwoods also had little hope of permanence. In this way, waste industries only brought a veneer of permanence to the southern environment. Even where waste industries gained a foothold they were not enough to completely rationalize the use of timber and minerals and often hastened the development of valuable resources or contributed to other types of environmental degradation. Waste industries gave boosters a myopic idea that environmental permanence could be had simply by maintaining stocks of profitable resources, despite a host of other environmental issues. The ultimate legacy of waste industries, then, is not environmental permanence but the wave of air and water pollution that tagged along with these industries—problems that would lead to a Progressive Era backlash over whether the benefits of permanent industries were worth their steep environmental costs.

CHAPTER 4

The Costs of Permanence

IN THE MIDDLE OF THE NIGHT on February 22, 1873, a flour mill and a sawmill owned by George Washington Rankin in Anderson County, South Carolina, were "sprinkled with spirits of turpentine" and burned to the ground. Rankin was a miller and small-time wheat farmer in the upstate. He had a substantial sum invested in his mills, which were powered by a dam across Twenty-Three Mile Creek, near Slabtown.[1] Authorities promptly arrested James and Frank Babb, African American brothers who lived just one mile from the mills, on charges of arson. Within months, the Babbs had been convicted and were sentenced to ten years in the state penitentiary "at hard labor."[2]

For years, Rankin's dam had been a flashpoint for the community. Although Slabtown was initially renowned for being healthy, in the early 1870s it was swept by a series of malaria outbreaks, which a vocal group of residents blamed on the dam. Three years before Rankin's mills were burned, citizens from Anderson County had petitioned the state legislature to have his dam removed, though another group of residents petitioned to keep it standing.[3] By 1871 the dam was enough of a problem that Rankin was indicted for maintaining a public nuisance by impeding the flow of Twenty-Three Mile Creek, overflowing lands of other property owners, and causing air and water to become "corrupted"—spreading malaria and other dangerous diseases. A local newspaper commented that "the vicinage was unusually sickly the past season," with "scores of persons suffering from chills and fever, and bilious fever."[4] Rankin's trial was one of the most sensational ever held in Anderson County. The *Anderson Intelligencer* dubbed it the "great mill-dam case" and noted that it "will be long remembered by the citizens of Anderson."[5] After days of testimony, including from several physicians about the causes of malaria, the jury ruled that Rankin was guilty of maintaining a public nuisance. On appeal, however, the South Carolina Supreme Court overturned the verdict and sent the case back to the lower court for another hearing.[6] Although the solicitor again indicted Rankin, a grand jury determined that there was not enough evidence to proceed.[7] Just months before Rankin's mills burned, then, he managed to evade criminal charges that threatened to shutter his mills and remove his dam.

The conflict over Rankin's mill dam started a sustained push for drainage legislation that would give recourse to residents who were affected by health problems in cases like this. For the next year, local newspapers were inundated with editorials on the drainage issue, and residents held community meetings to find a solution to their health woes. In January 1873 a resident calling himself "Reform" wrote that the "obstruction of mill dams" was one of the biggest problems hindering agricultural development because dams rendered fertile lands unusable for farming, damaged public health, and drove residents away. He argued that the state needed to find a solution that would not impair the property rights of dam owners but would "open up these fertile bottom lands to the skill of the agricultural laborer, whether white or black."[8] Within days, drainage supporters were cheered when the governor's annual message supported a "flowage act" that would provide a mechanism for the removal of mill dams, and a correspondent from Anderson wrote that this was a "step in the right direction."[9] Even as politicians prepared to act, however, Slabtown was visited by a series of devastating epidemics, which residents publicly attributed to the swampy lands created by Rankin's dam. One "refugee" even described how "one of the physicians who waited on the sick and dying in that neighborhood, said that it possessed the symptoms and virulence of the yellow fever, even to the black vomit," and urged "the Christian, the patriot, the legislator, and citizen" to act before these problems got worse.[10]

After the devastating summer of 1873, nearby communities also organized to promote free-flowing rivers when public health was threatened. At a meeting in December, residents of Pickens, thirty miles north of Anderson, drew up a petition asking the state legislature to give county commissioners the power to determine if mill dams were a health nuisance and have them removed after compensating the landowner. They linked their efforts with the struggles of people in Slabtown, noting that they "sympathize[d] deeply with our suffering fellow-citizens of Anderson" and "desire[d] to unite our efforts with theirs."[11]

This is not to say that critics of Rankin's mill dam were opposed to industrial development. Residents who supported drainage legislation were quick to note that they intended to "make no war upon mill-dams or mill-dam owners" and only supported criminal charges if an owner allowed a dam to stand knowing that it was creating health problems.[12] Thomas Russell, a resident who had been forced to move out of Anderson to improve his health, surprisingly credited mill owners for being willing to remove dams or otherwise alleviate problems. He named half a dozen property owners in Anderson who would supposedly remove their dams if they received proper compensation, though notably Rankin was not among them.[13]

By the spring of 1874, legislators were debating a drainage bill specifically for Anderson County that empowered county commissioners to hear complaints about health and drainage nuisances from aggrieved residents—provided that one-third of nearby landowners petitioned for a hearing. Commissioners were granted the power to hire workers to drain land and remove obstacles, as well as the right to force mill dam owners to install floodgates to abate flooding or health problems. In March 1874 the Anderson drainage act was signed into law, and one of the first nuisances reviewed by county commissioners was Rankin's mill dam.[14] After visiting the dam, the commissioners determined that it was a nuisance that needed to be destroyed. They paid Rankin's wife $2,850 as compensation and ordered that the dam had to be removed by November 1874. Although this put an end to critiques of Rankin's dam, at least one resident was outraged—not by the dam's removal but by the "enormous amount" the county paid for a site with no functional mills or machinery. This Carolinian, "Three-and-Twenty," concluded that such an excessive payment would fall most heavily on Slabtown residents, who were already spending vast sums to drain bottomlands and bring them into cultivation, when they were taxed to pay Rankin.[15]

While it is clear that health problems allegedly caused by Rankin's mill dam prompted upstate residents to think deeply about the consequences of obstructing rivers, it is less clear what role James and Frank Babb played in this movement, if any. Anderson County was not in the state's most intensive plantation district, but after the Civil War opportunities for African American freedpeople were often circumscribed by increasingly exploitative sharecropping or tenant farming contracts, and black farmers had to find creative ways to get better working conditions and contract terms. In this context, it is not outrageous to suggest that the burning of Rankin's mills was related to his continued refusal to ameliorate this deadly nuisance—especially given the short time that elapsed between his court victory and the destruction of the mills, the community-wide criticism of his dam, and the close proximity of the homes of James and Frank Babb to the dam. Yet the involvement of the Babbs raises more questions than it answers. Were they actually responsible for burning Rankin's mills, or were they just targeted because of their race? If they did burn the mills, what was their motive? Was this a form of protest against Rankin's public health nuisance, or was this about other issues entirely? The answer to these and other questions is unknown. Almost as soon as the Babbs entered the historical record when they were arrested for arson, they disappeared into the depths of the state penitentiary and were lost to history.

Whether or not James and Frank Babb were responsible, the case highlights the degree to which debates over environmental health, mill dams, and industrial growth were connected to the existing labor and social systems of the South. Residents who spoke out against the dam worried that poor health would contribute to labor instability by forcing residents to leave the area, which would prevent bottomland from being opened up for farming. At a time when the future of agriculture was still up in the air, malaria posed a threat not just to life and limb but to labor. Residents worried that disease would drive away black laborers and inhibit agricultural development. Environmental health problems also afflicted black and white southerners at different rates, especially as black southerners were increasingly consigned to poor lands and segregated living on farms that were often closest to environmental hazards. Although black South Carolinians had some legal and political options for dealing with these issues under radical Reconstruction, within a few years the state would be firmly in the hands of white "Bourbons," who worked to reverse the gains made by African Americans and limit their civil and political rights, circumscribing opportunities for black southerners to contest environmental health problems and other environmental injustices. This process was mirrored throughout the region, so that by the twentieth century the environmental impact of industrial development fell most heavily on black southerners, who had no formal channel for protest.

At heart, then, the conflict over Rankin's dam was about whether the benefits of industrialization were worth the environmental costs. Although one scholar argues that rural watermills in the South were important in "maintaining quasi-premodern local cultures" and did not reflect the emerging industrial economy, struggles over Rankin's dam mirrored debates that played out for decades as southerners of all stripes struggled to come to terms with the wrenching environmental changes of industrial growth.[16] New manufacturing industries may have been held up as the key to permanent growth by outspoken boosters, but these enterprises used resources in new and troubling ways. The environmental effects of manufacturing industries were scattered far and wide, and air and water pollution had a serious impact on all southerners. Just like residents of Slabtown, black and white southerners articulated different ways of using these industrial resources permanently and tried to modify industrial operations to accord with their vision for the future.

ᛰ

Historians have spent a lot of time examining the social, economic, political, and environmental effects of industrialization, which began in earnest during the New South era. Despite the preference of most public officials, businesspeople, and community boosters for manufacturing, the scholarship on the

South is overwhelmingly focused on resource extraction. Countless studies chart the environmental degradation wreaked by mining and lumbering, so narratives of declension have become emblematic of the New South itself.[17] Although parts of the region were tied up in this extractive economy, it was never the experience of all southerners. The New South economy was considerably more diverse, and looking at manufacturing uncovers a different narrative. While Edward Ayers is right to note that industrialization "touched the lives of a million people" and "shaped the histories of hundreds of counties," he might have also noted that the environmental problems spawned by the manufacturing economy touched the lives of far more people than just those who worked in southern mills.[18] Pollution has never respected human boundaries, and as New South industrialization ramped up, it was difficult to escape industrial by-products anywhere.

Scholars have recently shed light on critics of New South industrialization and have deepened our understanding of race, labor, and economic development in the New South. Historians have spent less time, however, understanding the voices of southerners who expressed concern about the environmental changes brought about by industrial growth and who sought out alternate paths. Yet just as workers did not silently accept the often-exploitative conditions of industrial labor, neither did southerners fully embrace exploitative uses of resources in an industrializing economy. Boosters may have portrayed manufacturing as a more permanent alternative to extractive industries, but it was undeniable that the new manufacturing economy came with a bevy of environmental problems. Smoke, chemical waste, water pollution, and flooding were often easy for businesspeople concerned with the permanence of industrial resources to just write off. But working-class black and white southerners—eventually even some businesspeople and urban professionals themselves—rejected the idea that manufacturing required putting up with the environmental side effects of these enterprises. Rather than simply accepting environmental degradation, these stakeholders fought the growing power of corporations over natural resources and articulated different ways of using these resources. Virtually every community affected by this wave of manufacturing—and many downstream and upwind of new industrial centers—witnessed a protest in the years following the Civil War. These protests raised difficult questions that challenged advocates of permanence: Was permanent economic growth worth the environmental hazards of industrialization? Was it possible to achieve permanence without industrial pollution? How should corporate and municipal officials work through competing claims to resources? What were the effects of permanence on ordinary people? Working through these questions forced southern boosters to confront the human costs of environmental permanence.

⁂

Nothing defined the New South Creed like manufacturing. For decades after the Civil War all that most boosters could talk about was industrial development. Industrial promoters like Richard Edmonds and Henry Grady called for a manufacturing revolution that would offset staple crop agriculture and extractive industries like lumbering and mining, which had mired the region in a colonial dependency on the North. Only through manufacturing could the South become independent.[19] This was an old sentiment. Decades before the Civil War industrial boosters like William Gregg and J. D. B. DeBow had advocated for manufacturing as a way to promote regional autonomy, and in 1861 Gregg even asserted that "the permanent prosperity of the commerce of the South" was dependent upon "the success of [the] manufacturing industry."[20]

Industrialization was sporadic before the war, but during Reconstruction a new generation of journalists, public officials, and businesspeople latched onto manufacturing as a panacea for the region's most pressing economic woes. These boosters believed that the South had unique advantages that their antebellum predecessors had overlooked, including its proximity to abundant raw materials like iron ore, coal, and waterpower that could fuel manufacturing and cut down on transportation costs. To take advantage of these resources, boosters promoted "home industry" as a way to ensure economic independence and prosperity by attracting factories directly to raw materials. In theory, home industry provided local markets for resources and finished products, did not challenge the racial status quo, and allowed agriculture and industry to thrive in symbiosis.[21]

All these qualities added up to economic permanence. Postbellum boosters claimed that manufacturing products out of southern raw materials at home would lead to permanent economic growth in a way that agriculture and extraction could never do on their own. In 1867 DeBow framed manufacturing as the key to sustained growth, noting that "every new furnace or factory is the nucleus of a town, to which every needed service is sure to come from the neighborhood or from abroad."[22] While discussing a new cigar factory on Marietta Street in Atlanta, the *Atlanta Constitution* commented in 1890 that it was "always an agreeable duty to chronicle a new enterprise, particularly if it be in the manufacturing line, for upon such industries depends the continued advancement of our sterling city upon the road that leads to permanent wealth and prosperity."[23]

Manufacturing also had environmental characteristics that made it seem like it could be a long-term addition to the South. As we have seen, boosters believed that siting manufacturing plants near raw materials would make it easier to use by-products and wasted raw materials to spur further industrial growth. Boosters also touted the South's untapped waterpower, which seemingly guaranteed that manufacturing could be a permanent enterprise. Because "white coal" flowed continuously, it was a renewable source of energy that could turn turbines to generate industrial power perpetually.[24] As Christopher Manganiello explains, utility providers and waterpower enthusiasts saw water as a more "reliable" solution for power than coal, which was subject to changing freight costs and availability problems and could be disrupted by struggles over labor in the mines.[25] Even well into the twentieth century, industrial boosters decried the fact that waterways were flowing to the sea without being harnessed for power. In the words of a waterpower enthusiast from the Palmetto State, "the people of South Carolina have little realization of the almost limitless power at hand—the power that is literally running to waste."[26]

The idea that free-flowing rivers were inefficient was a hallmark of the thinking of bureaucrats and scientific conservationists nationally. The very term "conservation" first became popular as a way to describe the impoundment of water for efficient and continual use, mostly in the arid West.[27] These ideas may have taken root in a western context, but southern boosters realized that water was a renewable resource that they had in abundance and claimed that it could fuel manufacturing enterprises perpetually.

Because water was the fuel for industrial growth, it provides the best vantage point for seeing how stakeholders worked through divergent visions for economic development, resource use, and permanence as the region industrialized. Industrial use transformed water into a commodity and changed the way people related to rivers—sometimes in dramatic fashion. The environmental effects of factories, as well as growing urban areas, showed up starkly in the rivers and streams that carried pollutants far beyond the boundaries of industrial centers. Even though water had been an important resource for generating industrial power for more than four decades, it was also necessary for a range of other competing economic activities. Debates over permanence, then, were always bound up with determining the best uses of the South's limited "white coal." Conflicts over lands and skies reflected similar dynamics, but the ways that stakeholders weighed the costs and benefits of industrial permanence are clearest in struggles over water, which was always at the center of industrial development in the New South.[28]

❧

The most striking changes caused by the burgeoning manufacturing economy were water pollution and the obstruction of rivers and streams by dams. Since the seventeenth century, waterways had served as a sewer for household and industrial wastes, but the dispersed rural population mostly kept the effects out of sight. Industrialization brought changes in both kind and degree of pollutants being dumped into waterways, making pollution more visible and conflicting with other water users. Farmers, city folk, health reformers, and eventually even some public officials expressed alarm at how sawmills used waterways to dispose of sawdust, mining companies used waterways to wash ores, textile mills used waterways to dispose of dyes and chemicals, and growing cities used waterways to whisk away human waste. Mill dams built to generate power exacerbated these problems by obstructing rivers, flooding productive land, and preventing the dispersal of pollutants downstream—inhibiting other uses like transportation, fishing, and irrigation. As they fought back against polluted and dammed waterways, southerners argued that manufacturers and utility companies needed to be restrained so that others could also enjoy the right to water. In doing so, they questioned whether the benefits of permanence were worth the environmental costs.

Common law traditionally allowed nuisances like dams to be removed by the affected parties, and during the antebellum era mill dams were occasionally destroyed to maintain access to water.[29] Free-flowing rivers were given priority into the 1880s, especially to promote navigation, which limited the construction of mill dams.[30] Public officials even worked to restrain the right of dam owners, and states like South Carolina acted to prevent health problems caused by mill dams, often by giving county commissioners the power to hear complaints and remove dams or other obstructions that injured the public health.[31] Alabama, for instance, had elaborate bureaucratic hoops to jump through before constructing a mill dam, which required community meetings and gave the sheriff the power to survey the potential for flooding, health risks, or other effects on nearby property owners before signing off on construction.[32] In Mississippi local juries had the authority to examine proposals for new dams and determine who would be impacted, whether navigation or fish migration would be obstructed, and if "the health of the neighborhood will be damaged."[33] Virginia's code deemed "any dam or other thing in a water course" that hindered the migration of fish or transportation to be a nuisance, "unless it be to work a mill, manufactory or other machine or engine useful to the public." To maintain navigability, the code also prevented courts from granting property owners the right to build a dam and provided a legal mechanism for removing dams or installing locks.[34] These and similar laws reflected the persistence of antebellum traditions toward mill dams. Even into the Reconstruction era, it was not guaranteed that industrial users would automatically be given priority access to southern waters or a license to use waterways however they wanted.

Despite efforts to maintain the navigability of waterways, by the 1870s public officials and industrial boosters were working to attract capital from the North to develop manufacturing. Republican state administrations encouraged the construction of railroads, promoted immigration of capitalists and laborers, and provided corporations with sweeping rights to natural resources, as well as the power of eminent domain. As southern states fell into Democratic hands in the 1870s, the probusiness policies of Reconstruction governments were often adopted by Democrats, whose ranks included many former Whigs predisposed to favor state efforts to promote economic development. After the economic depression of the 1870s, Redeemer administrations doubled down on their commitment to attract new industries by funding and publicizing surveys of raw materials for potential manufacturers, providing tax breaks for manufacturers, disseminating advice about labor and supplies, and promising easy terms of incorporation for companies who wished to come south.[35] In the 1890s the town of Greenwood, South Carolina, even had a "standing offer of a desirable site" that it would give to "any manufacturing establishment" looking to relocate there—largely because municipal leaders reportedly believed that manufacturing was "necessary to the permanent growth of a community."[36] Public officials and businesspeople also worked to develop hydropower and later hydroelectric infrastructure to provide cheap power to mills. Between 1880 and 1925 private utility companies harnessed "white coal" and regularized the flow of water by constructing dams capable of generating vast amounts of electricity and stringing transmission lines across the region. Utility providers like James Duke cut deals with manufacturers or provided financial backing for building factories or converting mills to electric power. The resulting "Super Power system" provided cheap power for urban and industrial customers and helped to fuel a manufacturing boom in the Southeast.[37]

Manufacturing surged as these efforts coalesced after 1880, especially in parts of South Carolina, North Carolina, Georgia, Tennessee, and Alabama. Between 1880 and 1920 the capital invested in manufacturing increased by almost 200 percent each decade, and after 1879 the region had a sustained value-added economic growth of 6 percent for fifty years—a rate of growth consistently higher than the rest of the nation. The manufacture of textiles, iron and steel, and furniture overcame significant challenges to achieve national and international significance, and by 1927 the southern textile industry had even surpassed New England in total production.[38] These gains carved out important industrial centers within the South. After 1879 Birmingham emerged atop Alabama cornfields to become one of the nation's leading producers of iron and steel. As consumer demand for cigarettes increased, the Duke-owned American Tobacco Company made Durham, North Carolina, the largest producer of tobacco products in

Hydroelectric dam at Parr Shoals, South Carolina. Constructed in the second decade of the twentieth century, the dam at Parr Shoals on the Broad River generated electricity for the city of Columbia, just twenty-five miles away. Hydroelectric dams like this became common in the twentieth century, providing cheap power for urban and industrial customers, fueling a manufacturing boom in the Southeast, and in the process transforming ideas about the best use of southern waters.
CREDIT: Courtesy of the South Caroliniana Library, University of South Carolina, Columbia, S.C.

the nation. By the twentieth century, Roanoke, Virginia, had become the hub for one of the nation's most sprawling transportation providers, the Southern Railway. Yet no other area was transformed as much as the "Piedmont Crescent of Industry," a territory of fifty thousand square miles between the Appalachian Highlands and the coastal plain that ran from Birmingham to Danville, Virginia.[39] The emergence of the Piedmont as a manufacturing center was one of the most dramatic changes of the New South, and the success of industry there was a testament to just how closely manufacturing and control of water were linked. Swift-flowing Piedmont rivers sat just above the fall line, making them perfect for generating industrial power or electricity, and by 1900 few Piedmont watersheds had been left untouched by some form of industrial development.

The expansion of manufacturing stressed the South's waterways more than ever before. Manufacturers relied on waterways not only for power but as an industrial sink that could transport wastes far away. As industrial uses of water became more common after 1880, concerned southerners had to find new ways of resolving conflicts over water, and many stakeholders turned to the law. They drew on what historian Christine Rosen calls "the first significant wave of industrial pollution litigation in American history," which was sparked by the industrialization of the antebellum Northeast.[40] American courts initially prioritized nonindustrial uses of water, but by the beginning of the nineteenth century, manufacturing industries were securing their hold on water resources. In Rhode Island a series of mill acts made it difficult to challenge industrial uses of waterways under common law, and these measures quickly spread to other states in New England. These mill acts were not just a legal change. As historian Ted Steinberg contends, they were a "stunning cultural transformation . . . [and] a shift in people's very perception of nature" so that "it was commonly assumed, even expected, that water should be tapped, controlled, and dominated in the name of progress."[41] New Englanders who were affected by pollution and damming found ways to challenge the monopolization of water resources by manufacturers, mostly by turning to nuisance law. Even as judges were interpreting the law to favor industrial development, they remained inclined to view any use of property that injured another property owner as a nuisance. Indeed, Rosen shows that attempts to halt "traditional" polluting industries like distilleries, tanneries, and slaughterhouses were often successful using nuisance challenges even into the mid-nineteenth century.[42]

The antebellum South did not have the protracted legal debates about manufacturing that were occurring in the Northeast because industry was limited to only small pockets of the region. As industrial users expanded their hold on water in the 1870s and 1880s, however, affected stakeholders also turned to the courts. There were thousands of damage suits filed during this period, which gave concerned white southerners a formal avenue to fight back against pollution or flooding caused by the construction of mill dams.[43] These cases shed light on the transformative effects of the new manufacturing economy, especially in the southern Piedmont, and the ways that southerners worked to blunt the harmful effects of factories and control their own water. Not all southerners could engage in litigation when they were affected by pollution or monopolization of water by manufacturers, however, and lawsuits were skewed toward those who could afford a lawyer and a defense. Unlike water control in the West, which prioritized agriculture, southern waterpower development benefited urban and industrial interests, and conflicts over water frequently pitted agricultural and industrial interests against each other, especially after dams became big business.[44]

Property owners who pushed back against industrial uses of water and sought recompense through the law forced jurists to work through competing claims by deciding what constituted a "reasonable use" of water. Reasonable use was a legal standard that gave each property owner a right to use his or her property in any way he or she wanted as long as those uses did not unduly interfere with the rights of other people to do the same. In conflicts over water, reasonable use required weighing factors like "whether a diversion or pollution of water is temporary or permanent and the extent of injury caused to other riparian landowners."[45] Damage cases did not necessarily challenge the logic of development, but they underlined that industrialization brought dramatic changes in the way that people could use land and resources and gave property owners a way to modify the effects of industrial development. In 1873, for instance, a Georgia landowner filed suit against the Athens Manufacturing Company for heightening its dam on the Oconee River, which overflowed his land and made the soil too wet for farming. A jury awarded the landowner $5,000, and a jurist later noted, "If this company raised their dam, thereby causing water in the creek to run over the plaintiff's land and thereby injuring and damaging him, that was an invasion of his rights."[46] Alice Hamilton, an Alabama landowner, filed suit in 1890 against the Tennessee Coal, Iron and Railroad Company for using the waters of Caffee's Creek, near Woodstock, to wash its iron ore, polluting the water and making it unfit for watering her livestock. She was awarded $475 in damages, just one-third of what she requested, though even this was deemed to be "excessive" and was reversed by the Supreme Court of Alabama.[47] After a particularly heavy gullywasher in 1896, South Carolina's Pelham Cotton Mills was forced to open the floodgates on its dam on the Enoree River to keep it from being destroyed by rising water. Eleven downstream landowners filed suit against the company for flooding their property. The company's actions had covered the corn of one farmer under ten feet of water and mud, destroying the crop and making the land less valuable for cultivation. Although the company claimed that its actions were caused by an "act of God," a jury awarded the landowners several hundred dollars each in payouts.[48] A Georgia landowner sued the Pine Product Company, which extracted gas and other chemicals from the wood of pine trees and used water from a local creek to wash it, preventing him from watering his stock in the polluted creek. The superior court dismissed the case, but on appeal the Georgia Supreme Court ruled that the damage was significant and the landowner was eligible for compensation.[49] People who relied on water for fishing also challenged industrial uses of rivers, and at times sport and subsistence fishermen used the law to force mill owners to build fishways.[50]

Lawsuits against industries were not just limited to water. As railroads expanded throughout the region, they spawned a flurry of legal challenges when coal-fired locomotives set fire to fields and ran over valuable livestock.[51] Landowners also brought suit against businesses like cotton gins, iron furnaces, and fertilizer manufacturers for polluting the air with particulates and smoke. Atlantan Mary Farley, for instance, filed suit against the Gate City Gas Light Company over gases that escaped during the process of manufacturing and distributing gas for light throughout the city, damaging her family's health, limiting their access to clean water, and killing off vegetation at their home. She received $1,000 in damages, though the company did not have to change its ways.[52] In the Ducktown Basin of Tennessee, industrial copper smelting spewed dangerous chemicals into the air, severely damaging land, air, and water and creating a moonscape where there had once been a hardwood forest. In the early twentieth century, groups of farmers and other Georgians convinced the state to institute a cross-border nuisance suit against the Tennessee Copper Company, and the 1907 U.S. Supreme Court decision supporting the state's injunction set an important precedent that states could sue industries in other states for pollution.[53]

As these examples suggest, property owners who were affected by air and water pollution or flooding could be successful at obtaining damages in court. Juries were often sympathetic to the interests of local landowners over industries. By challenging exploitative uses of water and air in the courts, litigants showed that manufacturing enterprises—even those deemed permanent—had significant environmental effects. Stakeholders who sued industries and forced them to pay damages were not necessarily signaling that they were opposed to industry, however. Litigants were often businesspeople who sought access to water for their own uses. Indeed, damage cases against polluting industries were not a very effective way to maintain clean water and undammed rivers, but they did offer southerners a way to get recompense for the destruction of their property.

Even when courts acknowledged that landowners should be paid for damages, jurists were careful not to do anything that could hinder industrial growth. Although antebellum courts did not cling to an "instrumental conception of the law" that promoted and maintained economic development, in the second half of the nineteenth century, southern lawyers and judges had become key promoters of industrial development. Judges in the South came from the class of urban professionals most likely to benefit from industrialization, and, like jurists throughout the nation, they used the law as an "instrument" of economic development.[54] A good example is a suit between J. M. Kirk, an Alabama landowner, and Birmingham's Lady Ensley Coal, Iron and Railway Company. Kirk sued the company for washing brown iron ore in a local stream, which left the water running through his property "ladened with red clay, refuse ore, and debris, rendering it unfit for stock and drinking purposes." "In some places a thick sediment or 'slush' was deposited upon portions of the farm impairing its fertility." Kirk's attorneys claimed the sediment was "so deep as to destroy [the land's] usefulness for cultivation." Although a jury initially ruled for the company, on appeal the Alabama Supreme Court acknowledged that company officials had not installed holding tanks that would allow the sediment and pollutants to sink out of the water before it was returned to the stream and argued that the damage to Kirk's land appeared in places to be irreversible. The court ruled that Kirk's full damages could be considered. The judge explained that courts were "not the 'masons' to 'chisel' away vested rights of property of private individuals, however humble and obscure the owner, for the benefit of the public, or great corporations" and claimed that the law provided even "the poorest citizen" an opportunity to receive "redress for an unlawful injury caused by his wealthy neighbor." This did not mean that the court was totally opposed to industrial development, however. The judge suggested that in cases where a business was threatened with an injunction, jurists had to abide by a different standard, one that took into account precedent to not "impede rightful progress" or "hinder industrial enterprise."[55] While the Alabama Supreme Court protected the interests of the farmer by allowing significant damages for the destruction of his property to be considered, the justices did not prevent the Lady Ensley Coal, Iron and Railway Company from continuing to dump wastes from washing iron ore in the stream. As industrialization geared up in the 1880s and 1890s, the use of water to dispose of manufacturing wastes became more common. In this context, jurists were careful not to do anything that would permanently limit corporate access to water, believing that this could discourage improvement and set back southern economic growth.

The judicial preference for manufacturing made it difficult to halt pollution through the courts, which was especially clear in efforts to obtain injunctions against polluting industries. When property owners filed for an injunction, corporations also pulled out all the stops to win. The traditional method of determining whether an action was a nuisance under common law—whether a use of one's property injured that of another—was unsuitable for industrial operations with unavoidable and widespread effects. Beginning in the mid-nineteenth century, jurists nationwide adopted the "balancing-of-interests test," with which they decided nuisance cases by weighing what was best for the public good. By defining the public good as industry, judges wrote off the environmental consequences of industrialization as the price of prosperity and used the law to promote economic development. The balancing test, as one scholar notes, allowed "local and regional economic concerns to rise above personal property rights."[56] In short, the balancing test vested jurists with the power to determine what constituted harmful forms of pollution and what was an acceptable hazard, though these decisions were rarely anchored only to environmental quality. The balancing test also forced judges to decide between two competing paths, and their efforts to determine the public good were always closely linked to the perceived relationship between manufacturing and permanence.

No industry was more emblematic of the New South than iron manufacturing, which had widespread environmental effects, especially on water resources. Even though Alabama planters were not opposed to industry per se, they threw up staunch opposition to the expansion of iron manufacturing.[57] This was evident in the outcries against the way that iron manufacturers polluted waterways, and conflicts over the burgeoning iron and steel manufacturing industry in Alabama were some of the most high profile efforts to weigh competing industrial paths. The Clifton Iron Company, founded in 1880 near Talladega, Alabama, provides a good example. The company constructed two fifty-ton charcoal furnaces, which refined iron ore mined from local holdings and used local streams to wash the recently mined iron ore and rid it of impurities.[58] This caused problems for landowners downstream of the furnaces, including James Dye, a former Confederate officer, substantial property owner, and farmer. Sediment and "refuse materials" flowed onto Dye's property, and in 1886 he filed suit against the company, seeking a perpetual injunction that would bar the use of its three washers. A local chancery court ruled in Dye's favor and prohibited the Clifton Iron Company from washing its ores in the stream, throwing the viability of the company's entire operation into question. The Supreme Court of Alabama overturned the perpetual injunction by applying the balancing test. The justices claimed the injunction should be thrown out mainly because "the great public interests and benefits to flow from the conversion of these ores into pig metal should not be lost sight of." In effect, they ruled that iron manufacturing was more important than agriculture and justified the "invasion of the rights" of this landowner to protect the "large sums of money . . . invested" in the mineral industries of Alabama.[59] Because both courts used the same legal reasoning by employing the balancing test, at issue here were two visions of what constituted the public good. The chancery court interpreted the public good in terms of agriculture and traditional uses of water resources. The Alabama Supreme Court interpreted the public good in terms of manufacturing, claiming that, despite pollution, the iron industry was a better use of resources than agriculture. The court's ruling stood as precedent for decades, helping to make the South's legal system into a potent tool for promoting economic development. Even as late as 1920 an Alabama justice would cite this case, noting that it had "never been overruled," and the court's decision paved the way for a massive industrial expansion in Alabama by providing iron industries with sweeping rights to the state's waters.[60]

This was just one of many cases where judges had to decide between competing paths, and these rulings suggest a preference for newer manufacturing industries over smaller enterprises. Through these rulings, jurists also allowed manufacturing industries to have priority access to southern waters, access that was contingent on defining certain forms of water pollution as acceptable. While damage cases and injunctions offered southerners a way to blunt the effects of manufacturing or at least recover damages, they rarely had much effect on actually changing the course of industrial development or halting it. The southern judicial system not only was an important avenue for challenging pollution but also played a crucial role in determining just what industries would have access to choice resources.

Legal challenges provided a way for white southerners with the funds to get compensation from, or sometimes to halt, polluting industries. But these cases also reinforced the racial disparities over resolving problems like industrial pollution. Black southerners had little recourse for water pollution, health problems, or flooding caused by manufacturing industries. As state governments in the 1880s and 1890s disenfranchised black voters and extended segregation, black southerners were effectively denied access to the judicial system—even if they had the money to pursue litigation. The exclusion of African Americans from the legal system perhaps opened up space for white southerners to challenge industrial pollution, since these acts did not challenge the racial hierarchy. But it also meant that the groups most affected by pollution were the least able to formally protest. This does not mean that black southerners simply accepted the consequences of pollution and the monopolization of water by industries. As we will see, black southerners found ways to challenge exploitative uses of water and other industrial resources, but these efforts were rarely through the law.

❧

The balancing test provided a legal mechanism to weigh whether the costs of industrial development were worth the benefits, but it was simply a formal codification of the process that communities throughout the region used to weigh the benefits and drawbacks of development. These questions were made more complicated by urban growth after the 1880s. Although industrial cities like Atlanta and Birmingham are most identified with the New South, towns with fewer than 2,500 people were more typical, and by 1900 approximately one out of every six southerners lived in one of these smaller population centers.[61] Even small towns ratcheted up pressure over industrial uses of water by concentrating pollutants and bringing priorities like public health and clean water to the fore, in the process changing the terms of debate on manufacturing and water use. If industry had built-in legal advantages, it could be hemmed in by local statutes and risked its well-being when environmental degradation fostered community resentment.

The similarities between legal balancing tests and community debates over economic development can be seen in an 1891 conflict over mill dams, water pollution, and urban health in Big Stone Gap, Virginia. Big Stone Gap was located in the heart of a coal-mining region in the southwestern corner of Virginia, and the fast-flowing Powell River had attracted several textile mills that used the river for power.[62] In the 1890s a vocal group of residents argued that these dams should be torn down for harboring disease, and the fate of the dams—and the town's industrial future—was debated at municipal meetings and in the pages of the town's weeklies. One resident, E. T. Short, claimed that the dams "should be declared a nuisance and removed at once regardless of the owners' wish."[63] The local newspaper urged the city to take action before the summer heat spread illness, declaring, "Blow it skyward, and if the dam owners . . . think they can recover damages from the city, let them try it."[64] A local businessman argued that an environment brimming with disease would hurt the business prospects of the town. He claimed that the dams should "come out by all means," because "people will not stay here at a risk of their health. They will be looking for more healthy localities." John Fox Sr., father of novelist John Fox Jr., similarly commented that "the health of the town is certainly more important than a little old woolen mill." In the eyes of these residents, the economic benefits of mills were not worth the price of an unhealthy living environment, and they argued that health and economic development would both benefit from destroying the dams.[65]

The argument for keeping the Powell River flowing freely was bolstered by the fact that the owner of one of the offending dams, a wholesale clothier named Abraham Longini, was a native Chicagoan and full-time resident of the Windy City. Because he lived far from Big Stone Gap, it was easy for residents to paint him as an outsider with little interest in the community who was profiting at the expense of residents.[66] The *Big Stone Post* reported that Longini and his family were "far removed from the peril to which they wantonly expose us" and declared, "The people of Big Stone Gap must have a poor spirit in them if they allow persons at a distance, or even at home, to keep a death dealing nuisance almost in the heart of their city." The crux of the argument was that municipal officials knew what was in the best interests of the town. Outside capital was necessary for development and was actively courted by New South boosters, but it also spawned tensions over whether the region was becoming a colony of the North—tensions that were evident in clashes over the best use of resources. In Big Stone Gap, officials rejected Longini's outside involvement and claimed that only they should be able to call the shots on how the Powell River was used.[67]

Longini vehemently denied that his dam was causing the community's health woes, however, and claimed that a manufacturing economy was in the best interests of the citizenry of Big Stone Gap. In a series of letters to the town newspaper, Longini insisted that manufacturing contributed to the town's prosperity and was a necessary stage in the growth of Big Stone Gap. He insisted that attacks on his dam would cool enthusiasm for manufacturing, hinder investment by throwing the rights of private property into question, and cause the economy to stagnate. "If this is the way to encourage outside capital to invest in your beautiful city," Longini concluded, "I am at a loss to understand such a policy." "Because I advocate keeping the stream free from sewerage," Longini insisted that "the future will bear me out that my judgement may be as good as the views of those who are ready at all times to sacrifice their neighbor's property for public benefits." He concluded that "there are other means besides dynamite, to overcome what to some of your readers may seem obnoxious."[68]

In Longini's view, the town's health problems were caused by an entirely different use of the river, and he accused residents of dumping their own wastes into the river for disposal just above his dam, where their journey stopped. Although the water of the Powell River was "the best and purest of God's gift," it was polluted "by the carelessness and recklessness of certain people who throw their refuse" into the water above his dam.[69] The editor of the *Big Stone Post* did not deny Longini's accusations but shot back that residents were entitled to throw their wastes into the river. It was "not possible to prevent people from throwing garbage" into the waters of the Powell River, "nor is it desirable." Because the river served as the "natural drainage of the town," it needed to be unobstructed to carry away "all the slop and refuse matter of a large population." Changing traditional ways of using the waterway "merely because the owners of a cheap mill-dam wish to preserve the obstruction," in short, was "simply rediculous [sic]."[70]

The conflict over Longini's dam was not simply about whether using the water of the Powell River was preferable to leaving it pure and free-flowing. It was about whether industrial uses of water conflicted with traditional ways of using these same waterways. The issue forced residents and town officials to use a mental balancing test similar to that used by jurists to decide what was in their best interests. Although residents were outspoken about destroying the dam, town officials were quick to note that this did not mean that Big Stone Gap would shun future business. One correspondent concluded that the town still welcomed economic development, but only on favorable terms. "We are, of course, glad to have foreign capital invested here," but he argued that "if the owners of this capital do not think proper to build anything but mill-dams, and insist on keeping them in the river to collect the filth, mud and refuse in the heart of the city—garbage that should be passed off as quickly as possible, and must breed disease as long as it is allowed to accumulate—we had better do without it." He concluded simply: "The entire city cannot be sacrificed to save a thousand dollar mill-dam."[71] In the spring of 1891 municipal officials decided that Longini's dam had to go. The town council ordered Big Stone Gap's Street Committee to "abate the nuisances of the dams by blowing them skyward," though the committee does not appear to have ever taken action.[72]

Like citizens of Big Stone Gap, communities throughout the South considered the benefits of manufacturing alongside threats to health, changing uses of resources, and industrial pollution. At issue were competing definitions of the public good, and residents used the same process as jurists to make their own determinations about what was in the best interests of the public. The decision to destroy Longini's dam was based on the value of continuing traditional uses of the river, and it suggests that debates over the use of rivers rarely turned on simple questions of preservation or development. Few southerners could afford to challenge all forms of economic development, and many employed a kind of mental balancing test to decide between two paths. In this context, pollution was weighed on a sliding scale that often hewed to economic needs, not environmental quality. Few towns followed the path of Big Stone Gap in deciding that public health was more important than manufacturing, but the calculus of development used by residents and officials there mirrored regional debates over industrial development. Whether considering iron and steel in Alabama, textile mills in the Carolina Piedmont, or fertilizer manufacturing in the Cotton Belt, the process was the same. In one way, though, Big Stone Gap was unique. The town was in the middle of a coal boom and could afford to seek other options. By 1894 Longini's clothing business had folded, and the town's economy continued to be dominated by coal mining.[73]

The challenges that stakeholders posed to water pollution and damming of waterways fell short in bringing about widespread change until the beginning of the twentieth century. While some stakeholders were successful at getting damages, the "instrumental" nature of the judicial system favored economic development through industrialization and headed off far-reaching reforms. People who brought suits against corporations were at a serious disadvantage because they lacked the finances, access to scientific or pseudo-scientific expertise, and legal skill of corporate lawyers who were experienced in hanging up cases on technicalities. Entire groups, notably African Americans, were written out of legal conflicts over water resources even though the environmental effects of industrial growth fell heavily on them. While some communities tempered manufacturing to maintain clean water, free-flowing rivers, or public health, this did little to hold back industrial development regionally.

⁂

By the Progressive Era, the health concerns of municipal officials in places like Big Stone Gap were being codified into state and municipal regulations of water use and infrastructure projects designed to protect clean water. Even though municipal officials came from the classes of professionals most likely to support industrialization, they emerged as outspoken proponents of clean water, which sometimes pitted them against businesspeople who wanted to continue to use rivers for disposing of wastes. Beginning with the Virginia Board of Health, which was organized in 1872, states and cities established commissions tasked with maintaining public health by eliminating nuisances like standing water and imposing quarantines. After major epidemics of mosquito-borne diseases like malaria and yellow fever in the late 1870s, municipalities and boards of health feverishly worked to maintain public health. Progress was slow, especially before the germ theory of disease was popularized in the 1880s, and city-controlled boards of health became mired in politics and were often ineffective at providing needed services. By the twentieth century, states began taking over these roles and were more successful in protecting urban health. As Progressive reformers became concerned about quality of life in the 1910s, states allocated more money to boards of health and granted them broader powers over urban spaces. Regulating water was always an important part of preventing disease, and states gave public health commissions augmented powers over determining how waterways were used—powers that had formerly been reserved for the courts.[74]

To maintain clean water, state officials passed pollution control ordinances in the late nineteenth century that took aim at various forms of water pollution. In a federal review of pollution control laws, North Carolina, Virginia, Tennessee, and Texas were recorded as having partial statewide protections, though Arkansas, Louisiana, Mississippi, and Alabama also had laws on the books. These regulations were mostly about preventing the dumping of wastes into waterways to protect drinking water and health, and industrial pollution was not a major concern. In the 1880s and early 1890s Virginia made it a misdemeanor to throw animal carcasses into any waterway used for drinking water or to otherwise "render impure, turbid, or offensive" municipal drinking water. The North Carolina legislature created a regulatory apparatus for testing and preventing water pollution where it affected drinking water, though legislators mostly took aim at human wastes. Texas made it illegal to "in any wise pollute" waters, making them "unwholesome or offensive" to residents, and Tennessee made it a "public nuisance" to "corrupt or render unwholesome or impure" watercourses and a misdemeanor to pollute water used by water companies. The law primarily prohibited using rivers to dispose of farm or livestock wastes, and the legislature even specified that it would be illegal to make water "unfit" for manufacturing as well. These states were ahead of the rest of the region in having statewide statutes, but as this legislation suggests, they mostly targeted agricultural or personal uses of waterways, not industrial pollution. Only a few states cracked down on industrial pollutants. The code of Virginia, for instance, specified that it was illegal to pollute water with "the refuse of any mine, manufactory, or manufacturing process." In North Carolina, the state outlawed dumping sawdust into streams, though this only applied to one county in the western part of the state. Louisiana took aim at industries that dumped "bagasse from sugar mills, ballast from vessels, sinking timber of any kind," and other items into waterways if they hindered navigation. Some states were clearly beginning to view industrial pollution as a problem, but these examples also suggest that farmers and stock raisers were often targeted for water pollution. Regulating waterways generally maintained corporate access to water and brought the use of water by farmers and stock raisers under strict supervision. By 1904 other southern states had also taken halting steps to prohibit water pollution, but they primarily left pollution control to local officials. Even with these laws, however, experts conceded that the region had some of the weakest pollution control laws in the country. While the lack of "severe" restrictions on water pollution perhaps signals a reluctance on the part of public officials to regulate profitable industries, it can also be chalked up to the delay in southern industrialization. The South was confronting the costs of industrialization after every other part of the nation and did not develop comparable statutory regulations until relatively late.[75]

As municipal officials redefined water pollution as a threat to public health and quality of life, southern cities also moved to construct limited waterworks and sewerage infrastructure. Until the 1870s few cities had developed infrastructure for issues like preventing pollution and providing access to clean water.[76] After the massive yellow fever epidemic in the Mississippi River Valley in 1878, municipal officials in Memphis funded the construction of a new sewerage system to eliminate standing water, dispose of garbage more effectively, and provide access to clean water. The famed "Memphis system" crisscrossed the city with six-inch pipes that provided sewer connections for businesses and private dwellings. Even with these measures, the city still struggled to provide clean water for residents. Until the 1880s the only private water utility, the Memphis Water Company, would not filter the water it supplied from the Wolf

River, which was polluted by nearby factories. The city tried to force the company to draw its water from the Mississippi River, but it was not until another company promoted artesian wells in the late 1880s that Memphis found a more reliable source of clean water.[77] Few cities went as far as Memphis, where officials built a sewerage system from scratch, but other municipal officials did work to develop more limited infrastructure for sewerage and drinking water, though they always struggled to keep up with urban growth.[78]

Despite a growing interest in protecting water from pollution and maintaining public health, the benefits of clean water never extended to everyone. African Americans tended to live near pollution and to be underserved by sanitation and clean water infrastructure more often than white southerners, though economist Werner Troesken is right to note that this could vary a great deal depending on the city.[79] Cholera was a constant threat, and it afflicted black neighborhoods at high rates, especially in Richmond, Nashville, and Atlanta.[80] This was a pattern throughout the region, and African Americans typically had to live near waterways prone to flooding and pollution because they were the cheapest places to live. Urban segregation, which was written into law in the 1910s and 1920s, exacerbated problems of pollution and ensured that these problems continued to fall heavily on black southerners. In Atlanta, black neighborhoods like Shermantown and Summerhill were sited in low-elevation areas that were disproportionately affected by flooding, as well as by industrial and municipal wastes. Even after the city built its first sewerage system in the 1880s, the pipes typically dumped unfiltered wastes into waterways that bordered black neighborhoods, bringing residents into contact with human and industrial pollutants. After decades of scrambling for clean water, the city government began piping water from the Chattahoochee River that was not tainted with industrial pollution and sewage in 1893. But this infrastructure did not service many of the predominately black neighborhoods in the city, which still had to obtain water from polluted springs.[81] Memphis was better than many cities at distributing sanitation infrastructure, but despite its state-of-the-art Memphis system, residents of the predominately black Ninth and Tenth Wards still did not have sewer connections seven years after construction started.[82] Neighborhoods in Savannah like Yamacraw, which fronted the Savannah River, lacked access to clean water and sanitation infrastructure at a higher rate than white neighborhoods even into the 1910s. By the turn of the twentieth century, white residents in Savannah lived on streets with a sewer connection 88 percent of the time, but only 59 percent of black households had access to the same utilities.[83] Racial disparities in access to clean water are perhaps clearest in the wildly different rates at which black and white southerners suffered from waterborne diseases. Between 1880 and 1890 waterborne disease killed more Atlantans than any other affliction, and black Atlantans were particularly susceptible.[84] Black mortality in Charleston and Richmond in the mid-1890s was twice that of whites.[85] In Anniston, Alabama, where death rates for black residents were lower on average, African Americans still died from disease at a rate that was 75 percent higher than white residents.[86] Black public health problems did not strictly cling to the boundaries of the South, and African Americans nationwide died from typhoid fever, caused by dirty water, twice as frequently as whites in the first two decades of the twentieth century.[87] These statistics do not directly reflect the effects of industrial pollution, but they do shed light on the ways that polluted water, whether contaminated by human or industrial wastes, affected African Americans most heavily.

Municipal leaders justified the disparity in access to public utilities and clean water by blaming African Americans for the health problems plaguing cities, which leaders used to take aim at black southerners and to justify segregation. Diseases like cholera and tuberculosis were even defined in racial terms, and white elites speciously argued that the prevalence of these diseases in black bodies was a function not of the poor living conditions available to African Americans in the segregated South but of racially inferior characteristics that made them more susceptible to diseases. In Atlanta, for instance, white elites defined tuberculosis as a disease that was endemic to black Atlantans and worked to limit the mobility and police the bodies of working black women domestics. By defining tuberculosis as a racially demarcated disease, historian Tera Hunter explains that white southerners worked to "sanction racial inequalities" and to "reaffirm their assumption that nature had ordained the relegation of African Americans to the mudsills of Southern society."[88]

Black leaders, especially by the twentieth century, fought back against these problems, though their efforts were hemmed in by Jim Crow. African American elites cast urban health problems as a crisis of conservation—not of resources, but of human life. Booker T. Washington admitted that "without health, and until we reduce the high death rate, it will be impossible for us to have permanent success in business, in property getting, in acquiring education, or to show other evidences of progress" and declared, "We must reduce our high death rate, dethrone disease, and enthrone health and long life."[89] Although black leaders like Washington understood how important it was to conserve health, they often missed the key relationship between environmental problems and black public health and promoted elitist solutions that did little to help African Americans struggling with poor living conditions. An 1897 study of "excessive mortality among Negroes" by researchers from Atlanta University, for instance, concluded that it was not due to "unfavorable conditions of environment" but to the "ignorance of the masses of the people and their disregard of the laws of health and mortality." Because health problems were supposedly grounded in poor choices, they were solvable. The researchers concluded, "If poor houses, unhealthy localities, bad sewerage, and defective plumbing were responsible for [African Americans'] high death-rate," then "there would be no hope of reducing the death-rate until either the colored people become wealthy, or philanthropic persons erected sanitary houses, or municipalities made appropriations to remove these conditions." Rather than stressing the need for "sanitary regulation," then, they focused on "social reconstruction and moral regeneration." Researchers urged black southerners to abandon city residences "over stables, in dark, damp cellars, and on back alleys, in the midst of stench and putrefaction" for living spaces in the "suburbs," where they would have access to "purer air and water, and had a garden spot besides." The researchers concluded that "convenience to the heart of the city often overrides considerations of health, and that the white people offer them hot-beds of disease for homes is no excuse for their taking them."[90]

Black intellectuals promoted education as the key to solving these pernicious health problems. Booker T. Washington was especially outspoken on this issue. Besides incorporating public health into the curriculum at Tuskegee by promoting sanitation, waste disposal, and clean water, Washington called attention to public health concerns at the Tuskegee Negro Conference in 1914 by hosting speakers on various aspects of the issue who taught about everything from pure food to caring for children. In 1915 Washington even established National Negro Health Week, which was cosponsored by the National Negro Business League, to raise the profile of public health problems in the black community. The event, which was held for more than two decades, distributed information on keeping wells and other water supplies free of pollutants, cooking healthy food, cleaning homes, and eliminating habitats for mosquitoes. One entire day in 1915 was devoted to community efforts to clean up black neighborhoods throughout the nation in order to give participants experience putting what they learned into practice.[91] Negro Health Week was a high-profile event, but other schools and universities used similar methods to tackle health problems afflicting black southerners. These campaigns rarely yielded much change, especially given how badly they misunderstood the root of these problems. Yet at a time when black southerners were cut out of formal policy-making channels, these efforts called attention to the racial differential in access to a clean environment, and they show how black leaders rejected the idea that permanence had to come at the cost of environmental and bodily health.

Sewerage infrastructure was not intended to prevent industrial pollution. But the growing power of public health commissions, substantial municipal investments in sanitation infrastructure, and the need to maintain a steady supply of clean water for white residents brought municipal officials into conflict with manufacturers. Unlike conflicts between agriculture and industry, which courts often adjudicated to favor industry, conflicts between urban and industrial interests stemmed from the same impulse. Urban businessmen were integral to organizing, supporting, and participating in public health crusades. They were also the most outspoken advocates of manufacturing. Even when municipal officials did promote clean water by taking aim at manufacturing enterprises that were polluting, their actions were not an attempt to challenge the logic of industrial development because clean water was just another selling point for their community. In 1903, for instance, the owner of the Blue Springs Company tried to get Columbus, Georgia, to adopt its water system by claiming that "impure, or even water that is suspected of impurity, is the worst thing in the world for a city's prosperity."[92]

The efforts of public health officials and businessmen to protect drinking water sometimes ran headlong into industrialists with different visions for water resources, even though their broad economic vision often aligned. Municipalities occasionally had to go after polluting industries to maintain their access to clean water. Perhaps the best example of how urban development complicated choices about economic development and water resources can be seen in a notable 1906 legal clash between the city of Durham, North Carolina, and the Eno Cotton Mills. The chief health officer of Durham filed a lawsuit for the city against Eno Cotton Mills, a textile mill on the Eno River near Hillsborough. Along with industrial wastes like dyestuffs, the cotton mill funneled human waste from water closets in the houses of its three hundred employees directly into the river. Because the city obtained its drinking water just downstream from the cotton mill, officials claimed that the company's actions had made the water "polluted and made unfit for drinking purposes," causing "the health of the inhabitants of the city of Durham" to be "seriously menaced." The city asked for a perpetual injunction to halt this pollution until the mill could "provide some other method of disposing of its sewage and dye waste, and other dangerous and foul matter."[93]

The mill owners did not deny that they were using the river as an industrial sewer, and the case hinged on which use was more important: the mill's business or the town's health. Company officials claimed that their pollution did not extend to the water supply intake and made technical arguments to show that the pollutants put into the river had diluted enough to be harmless—that the river could cleanse itself. They even claimed that there were other places more suitable for getting clean water and urged the Durham Water Company to look elsewhere.[94] The company's arguments ultimately came down to business, though. "God Almighty had provided the Eno river as the natural power for disposing of filth and other deleterious substances deposited on the earth by man and beast," as one observer put it, and "the cost of its destruction by any purifying process would be tantamount to a confiscation and ruination of the Eno cotton mills."[95]

Though he gave the mill time to construct a treatment system, the superior court judge granted the city an injunction halting the "flowing or discharging any sewage into said Eno river" unless it had "passed through some well-known system of sewage purification approved by the State Board of Health," a decision that was upheld by the North Carolina Supreme Court.[96] Even with this landmark ruling, justices on the North Carolina Supreme Court were quick to note that they were not antidevelopment and that "the injunction should operate so as to produce the least possible injury to the defendant's property and business consistent with the maintenance of the rights and interests of the public."[97]

This case received much publicity, and an official with the North Carolina Board of Health commented that it was "a matter of very great and far-reaching importance involving a new question in our State."[98] A correspondent in Richmond, a city that was concurrently fighting its own battles against polluting industries, editorialized that "legitimate enterprise is to be encouraged, but not at the expense of the public health. The streams of Virginia are nature's own gifts, and they belong to the people." While "they may be used by private enterprise so long as there is no trespass," he concluded that "when they are so employed as to deprive the public of its rights, the restraining power of the law should be exercised."[99] Not everyone believed that the decision set a good precedent for attracting industry to the South, however. Although the North Carolina Supreme Court framed its ruling in a way that continued to encourage industrial activity, outside observers believed that the ruling would set a precedent for the regulation of manufacturing. A sanitation engineer from New York claimed that arguments about "riparian self-purification" made by the cotton mill were true and argued that the decision had been made on the basis of "legislative enactment . . . not scientific investigation." It had set a dangerous precedent, because "the laws, while compelling the removal of nuisances and the protection of public water supplies, should be of such scope and latitude as to enable each case to be considered scientifically upon its merits."[100] A Georgia citizen, writing under the pseudonym "A Tax-Payer," noted that although Eno Cotton Mills was dumping the refuse of only three hundred operatives into the Eno River, "the defilement of the water shed of the Chattahoochee river, including Atlanta down to Columbus, consists of fecal matter, excrement, sewage, etc., from about 250,000 people." The North Carolina mill was less "threatening to the health of the inhabitants" of Durham than Georgia textile mills at West Point, Langdale, and Riverview. Durham's victory had set a dangerous precedent for future economic development by opening the door for complaints about nuisances on the Chattahoochee, and he worried that the city of Columbus could also be held liable for "damages for injuries by sickness and death." This "Tax-Payer" lamented, "If the cotton factories at and above Columbus can be stopped from the use of the Chattahoochee river as a sewage and natural drainage for all cotton mill waste and filth, then Columbus' present and greatest coming industries are stabbed in the heart."[101]

The struggle over industrial pollution and human wastes in the Eno River did not set the precedent for clean water that many municipal officials wanted, however. In the first decade of the twentieth century, other cities also had to fight to keep their water free from industrial pollution. This was especially evident in Richmond, which had some of the strongest pollution control laws in the region by the turn of the twentieth century. In 1901 an editorialist wrote to the *Richmond Times* lauding the state for its oversight of the city's water. "Nothing is more important than to prevent pollution of a water-supply," he claimed, because "it is far easier to require factories to take proper precautions when they are built than to have them removed by injunction or to have their business seriously impaired in order that the health of the community may not be placed in jeopardy." He urged the Virginia Board of Health to be given more power over preventing pollution, hoping that the city would not allow future "pollutions of the James to occur as have been such sources of trouble and expense to other cities."[102] In 1905, however, Ernest Levy, the city's chief health officer, reported widespread pollution of the James River from upstream factories. Levy focused on sulphite waste, which was a by-product of the pulp and paper factories at Covington, Virginia, more than two hundred miles upstream. Dumping sulphite into the water turned it "dark brown and later a purplish black," and Levy observed that "this appearance can be noted for the entire distance from Covington to Richmond." This was an alarming discovery, but Levy assured the city council that the problems were more aesthetic than real. Industrial waste from pulp and paper mills did not facilitate bacteria growth and only was problematic when water levels were low. Levy explained that "the water is rendered objectionable in appearance by this waste" and was "not relished by the consumer, even if he knows that it is probably safe to drink it."[103]

Levy's report prompted a years-long debate over whether industrial polluters should be regulated. The issue did not come to a head until 1911, when the pollution had reached a point where the city council lobbied the Virginia General Assembly to stop the "manufacturing establishments emptying noxious waste material into the rivers and streams of the Commonwealth" from dumping wastes or to force them to install treatment systems.[104] Council members cited Levy's study to argue that the James River and the city's water supply were "seriously contaminated by the flowing therein of waste material from pulp and paper mills, tanneries and other manufacturing establishments." This had made the water "undesirable, if not unfit for use for domestic purposes," and was a "nuisance, and also a serious injury to all riparian owners upon the said rivers and streams." Citing the legal principle "sic utere tuo ut alienum non laedas" (use your own property in such a way that it does not harm others), the council argued that "the owners of the adjoining soil and the next owner has [sic] precisely the same rights therein as every other owner, and that no riparian owner of a stream may so corrupt or pollute it as to injure the other owners by diminishing the value of their property in the natural stream."[105]

Within a year the legislative delegation from Richmond had introduced several bills calling for an end to industrial pollution by pulp and paper mills in the James River. The bills mandated that any factory "from which deleterious, noxious or unhealthy waste material may flow" into waterways used for drinking had to make plans for the "purification of said waste material" under the oversight of the state Board of Health.[106] Besides the public health benefits, public officials predicted that this would save the city between $10,000 and $12,000 per year for "coagulants . . . to remove the discoloration and impurities not natural to river water."[107] The city attorney outlined how much was invested in the water purification plant and concluded that this "seemed to be a case . . . of life and health and happiness against an industry." This mimicked the balancing test that jurists had used for decades to decide if permanent manufactories were worth the cost, but with a twist. Now the question turned on quality of life, rather than just economic gain. The city attorney answered this question by arguing that Richmond's priority should be clean water, and he concluded that the city "requires the protection of water used for domestic purpose as the prime necessity."[108]

The proposal to regulate polluting industries on the James River had strong municipal support from the Richmond City Council, the Committee on Water, the Board of Health, the city attorney, and the entire delegation in the House of Representatives. The *Times Dispatch* even claimed that "other cities of the Commonwealth interested in the protection of their water supply from pollution are joining in the fight Richmond is making," and the events were covered throughout the state.[109] Yet the city attorney rightly predicted that such legislation "would be bitterly opposed by pulp mills, iron furnaces and other industries which now empty all manner of refuse and coloring matter into the waters of the upper James River." At a committee hearing on the proposed regulation, it was apparent that industrialists responsible for the wastes were not thrilled about having their access to the James River curtailed. Several pulp mills had relocated to the James River from the Potomac River after the federal government cracked down on pollution to maintain the water supply of Washington, D.C., and the companies had already used their substantial influence to defeat similar pollution control legislation in Virginia just the previous year.[110] Representatives from the Chamber of Commerce and the city's Business Men's Club stood by the pulp mills, claiming that they "could find nobody, outside of the City Council, who wanted its passage." At the hearing "large delegations representing the pulp mills at Covington and tanneries at various points were present to oppose the bills." They argued that these regulations would stifle their productive industry, and one representative reminded the committee "how a mill had been brought to Virginia which came near going to West Virginia, where it was kept out by objections from small fishermen." Yet their main strategy was to blame the city's own discharges into the river. W. E. Allen, a spokesman for the manufacturers, argued that "it was strange Richmond was after the material discharged by plants, while neglecting sewerage in the streams, which really cause disease," and claimed that "the city avoids that subject because it would be itself affected." "Rather than destroy the industries which employ so many men," Allen concluded, "Richmond had better go elsewhere for water."[111]

By 1929 the city had negotiated a contract allowing it to take water directly from the Chesapeake and Ohio Canal, which George Whitfield, the head of the Department of Public Utilities, reported was starting to "improve the quality of that supply." Several of the worst offenders had also started cleaning up their acts, and the West Virginia Pulp and Paper Company had "spent a vast sum of money on improvements which upon completion will remove 85% of the sulphite waste from their plant at Covington." Yet pollution of the James River had seemingly gotten worse, largely because of the construction of a massive new pulp mill upstream of Richmond at Lynchburg. Whitfield lamented that "pollution from pulp mills is now so great that unless it is reduced by the time the river reaches a low stage it will be impossible to furnish the citizens of Richmond with water which is safe and at the same time palatable."[112]

The struggle over the water of the James River was just one of many struggles over the environmental effects of industrial development occurring throughout the region, which only increased as the region's industrial development boomed. By the 1930s these clashes had led to increased regulation of water resources, though it fell far short of what was necessary to prevent watersheds from becoming polluted. If a municipality could maintain public health and access to clean water, it was often willing to overlook industrial pollution. The *Atlanta Constitution* explained that pulp and paper mills—one of the industries deemed most permanent by boosters—spewed chemicals into the air, causing an "unpleasant odor," and also allowed "chemical and other wastes" to be "dumped into the stream," resulting in "contamination." Yet the newspaper noted that "communities in which paper mills are now established . . . consider these objections comparatively minor in view of the vastly stepped-up income the mill means to the community."[113] Permanence, ironically, was sometimes more important than environmental quality.

The New Deal arguably increased the dramatic environmental effects of industrial development and dam building on the South's waterways, especially with the massive Tennessee Valley Authority projects after 1933. It also made federal officials part of these decisions, but resistance to industrial changes to water resources persisted into the 1930s. Even major New Deal public works projects like South Carolina's Santee-Cooper Power and Navigation Project ran into significant opposition from conservationists and locals who argued that the massive environmental transformations were not worth the benefits.[114] These southerners no doubt would have agreed with historian Ted Steinberg's contention that "industrial capitalism is as much a battle over nature as it is over work," and they protested rapidly changing uses of southern waters as the industrial economy placed water resources into corporate hands.[115] Because a coalition of southerners—not just outspoken industrial promoters—believed that manufacturing was the best solution for continued underdevelopment, the stakes were high. Some stakeholders welcomed development and gave little thought to the environmental costs, but others, especially those in the path of mosquitoes, floodwaters, or industrial pollution, believed that there should be limits on how industries should be permitted to use water. These efforts did not help all southerners, however. Despite struggles to improve living conditions, African Americans were never able to fully gain parity with white southerners in carving out access to a clean living environment—a dynamic that laid the foundation for environmental justice struggles in the late twentieth century.

Nevertheless, black and white southerners often challenged corporations that had crossed the line into irresponsible use of resources. Their efforts did not repeat the antebellum pattern that Gary Kulik, Ted Steinberg, and other scholars sketch out, however, in which a largely subsistence population challenged industrial uses of resources. They did not reflect capitalism coming to the "countryside."[116] Conflicts over industrial development in the New South were about competing paths to capitalist development, debates that were always closely linked to different visions for using the South's resources. Critics of industrial uses of water did not shun industry or capitalist growth totally. They simply wanted to control the environmental effects of industrial development. In the first decades of the twentieth century, concerns about manufacturing's effects on the South's waterways had become part and parcel of the region's brand of Progressive reform, which did not challenge industry but affirmed it. Taken as a whole, these challenges did not halt industrial development, but they did supply cleaner water to urban residents, cracked down on the most overt forms of pollution, and provided a check on the power that corporations held over natural resources.

CHAPTER 5

Tourism's New Path

IF ANY SINGLE EVENT laid bare the perils of impermanence, it was the Florida land boom of the 1920s. Four decades earlier, businessmen like Henry Flagler and Henry Plant had transformed Florida into a popular destination for wealthy vacationers by crisscrossing the state with rail lines and building fashionable resorts that offered exclusive opportunities for recreation and social interaction. In the flush times of the 1920s, however, Florida became a tourist mecca for growing numbers of middle-class Americans who traveled to the state in their Tin Lizzies to enjoy surf and sun. As Florida became synonymous with tourism, a frenzy of speculative development was initiated by millionaire businessman Carl Fisher, who built Miami Beach on a precarious barrier island hugging the eastern boundary of Biscayne Bay and promoted it as a vacation destination in the years after World War I. In the wake of Fisher's success, hundreds of thousands of Americans flooded into Florida. Real estate prices skyrocketed, and suburban cities like Coral Gables, which appeared almost overnight, drew tourists, developers, and speculators eager to experience or profit off the surge of enthusiasm for coastal Florida. As land prices boomed and credit loosened, risky speculative ventures became the norm. The sandy foundations of the Florida boom were exposed when transportation difficulties and a financial downturn in 1926 burst the real estate bubble and brought a swift end to the boom—all capped off by a devastating hurricane that tarnished Florida's image as a national playground.[1]

The dramatic rise and fall of Florida's tourism empire was not a shining example of the permanence of tourism-based enterprises. Yet in 1932 University of North Carolina sociologist Rupert Vance praised the boom for showing that tourism could be a permanent solution to the South's economic and environmental problems. Vance was one of the leading proponents of "regionalism," an approach to building up the southern economy, solving persistent social problems, and bringing the region up to the standards of the rest of the nation through careful planning and a collaboration between academic, governmental, and business partners.[2] It is curious that Vance, an advocate for regionalism, would praise the Florida boom, which even he admitted was "at variance with regional planning." Although Vance characterized it as a "boom run riot," it also proved that natural beauty and a mild climate could be valuable and renewable resources for communities on the make. Vance explained that the boom showed "of what grace and charm the southern shoreline is capable in landscaping and architecture" and "has left some of the most beautiful and civilized spots in America" in its wake. He praised developers like Carl Fisher, George Merrick of Coral Gables, and Hollywood's Joseph Young, who had reshaped Florida's natural landscape into more enduring examples of "earthly beauty" and "landscape artistry" by creating an "American Riviera" atop "mangrove swamps and sandbars." While this process was "chaotic, speculative, exploitative," it also showed the ability of tourism-based industries to bring "the beauties of nature and man-made beauty in harmony." "There is much of charm and artistry that regional planning may learn from the plans of the ill-fated promoters of the Florida boom," Vance admitted, and he explained that in Florida "the core of development remains," because "high pressure salesmanship cannot permanently despoil the region of its natural charm." The boom may have gone bust, but "the impetus of the movement has remained and will be permanent."[3]

Vance was one of the few people to see permanence in the Florida land boom, but he was not alone in believing that tourism could be a permanent enterprise for southern communities. By the 1930s, well before tourism had become one of the Sunbelt's leading industries, a "growth coalition" of regional officials, business leaders, and planners had embraced tourism as a strategy to bring economic and environmental permanence to the still-developing South.[4] Tourism has rightly taken its place in the historical literature alongside other enterprises, but scholars have been more interested in how tourism transformed perceptions of people or culture than southern landscapes.[5] Scholars who do consider the environmental impacts of tourism typically only look at the practical effects of tourism-based enterprises on the landscape or at the ways tourism boosters sold romanticized images of nature to attract vacationers to a range of different destinations.[6] There has been little consideration of how tourism's perceived environmental footprint—one founded on a perception that it was the quintessential permanent industry—shaped its place in the political economy of the New South and ultimately laid the foundation for the region's post–World War II tourism boom.

If we truly want to understand how tourism shaped the South, however, we have to take seriously boosterish perceptions of the industry's environmental permanence, even if this was myopic and did not reflect reality. Vance suggests that tourist enterprises had the potential to draw continually on renewable resources like climate, scenery, and salubrity—resources that had been overlooked in the New South rush to develop agriculture and industry. As opportunities for travel became available to a wider group of Americans, the success of tourist enterprises also demonstrated that the industry had the financial legs to contribute to lasting growth, even to spur further development. In a region still leery about the expansion of federal power, private tourism initiatives promised to address the most glaring examples of resource depletion without having to turn to state or federal regulation. Finally, tourism maintained the racial hierarchy by carefully policing who could and could not benefit from the South's leisure resources.

Defining tourism as a permanent industry was a contested process, however. As tourism grew into a stand-alone industry in the twentieth century, boosters, businesspeople, public officials, and other stakeholders had to decide how it fit into long-established ideas about the best uses of the South's natural resources. Was tourism the highest use of these resources, and could it bring permanent prosperity? Or would tourism stunt development by inhibiting the use of valuable resources simply for the sake of scenery? The long-term success of permanence hinged on these vital questions.

☙

Tourism was not new to the postbellum South. Since the late eighteenth century, wealthy southerners had traveled to resorts at the seashore, mountains, and natural springs to escape diseases that scoured plantations and cities in the summer.[7] Health resorts like Flat Rock, North Carolina, and Aiken, South Carolina, were refuges for planters from Lowcountry South Carolina and Georgia, and natural wonders like Kentucky's Mammoth Cave and Virginia's Natural Bridge were popular destinations for travelers north and south. Tourism was completely halted by the Civil War, and travel accommodations remained primitive for years afterward. As late as 1870 author Edward Pollard observed that tourists were scarce at mountain resorts and mineral springs in Virginia, despite their popularity before the Civil War. Pollard lamented that "scenes . . . once referred to as wonderful and interesting, have fallen into comparative obscurity, and have for years since the war failed to make their appearance, even in the advertisement columns of the newspapers."[8] By the 1880s, tourism was slowly being reestablished in parts of the South. As wealthy Americans discovered the virtues of going on vacation, the postwar reconstruction and expansion of railroad infrastructure connected isolated resorts with national transportation networks, drawing northern tourists looking for milder climes to health resorts, sanitariums, boardinghouses, natural wonders, and other sites in the region. By 1890 seasonal tourism was so common that clergyman and travel writer Henry Field even reported that "migration to the

South at the approach of Winter, has become almost as regular as the migration of birds."[9]

Most early tourists came to the South looking for a salubrious environment. In the nineteenth century, Americans widely believed that landscapes could influence bodily health. The growth of cities, especially in the industrial North, spawned a class of urban travelers who sought out landscapes that would act as a palliative for a range of real or imagined maladies derived from urban living, from tuberculosis to neurasthenia. Southern sites in the mountains, natural springs, and coastal resorts became popular stops for vacationers who believed that these spaces had unique health benefits derived from their mild climate and salubrious landscape.[10]

The growth of health tourism in the 1870s and 1880s transformed the way that southern boosters perceived their environment by imbuing it with healthy attributes. Health resorts showed that there was economic value in seacoasts, hot springs, and scenic mountain vistas that had little use for agriculture or industry. Perhaps no part of the region was transformed as much as the piney woods, a belt of longleaf pine that hugged the fall line through the Carolinas and Georgia into northern Florida and southern Alabama and Mississippi. For more than 150 years, longleaf forests had been vital for producing turpentine, pitch, and tar. By the mid-nineteenth century, however, naval stores producers were migrating south after tapping out the forests of the Carolinas, leaving cutover or burned areas to stagnate. As regional tourism gained momentum after the Civil War, businesspeople latched onto these once-valuable forests and repackaged them as healthy landscapes, making cutover pine forests a valuable resource by linking them to the fortunes of tourism. At a time when prevailing medical theory held that certain maladies were miasmatic, or caused by impurities in the air, regional physicians touted the benefits of breathing the fragrant aroma of pines, as well as their role in keeping the air clean. Physicians joined with municipal boosters and local businesspeople to promote the healthy traits of cutover pine forests to attract visitors, in the process making it clear that tourism could be a profitable waste industry.[11]

The arrival of health tourists in the 1870s and 1880s transformed the piney woods into profitable landscapes once again. In the 1880s the Red Hills of Georgia abandoned cotton cultivation to become one of the most popular resort destinations in the entire country. By 1883 more than fifteen thousand visitors were staying in Thomasville's five hotels each season.[12] In South Carolina, health tourism transformed Summerville from a sleepy hamlet visited chiefly by Lowcountry planters to a booming health resort, especially after it was praised for its healthy reputation by officials at the International Tuberculosis Conference in Paris.[13] Even resorts based around natural springs like the

Hygeia Hotel in Citronelle, Alabama, and Abita Springs, Louisiana, successfully played up the health benefits of surrounding cutover forests that placed them in the "Ozone Belt" to attract a broader group of travelers.[14] Promoters were so successful in diverting health tourists to the piney woods that in 1896 the owners of the Lakewood Hotel, a resort in New Jersey, urged travelers not to "go South," because their hotel was only fifty miles from New York and still "Among the Pines."[15]

No part of the South was transformed as much as the Sandhills of North Carolina, in the heart of the state's piney woods district. After the naval stores industry picked up and left, the Sandhills languished until 1884, when entrepreneur and state immigration agent John Patrick purchased seven hundred acres just off the Seaboard Air Line Railway for under two dollars per acre. The sale price indicates that the area had few economic prospects, but Patrick gambled that there was still value in the pines. He cast the poor sandy soil, mineral springs, and cutover pine forests as unparalleled health assets and argued that these wasted resources would make his community, which he eventually dubbed Southern Pines, into a booming health resort. As one advertisement noted, the "latitude, perfect drainage, sandy soil, pure water and curative ozone, exhaled from long leaf pines," made Southern Pines "especially favored, both as a resort and a permanent abiding place."[16] Patrick organized the Southern Pines Resort Company and worked closely with Seaboard Air Line officials, who would later hire him as their industrial and immigration agent, to construct a resort and suburban village. By 1896 the resort boasted eight hotels, dozens of cottages, a modern railroad depot, a variety of stores and food markets, and even a nine-hole golf course with "some fine natural hazards."[17] Observers in the mid-1890s called Southern Pines "one of the healthiest and most desirable winter resorts in America," and it was one of the most popular tourist destinations in the state.[18] Even the unsightly presence of naval stores operators still trying to extract what little turpentine remained in local forests did not inhibit tourism, and physician George Saddleson explained that the "manufacture of spirits of turpentine and resin" there would "undoubtedly prove of great interest to most who shall come here, and . . . will be beneficial in a certain way, as many have received great benefit from breathing the fumes of the hot resin as it comes from the distillery."[19]

Black and white southerners shared an understanding of bodily health as connected to the landscape, but their access to healthy landscapes—or the profits that resort owners made off these landscapes—was not equal. Indeed, the health and leisure benefits derived from the Carolina piney woods were not equitably distributed. As Patrick transformed Southern Pines into an exclusive resort, he privatized pine forests that had functioned as a de facto commons by offering their health benefits solely to white visitors. The only access to these landscapes available to African Americans was through work as low-wage laborers, from golf caddies to restaurant servers. African Americans were deliberately excluded from the resort grounds unless they were working, and the town was strictly segregated on racial lines. Two decades after Southern Pines was founded, a local newspaper reported, "There are practically no colored people, the only exception being a narrow strip of territory lying adjacent to the colored settlement, from which the white people have almost wholly removed." Black residents were consigned to West Southern Pines, an arrangement that "gives the town ample colored help and allows each race to live its own life." For resort boosters, segregation was simply another selling point for tourists, who often craved encounters with locals as a glimpse of the "authentic" South. At resorts throughout the South, tourism promoters encouraged such opportunities but were careful to limit and carefully script these interactions.[20]

Even so, African Americans contested their exclusion from the resort's landscape of leisure by building the region's only sanitarium for black consumptives, the Pickford Sanitarium for Consumptive Negroes, just half a mile from the white resort at Southern Pines. Dedicated in 1897, the institution was the brainchild of Dr. Lawson Scruggs, a black physician who had been born into slavery before attending medical school at Shaw University in Raleigh. Scruggs decried that African Americans were cut off from health care and leisure available to whites. He explained that black sufferers had to "remain at home and be deprived of any of the benefits that might be gained by a change of residence," which was "in the great majority of cases, only a crowded, unclean, tenement house, too often unfit for the indwelling of so many cattle." Even if African Americans had the money to "change climate and residence . . . for the protection of [their] health and life from the ravages of CONSUMPTION," Scruggs noted that "all of the hotels . . . here in the South, as well as the special sanitary institutions for consumptives, are, by long-standing customs and laws, closed against the Negro." To build a sanitarium for black patients, he secured funding from charitable northerners and black mutual aid societies and used it to purchase land and construct health and leisure infrastructure there. An advertisement noted that the sanitarium was "favorably located in the healthful pine belt of North Carolina" and was the "only" sanitarium "in the South built and equipped for the special treatment of those diseases of the throat and lungs so prevalent amongst colored people." Visitors were welcome between November and April, provided they could afford to pay fifteen dollars each month—a hefty sum. The Pickford Sanitarium shows that black southerners found ways to gain access to resources that would improve health and provide recreation, placing limits on efforts to exclude them from white places of leisure. As the region's only sanitarium open for African Americans, however, Pickford also reveals the limitations on leisure for black southerners and the ways that tourism reserved valuable resources for white visitors. In fact, the sanitarium was promoted by white elites, including John Patrick, who served on the board. Because Pickford "isolate[d] the disease from the public" and protected white visitors, even the General Assembly endorsed the sanitarium.[21]

Health resorts like Southern Pines took seemingly worthless forests of tapped-out pine and transformed them into the glitz and glamour of a fashionable resort, and this made it seem like tourism could be a permanent enterprise in the South. The long-term nature of tourism was especially clear when contrasted with the migratory naval stores industry that had preceded it. In 1886 physician and visitor William Waugh admitted that "the first impressions on getting out at Southern Pines are decidedly discouraging" because "one looks out on a scene suggestive of a half burned, half-cleared Jersey barren" where "pines number from twenty-five to fifty to the acre—all the land will sustain—and as they have been repeatedly barked for turpentine, the trees have a rather ghostly aspect." Waugh concluded, however, that "a little reflection shows that this rather dreary region is better for our purpose than the ideal forest," because a cutover forest provided an environment that was not conducive to disease.[22] Two years later the Seaboard Air Line Railway noted that before the resort the area had been "a favorite field for turpentine invaders, who 'boxed' many of the finest pines for their resinous sap." The company described how "hundreds of these noble trees in their scarred, maimed and disfigured trunks bear mute and pitiful testimony to the ruthless savagery of the 'tar heelers,' who spared no 'long leaf' that could yield tribute to their rapacity," suggesting that tourism was a more responsible use of these forests than the "savagery" of the naval stores industry.[23]

The success of Southern Pines rippled through the tapped-out forests of the Sandhills. A few years after building Southern Pines, Patrick started another winter health resort called Pine Bluff, seven miles to the south.[24] Just to the west was another popular resort, Pinehurst, founded in 1895 by James Walker Tufts, a Boston entrepreneur, and built on the Southern Pines model. By the twentieth century, Pinehurst had become one of the most popular golfing destinations in the United States.[25] The success of winter resorts in the Sandhills was not just a testament to the allure of resort names that started with "pine." These resorts offered an experience based on the health value of tapped-out forests, and they showed that tourism could draw on wasted or overlooked resources to be a permanent industry, at least in parts of the region. Author Joe Mitchell Chapple concluded in 1911 that Pinehurst was "more than a winter resort." "It is a development and a study in economics and sociology," he explained, "which demonstrates how a great sandhill region, with incomparable climate and splendid water, has been transformed as if by magic into a thriving town settlement."[26] What happened in the piney woods was replicated in other places. By the twentieth century, mountain districts like Asheville and Linville, North Carolina, were able to market their scenic beauty and salubrious environs to become notable health resorts. Coastal cities like Charleston, South Carolina, and Savannah, Georgia, were transformed from stagnant ports that had been surpassed by interior New South cities into bustling resort districts. After entrepreneur Daniel Purse bought Tybee Island and connected it to Savannah by rail in the 1880s, a 1901 biographer remarked that his efforts had transformed Tybee Island from "almost a sand desert, into a popular summer resort."[27] Even promoters in Florida were able to convince tourists that the state was a desirable location—not a malarial swamp—for health travel by playing up its "climate or its tropical scenery."[28] Health tourism, then, took landscapes that were not useful for agriculture or industry and transformed them into profitable spaces. Besides providing a concrete demonstration that tourism was a quintessential waste industry, this process also cordoned off these landscapes for the enjoyment of only a select few.

☙

Even as health resorts laid the foundation for viewing tourism as an industry that could draw continually on scenery and climate, the region's growth coalition was not totally convinced that tourism had the economic legs to contribute to long-term growth. At a time when tourism was largely seasonal, skeptical boosters and public officials sometimes concluded that betting everything on visitors was folly. Because wealthy tourists in the nineteenth century had cash to invest in a region that desperately needed it, boosters worked to leverage tourist travel into agricultural or industrial development. In their efforts to market the South as a place of business and of leisure, New South promoters did not see tourism as a force for environmental preservation that was mutually exclusive from other enterprises. It was simply a keen way to hasten agricultural or industrial development.

This is at odds with standard historical narratives of tourism in the South. Scholars typically explain the popularity of southern tourism by characterizing the region as a place where visitors could escape the hustle and bustle of life in the industrializing North. As Rebecca McIntyre contends, tourism promoters cultivated a nonindustrial image by casting the South as "a refuge from the hectic pace of modern life where the tourist could relax in the calm soothing atmosphere of a pre-modern world"—an image tourists found "more exciting than the bland generic landscape of an industrial city."[29] Yet before the twentieth century, tourism was about promoting agriculture and industry as much as it was about promoting recreation and recuperation. Just as guidebooks in the West linked travel with Manifest Destiny, New South boosters linked travel with the New South Creed, not always in subtle ways.[30]

This was particularly true of railroad officials, who were the region's leading tourist promoters into the twentieth century. From the 1870s to the 1900s, railroad companies had sole discretion over which resorts would get rail access, and they invested in tourism infrastructure, advertised travel opportunities, and even purchased or constructed hotels, pavilions, or other infrastructure to promote passenger travel.[31] Even with efforts to increase passenger travel, railroad officials realized that it would never be their primary source of income. The profits from hauling freight were much greater than those from hauling passengers. An 1889 railroad manual estimated that on average 70 percent of all revenues came from freight, while only 25 percent came from passenger travel, and these figures skewed even more in favor of freight as far-reaching development programs promoted agricultural or industrial development.[32] In this context, tourism was less important as an end in itself than as a strategy to promote other kinds of development. Railroad officials used tourism to generate freight by inviting tourists to invest in other kinds of development. This strategy was also based on the realities of the railway journey. Because tracks were generally located close to business infrastructure, passengers stared out of their cars at what one scholar terms a "metropolitan corridor" of fields, forests, cityscapes, and industrial establishments. Tourists already had a window seat on southern development, and selling business opportunities to visitors was a result of railroad needs and an acknowledgment of the realities of the tourist experience.[33]

This strategy required putting the region's resources to work, but not in the ways we typically expect of tourism-based enterprises. Rather than trucking in nostalgia for the Lost Cause and playing up only the climatic, historical, or scenic elements of the South, railroad officials and other tourism boosters called attention to latent industrial resources and commercial infrastructure in the hopes of attracting investment. Railroads also encouraged resort owners to develop nontourist enterprises that could provide freight, sometimes in close proximity to tourists. In promotional literature published nationwide, railroad officials, tourism promoters, and community boosters marketed tourist activities alongside industrial development, "progressive" agriculture, and commercial development. "Instead of painting beautiful pictures of the delights of the winter climate, the rare sports, the seductive pleasures of the rod and reel," or "the 'overpoweringly grand' tropical scenery," a Florida agricultural journal urged promoters in 1892 to tell tourists about "our cow peas, potatoes, cane fields, tobacco farms, corn, cotton, peanuts, fruits, fibres, vegetables, stock, and a thousand other products that can be grown in profitable profusion on our now useless land."[34] Railroad officials and tourism boosters did tell tourists about these opportunities while also directing them to industrial or commercial sites. A guide published by the Virginia Midland Railway, for instance, claimed that "so much needs to be said about the picturesque that there is danger of overlooking the salt works, the marble, the iron works, the coal mines that one notices on his way," while another guide described attractions for sightseers in Charleston, South Carolina, including "the representative phosphate manufactories of the state."[35] In 1890 Walter Raymond and Irving Whitcomb, the leading travel agents in the United States, even organized a special "Grand Tour through the New South" that gave northern tourists an opportunity to visit the "centres of commercial and industrial importance" in the South.[36] By showing that the South was more than just a place to recuperate from illness or enjoy the outdoors, boosters attempted to convince tourists to invest in development or settle there permanently.

Although scholars show that tourism enterprises often prioritize aesthetic uses of resources that can conflict with other developmental priorities, in the nineteenth-century South, resort owners and boosters did not see tourism as mutually exclusive with other enterprises. Few municipal officials and town boosters wanted to be entirely at the mercy of tourist travel, and they worked to attract other industries as well, often alongside profitable resorts.[37] In the Shenandoah Valley of Virginia, railroad officials and local boosters worked to transform Luray, a sleepy tourist town, into a thriving industrial metropolis, always claiming that their actions would not drive away tourists. Luray had been a backwater until 1878, when a photographer discovered a series of large caverns that quickly became one of the most popular tourist destinations in the South.[38] By the 1880s the caverns were under the control of the Norfolk and Western Railway, and railroad officials worked with the Valley Land and Improvement Company to aggressively court tourism and develop their substantial land, timber, and mineral holdings. By the 1890s their efforts had attracted a number of new industrial enterprises, and one local writer explained that tourism had made visitors aware of Luray's "natural advantages" and "agricultural resources," which "led people to look at the town in other lights than as the resort for visitors to the caverns."[39] Thomas Grasty, a correspondent for the *Manufacturers' Record*, praised the vision of the Valley Land and Improvement Company and assured readers that industrial development would not drive away tourists. Luray's unique "topography" allowed company officials to "build hundreds of factories out of sight of the select residence section." Because factory sites were north of the town, he predicted that the "prevailing southern winds will carry their smoke away from the residences, south of the inn," a point "proved by the fact that no smoke or odor from the tannery has ever been perceptible at the inn, which is only half a mile away." Grasty also pointed to the nearby "large, swift-flowing stream" as a depository that would whisk away municipal and industrial wastes and concluded that "the charm of the land above the inn, even from the standpoint of the most fastidious and aesthetic of home-seekers, will not in the least be marred by the construction of furnaces and factories along the railroad on the other side of the present town."[40] Within two decades the town had successfully developed an array of industrial and agricultural enterprises that supported a population of three thousand, though it never became the industrial powerhouse that Grasty or others had hoped.[41] Although Luray did not live up to the visions of boosters, it provided a concrete example that tourism and other enterprises could be mutually reinforcing. Edward Ayers claims that Luray is evidence that "even a hole in the ground could be made to pay" in the New South, but for boosters, Luray proved that both tourism and industrial development were critical to sustained growth.[42]

It was not always easy to sell tourists on the benefits of living near heavy industries, however, which was evident even in Grasty's defense of industrial growth. Other resort owners and boosters looked to develop related enterprises that would be more compatible with the scenic or healthy landscape qualities that attracted tourists. At resorts in the North Carolina Sandhills boosters encouraged fruit cultivation as a form of compatible development. After Henry Bilyeu, a northern migrant farmer, made it clear that orchards could thrive in the Sandhills, John Patrick worked with railway officials to market Southern Pines for permanent residents or part-time hobby farmers. A visitor in 1886 suggested that the resort was ideal for anyone interested in "gardening for pleasure and profit," and within a year the Seaboard Air Line was advertising small plots for sale that ranged from five to forty acres for visitors who "desire a sufficient quantity of land on which to establish a fruit orchard (for which the land is specially suited)."[43] While artisans and truck farmers would find plenty of work at Southern Pines, an advertisement assured visitors that there were "no large factories for mill hands to find employment."[44] This real estate strategy paid off. In 1892 a physician from Pennsylvania described how the resort was "inundated" with tourists, who filled every available room. "Most of the citizens are persons who originally came from the North in quest of health, and, finding it here, concluded to make this their permanent home," which had resulted in "the development of several industries for which the sandy barrens were not previously thought to be suited," including the cultivation of grapes, strawberries, and other "small fruits and vegetables."[45] James

Tufts followed a similar strategy as he worked to build a profitable resort at Pinehurst. To make the resort self-sustaining, he established a peach orchard, sought to reduce transportation costs for local farmers, and worked to make it easier for outsiders to get involved in peach cultivation, hoping that orchards would beautify the landscape while serving as an incentive for permanent settlement.[46] Tourism and fruit raising, in short, were symbiotic. In 1901 the *Pinehurst Outlook* reported that lumber cutting and naval stores extraction had been replaced by "fruit raising," which was "almost equally as profitable and much more enduring."[47] In the 1920s the *Manufacturers' Record* even profiled how fruit cultivation had grown up alongside tourism at Southern Pines and Pinehurst. The author predicted that "while the fame of the Sandhills section is based on the remarkable resort development . . . the industrial development, especially along the lines of fruits and vegetables, is likely to become a feature of great and continually growing importance," and by the 1930s the Sandhills region was one of the leading fruit-raising districts in the South.[48]

In a national context, the melding of business and leisure evident at Luray and Pinehurst was not unusual. Between 1870 and 1900 tourism boosters in the West, as historian Earl Pomeroy explains, targeted the "potential investor."[49] Farther east, tourists were attracted to sites with industrial or technological meaning. By the late nineteenth century, Chicago's Union Stockyards, Richmond's Tredegar Iron Works, coal mines at Mauch Chunk, Pennsylvania, and waterpower infrastructure at Niagara Falls were popular destinations, and urban sites in New York, San Francisco, and Chicago were starting to entice travelers.[50] Although middle- and upper-class tourists still traveled to escape the rigors of urban life, visiting these sites provided a way to experience the "technological sublime" or to reconcile conflicting imperatives of work and leisure.[51]

Tourism boosters in the South drew travelers into the region to similar sites, but they cast these as places of business that offered a unique experience to witness and participate in the South's development. This was clear in a guidebook to Georgia and Alabama that downplayed the attractiveness of plantation ruins and other vestiges of the Old South and instead claimed that "the most interesting features of this section are found in the energetic industrial development of the new South, rather than in the decaying landmarks of the old *regime*."[52] A visit to the New South was, in short, a unique opportunity to witness the industrial rebirth of an entire region or maybe even to participate in this development by taking advantage of unique business opportunities in the South.

Making tourism into a strategy for achieving industrial or agricultural growth muddied the waters over whether it could be a permanent solution for the developing South. By tethering tourism to other enterprises, boosters worked to attract tourists who would become investors, and they placed tourism squarely within a vision for using natural resources chiefly as raw materials for industrial production. Scenery and health may have initially attracted tourists, but the end goal was to use these qualities to speed up a wide-ranging transformation of southern landscapes as they were remade into industrial and agricultural hubs.

⁂

As it became clear that tourism could be a stand-alone industry, however, it was more difficult for boosters to justify using it to attract other forms of investment. Medical science in the late nineteenth century showed that diseases like tuberculosis were highly contagious, leading health resorts to shift their focus from consumptives to travelers who were looking to improve their general health through contact with nature and a mild climate. This required opening up further opportunities for outdoor recreation by preserving scenic drives, building golf courses, maintaining stocks of sporting game, and developing a host of other leisure activities dependent on maintaining an aesthetically pleasing environment. These efforts sometimes involved far-reaching transformations of the landscape, but they also promoted scenic uses of resources that made it seem like tourism was incompatible with the agricultural and industrial enterprises that boosters had long promoted.

As tourism shifted away from its health roots, then, it assumed a more preservationist bent, touching off clashes between tourism boosters and other stakeholders over whether it was an acceptable means to bring about economic and environmental permanence. During congressional battles over early national parks, influential groups of outdoor enthusiasts joined with railroads to effectively argue that nature preservation at Yellowstone and Yosemite would serve as the foundation for a tourism industry in these places. By the twentieth century, outspoken proponents of conservation like the Sierra Club and the Boone and Crockett Club gave voice to recreationists and sportsmen and contributed to a perception that nature preservation and outdoor recreation were linked.[53] The belief that tourism used natural resources in ways that—at least on the surface—would leave them in better shape for future generations had become a hallmark of the conservation movement by the twentieth century. Writing about the value of national parks, Albert Hopkins, an editor at *Scientific American*, argued that tourists brought money to local communities and promoted the preservation of natural resources. Hopkins noted that the "tourist leaves large sums of money but takes away nothing which makes the nation poorer." Tourists gained "improved health, with a recollection of enjoyment of unequaled wonders of mountain, forest, stream and sky, of vitalizing ozone and stimulating companionship with nature" at no cost, and he concluded that "of the natural wealth he takes nothing."[54] Tourism, then, was the ideal waste industry, one that could continually draw on wasted scenic and climatic resources. As tourism gained a foothold in the New South, conservation gave it economic and environmental legitimacy, leading members of the New South growth coalition to consider whether they should prioritize it over other enterprises as they worked to build a durable economy.[55]

This reassessment of the environmental and economic footprint of tourism was also pushed by a host of new groups that were becoming involved in decisions about economic development. The growing popularity and availability of automobiles in the early twentieth century opened up tourism to middle-class tourists who never before had an opportunity to travel. It also unleashed community boosters, auto enthusiasts, good roads promoters, and others who never had much say over tourism development. As railroads lost their hold on deciding which resorts would get transportation access, local boosters no longer had to fit into the developmental priorities of freight and passenger managers. After 1900 progressive politicians and aggressive local boosters pushed for vastly expanded road-building programs. Southern boosters and other "business progressives" assumed a prominent place in the national road-building frenzy and promoted the need for good roads, lobbied state governments to establish state highway commissions, and used county bonds to fund road projects.[56]

Tourism was central to good roads campaigns, and "highway progressives" sought to build roadways that would display the scenic beauties of their community and state for outsiders. In defining roads by their scenery, they also provided a key impetus to preserve natural landscapes by limiting development along scenic corridors. Proposals for new roads often had important scenic elements. Joseph Hyde Pratt, the North Carolina state geologist, organized the Southern Appalachian Good Roads Association in 1909 to promote better roads, including an unrealized scenic highway along the "crest" of the Appalachian Mountains that anticipated the Blue Ridge Parkway.[57] The Dixie Highway, promoted by Carl Fisher to bring travelers to Miami Beach, also revealed the South's "wonderful scenery" to "owners of automobiles in the middle western states." The road set community boosters scrambling to sell the scenery of their municipalities, and a member of the Asheville Board of Trade even noted that "no other highway has such a diversity of climate, scenery, historical sections, manufacturing centers and tourist playgrounds as had the Dixie."[58] Other roads were sited to highlight scenic features, and by 1930 a newspaper editor in Anniston, Alabama, even complained that automobile tourism was too focused on scenery. "Hurrying through the State in automobiles," he claimed, "does not give tourists from other parts of the country sufficient acquaintance with Alabama to impress them with the many possibilities to be found here for industry and business." While tourists did "gain an impression of the beauty of Alabama scenery and enjoy the delights of Alabama's climate," the editor lamented that "they can gain only a fleeting impression of the advantages offered for business, agriculture, and industrial enterprises."[59]

Good roads gave black travelers a chance to enjoy scenic vistas, too. Road building provided middle- and upper-class black southerners with increased mobility that allowed them to resist white attempts to limit their independence.[60] A delegation of black business leaders from Savannah, for instance, took an auto tour to Chattanooga in 1917 and praised the highway through northern Georgia. They described the scenery as "surprisingly wonderful," aside from places where the "mountain side was bare and red from erosion or from the invasion of commercial and pitiless man in quest of the rich ores which lie embosomed there." The travelers concluded, "Unlike the railroads, the motor highway seems to have been laid out with a view to bringing before the tourist the full shows of the great natural features of that section."[61] Good roads also provided black entrepreneurs with more latitude to build their own resorts, flying in the face of white efforts to limit their options through tourism. As historian Andrew Kahrl has demonstrated, African Americans struggled—often successfully—to carve out their own spaces of leisure on seacoasts, rivers, and lakes, even in the face of Jim Crow. Kahrl shows that African Americans were an integral part of the phenomenon of "coastal capitalism" that swept through the Southeast, especially as new highways connected African Americans living in cities to the region's burgeoning black resorts.[62] By 1928 black southerners had developed a range of resorts, from the three-hundred-acre Piney Wood Country Club in Atlanta to Virginia's Buckroe Beach to Tuxedo Park, an amusement park in Birmingham.[63] Just like the Pickford Sanitarium, these resorts challenged the privatization of the South's landscapes for white recreation by giving African Americans their own unique spaces for recreation and claiming access to leisure resources.

Good roads may have given middle- and upper-class African Americans greater mobility and access to scenic nature, but roads afforded only slight benefits to the vast majority of black southerners who could little afford to purchase an automobile or travel. Indeed, Progressive politicians used good roads campaigns as yet another way to keep a tight grip on black laborers. Reformers in states like Georgia and North Carolina pushed to abolish the convict lease so that convict labor could be used for public works projects like road building. Although billed as a reform, this put chain gang labor, largely black, to work on southern roads. As Alex Lichtenstein argues, road building was part of a broader campaign to "check the chaotic tendencies of southern race relations" and maintain the racial hierarchy.[64] By stressing opportunities for tourism that helped to promote good roads, southern politicians may have opened up more space for African American leisure, but they also worked to tighten their grip on black laborers and uphold the exploitative racial hierarchy.

As tourism promoters became preoccupied with scenery, they began to perceive that it was incompatible with agriculture or industry, which used natural resources in far different ways. The sense that tourism could not coexist with these other enterprises stemmed in part from an impulse to beautify living spaces and to preserve the scenic resources that drew tourists to the region in the early twentieth century. In an effort to draw more tourists south, for instance, public officials and women's clubs joined hands to promote highway beautification in the 1920s, taking aim at billboards, trash, and roadside stands while also promoting landscaping to make roadways seem natural.[65] Nationally known highway beautification advocate Elizabeth Lawton told a group of North Carolina merchants and urban boosters that they should make roads not into "horticultural exhibits" but into spaces where "travelers may enjoy the state itself, the rollicking fields, the crops, the woods, the hills." Lawton explained that the state's roadways were "naturally lovely and interesting if they are left as nature made them" but argued that "they are no longer natural." She decried "raw shoulders and cuts," "long stretches barren of trees," and "an ugly rash of advertising" that "tells of the greed of the Billboard Blight."[66] Highway beautification was just one aspect of a broader focus on the South's "scenic resources," a new category of natural resources that needed to be maintained to draw in tourists.

In the first decades of the twentieth century, local officials, women's clubs, tourist promoters, businessmen, and other stakeholders clashed about the preservation of scenic resources on more than just highways. Often linked to the imperatives of the City Beautiful movement, these decisions turned on what enterprises would be the most permanent use of community assets and scenic resources. In 1905 William Banks, a writer for Columbia's newspaper the *State*, rejected industrial growth as the best path for the future of Aiken, South Carolina. Located in the piney woods in the western part of the state, the town had been a popular resort for members of the antebellum planter elite and their postbellum inheritors.[67] Just one year earlier, a group of industrialists had discovered nearby abundant deposits of kaolin, which could supply raw materials for manufacturing products like fine china and paper. A group of mostly northern investors had organized the Pope Clay Products Company to "develop" these deposits. Yet Banks rejected industrial development and declared, "Aiken's asset of greatest value is her beauty," and he urged that this "beauty" should be preserved. Banks claimed that "Aiken's loveliness is not alone of the present. It will be preserved as an asset. No tall chimneys will mar the beauty of this city of parks, and the blue of the sky will never be made vile with the smoke of sordid industry." This was possible because Aiken was not likely to become a center of manufacturing. "Aiken's asset of greatest value is not her manufacturing interests, not her fine farm lands in the back country, not her kaolins and other mineral clays which are being developed and will some day make this a distinctive industry"; instead, "Aiken is proudest of her beauty." The town could afford to be. By the twentieth century, Aiken had attracted some of the wealthiest industrialists of the Northeast, who spent months at this "winter colony." Banks claimed that these tourists were "worth more to Aiken than cotton mills or other enterprises would be" because along with "investing $1,500,000 in homes in the pine barrens, the cottagers often visit the shops and the stores and spend money freely, though not in a prodigal manner."[68] Banks's rejection of industry in Aiken shows how tourism was starting to redefine economic development by providing boosters with an alternative path that was less destructive to valuable scenic resources. Other communities worked through these issues using a similar calculus. In St. Petersburg, Florida, for instance, civic booster William Straub successfully convinced the municipal government to purchase and preserve the waterfront in the early 1900s to keep tourists coming to the area, arguing that the city's growth should be founded on tourism instead of industrial development.[69] Instead of promoting industries that would use up resources, mar the landscape with ugly infrastructure, and turn away tourists, tourism offered communities like Aiken and St. Petersburg an environmental and economic permanence that was founded on renewable resources like scenic beauty. Tourism, in short, was just as profitable as other enterprises but more permanent.

Despite the urging of people like Banks, not all boosters believed that relying on scenic resources was the best path. Other community promoters and businesspeople concluded that tourism was stunting opportunities for economic growth by tying up resources that could be more profitably used for agriculture or industry. A Florida newspaper editor lamented in 1906 that "this State has for many years catered to the tourist, to the neglect of almost everything else," while the state's "wonderful resources were lost to view."[70] In Jackson County, the heart of the mountains of western North Carolina, a local newspaper similarly declared, "We of this section have very naturally fallen into the habit of developing [scenic resources] to the partial exclusion of others that are equally, if not more, important" and concluded, "It is in harnessing the never failing and everabounding supply of power that flows ceaselessly down the mountainsides and through the valleys, and turning with it the busy wheel of industry . . . that our towns are to become industrial centers."[71]

These conflicting visions suggest that boosters were still struggling to determine what role tourism would play in the New South. As it became clear that tourism could be a stand-alone industry, community boosters clashed with businesspeople and other stakeholders over whether it was truly the best use of the region's scenic and industrial resources. While some promoters urged tourism as a way to preserve resources by drawing only on renewable scenic resources, others argued that tourism's need for scenery would hamstring industrial or agricultural uses of valuable resources and stunt growth. Over time, these opposing viewpoints fueled conflicts over natural resources, economic development, and the role of tourism in providing permanence for the South.

&

One of the biggest showdowns over the environmental and economic permanence of private tourism initiatives occurred one hundred miles north of Atlanta in Tallulah Gorge, where the Georgia Power Company planned to build a hydroelectric dam in the first decades of the twentieth century. For most of the nineteenth century, Tallulah Falls—a series of waterfalls running through a deep gorge carved out by the Tallulah River—had been the site of a bustling tourist industry where tourists could escape Atlanta to relax, enjoy the unique scenery, or take the waters. By the 1890s thousands of tourists were traveling there each week during the season. State legislators and tourism promoters sought to turn Tallulah into a state park in the early twentieth century, but their efforts failed, and in 1910 the Georgia Power Company purchased land and water rights at Tallulah for a hydroelectric dam.[72]

The company's plans spawned a backlash from tourists and community boosters and forced Georgia's businesspeople and public officials to decide between two competing paths to permanence: tourism or hydroelectricity generation. Opposition to Georgia Power was spearheaded by Helen Dortch Longstreet, the widow of famed Civil War general James Longstreet and the postmistress of Gainesville, Georgia. As a staunch Progressive reformer, Longstreet had been active in a variety of local and national campaigns in the first decade of the twentieth century. She decried that the natural beauty of the gorge was going to be destroyed just to line the pockets of a rapacious corporation and became involved in the struggle for Tallulah in 1911, just as Georgia Power was starting construction on the dam. At the helm of the Tallulah Falls Conservation Association, Longstreet raised money, built a statewide political coalition, lobbied public officials, led legal action, and published a slew of vituperative articles that took aim at the dam's proponents.[73]

Helen D. Longstreet, 1913. Helen D. Longstreet was a Progressive reformer who fought against the proposed construction of a dam across Georgia's Tallulah Gorge, a popular tourist destination, for producing hydroelectricity. Longstreet wanted to keep Tallulah Gorge as a tourist destination and argued that tourism would be a more permanent use of the natural beauty of the landscape than power.
CREDIT: Library of Congress, Prints & Photographs Division, LC-DIG-ggbain-13584.

Longstreet argued that tourism would be a more permanent use of Tallulah Gorge than hydroelectric power, trying to counter Georgia Power's claim that its opponents were "maudlin sentimentalists" out of touch in an age of development.[74] In 1912 she published a tract claiming that Tallulah Falls was the "Switzerland of America." Tourism contributed "upwards of two hundred millions of dollars yearly" to the economy of Switzerland, and there was "no reason why the matchless mountain scenery of the Blue Ridge, in which Tallulah is the unrivaled queen, should not attract to the mountains of Georgia larger travel than annually pours the yellow treasure into the lap of Switzerland." Taking a cue from parks out west, Longstreet predicted that Tallulah could be one of America's most popular national parks and that federal authorities "will build grand boulevards to Tallulah by which it may be reached and enjoyed by the republic's humblest toiler, and by the tourist from the remotest quarters of the earth." This would enable Georgians to permanently derive profits from the falls, which would "pour treasure into the lap of Georgians and their children and their children's children long after this day's vandalistic effort has been buried beneath mountains of oblivion."[75] Preserving Tallulah Falls would also keep capital in the state and prevent rapacious utility executives from taking the profits out of Georgia. She argued that "Tallulah Falls will be worth more than five hundred millions annually if preserved for its scenic value," but when "commercialized it will pay" Georgia Power only "about $300,000 annually."[76] Longstreet later reiterated this point by quoting a prize-winning essay sponsored by the Tallulah Falls Conservation Association. While the essayist noted that preserving the falls was necessary even if it brought in no money, he or she argued that "scenery is now an asset. . . . The uncommon beauty of Tallulah, its scenic and historic surroundings, its climate and ease of access should, in the nature of things make it a more paying investment, if exploited scenically, than for power." The author concluded that Tallulah "may safely be trusted to pay as much for scenery as for power."[77]

Georgia Power countered that its actions would not destroy the scenic value of Tallulah because there would still be water flowing through the gorge. A local newspaper editor, echoing the company, even claimed that the dam would "add very materially to the interest and beauty of the place" and would be "better than the virgin falls."[78] A representative of the Georgia Weekly Press Association who had just been treated to lunch by Georgia Power officials agreed, suggesting that "far from being robbed of its scenic beauty . . . this delightful country is now more attractive than ever" because "in addition to all its natural charms, it is now enjoying many comforts and an industrial prosperity" that were "impossible under old conditions."[79] As Longstreet's arguments about the economic and environmental permanence of tourism hit their mark and prominent Georgians joined her cause, the company tried to assume the mantle of permanence. Company representatives argued that the lake created by their dam would offer unique recreation opportunities and add to the area's scenic beauty, attracting more tourists than the gorge itself.[80] In a long advertisement published in the *Atlanta Constitution* in April 1911, the company explained its plans in technical detail but concluded that the dam would create a "beautiful artificial lake" one and a half miles long that would be "attractive" for "the inhabitants of the section about the falls."[81]

Longstreet's efforts to define tourism as a valuable business that could maintain scenery were not enough to stop the momentum of the company. Although she successfully convinced state officials to reexamine whether Georgia Power held legal title to the property, a jury ruled that construction should proceed. By the spring of 1913, Tallulah Falls was dammed.[82] While Longstreet's attempt to frame the conflict as an example of the permanence of tourism was not successful in deterring Georgia Power, this does not suggest that Georgians had no interest in permanence writ large. Rather, the controversy pitted two competing visions of permanence against each other. Even Georgia Power felt compelled to make a case as to why its proposed use of the gorge would be more long-lasting, and it touted the economic benefits of hydroelectricity, as well as the long-term recreational and scenic benefits of the artificial lake. What the clash at Tallulah makes clear, then, is how the emerging consensus that tourism could be a permanent industry of its own could fuel radically different visions for the future.

Waterpower was often at the center of debates over permanence because it forced communities to weigh two mutually exclusive visions for conservation: conserving water or conserving scenery. The fact that scenery was even part of the equation in cases like Tallulah shows how tourism's supposed economic and environmental permanence was reshaping the calculus of development in radical ways. Similar conflicts played out on a national stage, though in the South these conflicts always had a unique inflection. In fact, the showdown at Tallulah Gorge mirrored a controversy occurring simultaneously two thousand miles to the west in the Hetch Hetchy Valley of Yosemite National Park. In 1901 San Francisco officials asked the Department of the Interior for permission to dam the Hetch Hetchy Valley to supply the city with clean drinking water, setting off nearly a decade of debate over the best uses of the valley. These conflicts pitted John Muir and the Sierra Club against municipal officials from San Francisco and their conservationist allies, who supported dams as exemplars of water conservation. Like Tallulah, the struggle over Hetch Hetchy came down to competing definitions of permanence. Although Muir stressed the spiritual and aesthetic significance of the valley, his vision for Hetch Hetchy left room for tourists and recreationists. Muir and his supporters, who had been instrumental in securing national park status for Yosemite by stressing its recreational potential, made the case that Hetch Hetchy was needed for outdoor recreation, which would be far less destructive than damming. Writer Robert Pike noted that flooding the valley would destroy its "scenic assets" and predicted that without a dam it would "furnish needed recreation and pleasure of the finest sort to thousands of our citizens," who would stay at "hotels and camps on the floor of the valley."[83] Supporters of the dam argued that Pike and other opponents of the project were too sentimental. Damming Hetch Hetchy was a wiser use of a free-flowing river than preserving it as scenery for a few wealthy recreationists, they claimed, which would deny San Franciscans access to clean and available water. Although the Sierra Club fended off the city's early attempts, a devastating fire swept through San Francisco in 1906 and helped to sway public opinion and federal support for the dam project. Hetch Hetchy was approved for damming in 1913 when Woodrow Wilson signed the Raker Act, legislation that also limited recreational uses of the reservoir to maintain water purity. Within a decade the O'Shaughnessy Dam was complete and the valley flooded.[84]

The conflicts at Hetch Hetchy and Tallulah Falls signaled that dam projects had considerable political support nationwide and were viewed as an integral part of water conservation. Each side in these conflicts framed its role in terms of permanence, whether arguing for water conservation, hydroelectric power, pure drinking water for urban growth, or preserving scenery for recreation. Despite these similarities, the struggle over Georgia's Hetch Hetchy, Tallulah Gorge, was inflected by its southern context. At Hetch Hetchy, Muir and the Sierra Club tried to uphold the sanctity of a federally protected national park. At Tallulah, recreation was cast as a mostly private concern. Promoters did lobby state and federal officials to extend protection to the gorge, but the main impulse was simply to allow private businesspeople—the same businesspeople who had attracted visitors there for decades—to continue to rake in money from tourism. The struggle for the fate of Tallulah, then, was less about state protection than competing definitions of corporate permanence.

☙

By the 1920s, privatizing southern landscapes for tourism had become big business. This was most evident in the expansion of the sporting economy into the South. Hunting had long been a common means of sport and subsistence in the South, but in the 1880s and 1890s it was embraced by middle- and upper-class men nationwide who saw sport hunting as a way to cope with the rigors of urban living. By the 1880s, hunting for sport and market purposes—aided by the expansion of rail networks and new weapons technology—had decimated wildlife on popular hunting grounds in the Northeast and Midwest. While some hunters turned to conservation to restore game, others turned to the South, a region that still had plenty of wildlife, an abundance of cheap land, and a booming tourist economy. Railroad companies, chambers of commerce, and dozens of new sporting journals distributed information on hunting and fishing opportunities in the South for potential tourists, drawing large numbers of sportsmen into the region from the 1880s to the 1920s. By the twentieth century, sport hunting was booming in the South, and in 1902 the region was visited by the nation's most famous hunter, Theodore Roosevelt, who traveled to the Mississippi Delta to hunt the black bear that would give him his enduring nickname.[85]

No activity seemed to lead to environmental permanence—even to require it—like hunting. Sporting tourism depended on securing a permanent supply of game. White elites had worried since the eighteenth century that wildlife were declining and had supported piecemeal efforts to conserve game and fish. The influx of sportsmen in the postbellum era made this more pressing. Suddenly, overhunting not only inhibited the pastime of wealthy planters but also wasted a valuable and renewable resource. Theodore Palmer, an avid conservationist, explained to a gathering of North Carolina conservationists in 1904 that "game is really an undeveloped resource which under favorable conditions can be managed so as to bring in large returns."[86] Public officials joined hands with conservationists to protect this resource and promote tourism. Reining in overhunting, imagined or real, through state legislation was a tall order, however. White elites may have wanted to preserve game, but since the 1870s efforts to enact restrictive legislation had run into fierce opposition from poor whites leery about having their independence constrained to maintain game for elite hunters. Nevertheless, by the 1890s state officials were feverishly working to prevent overhunting of valuable wildlife to protect the sporting economy. Within a decade, southern states had started to enact closed seasons or make it illegal to hunt or fish on private property without signed permission—important steps in privatizing wildlife for conservation.[87]

After 1915 white public officials, conservationists, and businesspeople overcame legislative opposition among poor whites by linking hunting and fishing regulations with the maintenance of the racial hierarchy. White elites placed blame for the destruction of valuable game squarely on African Americans who used hunting to provide for their families, make money, or for leisure. Public officials and sportsmen cast African American hunting as a grave threat to game birds and to revenues from tourism and used racist appeals to promote the need for conservation legislation. As a number of scholars have demonstrated, efforts to limit the hunting and fishing activities of African Americans were as much about limiting their mobility as preserving game, and social restrictions and tourism promotion went hand in hand. In response to the supposed depredations of "pothunters," during the second decade of the twentieth century, state legislatures created state-level wildlife agencies, and some required licenses for hunting and fishing activities.[88] After the passage of a statewide game law in 1911, the *Atlanta Constitution* even reported that white farmers east of Atlanta were "using the new state game law as a club to drive indolent negroes back to the fields."[89] Promising to maintain the permanence of the racial hierarchy, then, provided boosters with a handy tool to maintain the permanence of the region's newest industry and the game needed to keep it profitable.

State officials and conservationists insisted that these game laws would maintain the raw materials for a substantial tourism industry that would contribute much-needed cash to the economy. Despite assurances that game laws would facilitate tourism, at times vocal groups of boosters expressed concern about this developmental path, harking back to long-standing unease about the permanence of tourism. Although Florida passed the "model law" that was developed by the American Ornithological Union for conserving game in 1901, the state provided no mechanism for enforcement for more than two decades.[90] After a proposal to strengthen the game law in 1913, the editor of the local newspaper in Estero, Florida, expressed concern that a strict game law would keep tourists away. He was roundly castigated by municipal boosters in Punta Gorda, who argued that the present law was already ineffective and predicted that game animals would be gone within a decade, taking the tourist industry with them. The editor of the *Punta Gorda Herald* was troubled more by the loss of game than by the loss of tourists. While tourists were "pleasant people," he argued that they "do not pay big dividends to anything except the three-month hotels and the moving picture shows" and were not "indispensable to the prosperity of the state." If "we are compelled to choose between them and the game in our forests," he claimed to be enough of an "arrant 'Cracker'" that he would choose game "and with tears in our eyes bid the tourists adieu." Northerners who were "hunting farming lands, home sites, business openings and investments and not deer, wild turkeys and quail will continue to come," he explained, "and help us build up the state." "Tourists are welcome," he concluded, but "permanent settlers are even more desirable."[91]

Even as state officials struggled to maintain game through legislation, businesspeople turned to privatizing wildlife. From the 1880s through the 1920s, northern sportsmen bought up thousands of acres, primarily in former plantation districts that had struggled to adapt to changing economic and social circumstances after emancipation. Throughout the Lowcountry of South Carolina and Georgia, the Red Hills of Georgia and Florida, southern Louisiana, and the Black Belt of Alabama and Mississippi, former plantations were remade into hunting clubs, hunting plantations, or private game reserves. These places privatized hunting by making land and wildlife off-limits to everyone except elite sportsmen, and owners maintained game populations by fencing their preserves, posting their land, seeding the ground to attract wildlife, and tightly controlling entry. By establishing large game preserves and cutting off public access, businesspeople made money, regulated who could pursue wildlife, and maintained populations of popular game animals. This process sometimes required far-reaching transformations of these landscapes that were geared toward making these places popular for game animals.[92]

Businesspeople, boosters, and conservationists cast private game preserves as a long-term solution to species depletion, one that could make hunting a permanent industry in the South. An article by *Atlanta Constitution* correspondent Julius Muller in 1902 even framed game preserves as an "industrial" activity that mirrored the drive for efficiency in other enterprises, and he claimed that they were a good fit in "the 'new south,' the south of industrial regeneration." By the time Muller was writing there had been little progress in getting restrictive legislation passed through state legislatures, but he was confident that "the suddenly alert power of business" would preserve game "almost at once"—especially now that businesspeople recognized that wildlife were "great sources of individual and communal wealth."[93] The supposed permanence of hunting was also clear in a 1927 guide to "manly sports" in the South Carolina Lowcountry published by the agricultural and industrial agent of the Charleston and Western Carolina Railway. This was one of the most popular hunting grounds in the South, and the guide boasted that species like "quail, deer, wild turkey, marsh hens, doves, fox and cat squirrels, rabbits and some bear" were plentiful, not to mention "millions of duck, many raccoons, opossums and minks, also some gray fox." This was a direct result of the privatization of the Lowcountry landscape through game preserves. The author, N. L. Willett, noted that there were more than one hundred separate game preserves totaling some 250,000 acres just in this three-county area. Most were former rice or Sea Island cotton plantations, and Willett suggested that the shift from agriculture to hunting was a shift to a more permanent economic base. He explained, "These game preserves, wire fenced and with keepers who keep out poachers, do not actually kill off wild life as fast as it comes into existence." Instead, private preserves functioned as "game sanctuaries," places where game "all flee in times of pursuit . . . seeming to know that their life is more sacrosanct here than on the outside." This made private preserves popular both for sportsmen and for their game. Each valued these places because they reflected a sense of the "original wild." Despite this unusual gesture at the intangible benefits of contact with wild landscapes, the company's primary logic for promoting game preservation was economic. As game increased, Willett argued that it would lead to more game preserves and a "continual enhancement in valuation." Game preserves had also brought permanent settlers to the area, who built houses and made other improvements. By purchasing former plantations, cutting off access to the public, and carefully policing hunting activity, northern migrants were creating "sanctuaries where wild life of the land and water is reproduced in large amounts and whose lives are perpetuated and whose forests in which never an axe is laid, are treated the same way," and Willett concluded that this was "a beautiful kind of ownership."[94]

The rapid growth of game preserves in the Carolina Lowcountry was mirrored throughout the Plantation Belt. Some of these preserves were indeed on an industrial scale. Few could rival Sportsman's Paradise, the 135,000 acres in Berrien County, Georgia, cobbled together in the 1920s by businessman J. Isom

Davis. Davis worked out agreements with private owners to use these lands for elite hunting and fishing and sold access by forming a hunting and fishing club for "northern and eastern millionaires." Two years later Davis was working to expand the preserve by nearly two hundred thousand acres after apparently being "besieged by large landowners in Ware, Pierce, Bacon and adjacent counties" who were envious of his success. This would make it "the largest hunting preserve in the civilized world," and local boosters cast it as a force for economic growth and environmental preservation. The *Atlanta Constitution* noted that the purpose was twofold: halting "promiscuous hunting through south Georgia woodlands, which threatened in time to reduce the amount of game," and interesting "rich eastern and northern sportsmen in the partially developed south Georgia region . . . which is not developed only because of lack of settlers and money."[95] Few preserves could match Sportsman's Paradise, but by the 1930s the region had been privatized on an astonishing scale, especially considering the legacy of an open commons. Just in the Red Hills area, historian Albert Way shows that by the 1920s there were more than three hundred thousand acres as private game preserves, and by the end of the decade there were more than two million acres that had been privatized region-wide.[96]

These transformations had dramatic social effects, especially in the Plantation Belt. Hunting clubs and game preserves prohibited black southerners from hunting on preserve grounds, backing this up with high fences, threats of violence, game wardens, and the law. While many of these clubs relied on the expertise of African American guides, they strictly delineated by race who could and could not hunt on their grounds.[97] This was happening throughout the nation in the early twentieth century as conservationists extended protection to all sorts of animals or landscapes, in the process redefining the long-standing hunting activities of poor whites, African Americans, immigrants, or Native Americans as poaching. The difference was that outside of the South these efforts were about extending the power of the state into rural communities through regulation and establishing an enforcement bureaucracy. They were not private business ventures. Despite significant state regulation of hunting and fishing, southern elites worked to create a landscape that welcomed wealthy white hunters while using game laws to restrict the independence of African Americans, an initiative that was policed and managed by businesspeople.

The privatization and conservation of wildlife and land were contested by black southerners and small landowners who wanted to continue hunting as they traditionally had. These groups did not have access to standard forms of political representation and could do little to halt private preserves or the flurry of game laws emanating from state legislatures. But black southerners pushed back against these exploitative conditions. Many chose not to abide by game laws that limited their independence, and they continued hunting as they traditionally had, even though these activities were redefined as poaching. The patchwork of fences, private lands, game laws, and threats of jail and violence did circumscribe the access of black southerners to game and fish, but never entirely.[98]

⁂

Even as struggles over the need for federal protection of the southern Appalachians in the early twentieth century showed the power of corporate permanence, they demonstrated that tourism was becoming a force of its own. Early national parks like Yosemite and Yellowstone attracted large numbers of tourists, and by the 1890s it was becoming evident to southern boosters that national park designation could be wielded to transform swaths of the region into productive and permanent tourist landscapes. The possibilities of scenic preservation seemed especially consequential in the southern Appalachians, where there was an already bustling tourist industry centered on Asheville. The expansion of commercial logging in the area in the 1880s threatened the scenery that attracted tourists, and Asheville boosters, under the aegis of the Appalachian National Park Association (ANPA), latched onto federal protection as a way to ensure the continued growth of tourism.[99]

The ANPA founded its case on the permanence that a national park would bring to the environment and economy of western North Carolina. In an 1899 petition to Congress, the ANPA noted that the southern Appalachians were already "one of the most deservedly popular health resorts of the world" and argued that this travel would continue if the area became a national park. It predicted that tourism would grow, especially given the proximity of North Carolina to major cities like New York, Chicago, and St. Louis, bringing large numbers of tourists to the state and providing continual economic growth for the region's economy.[100] The permanent growth of tourism, however, was dependent on maintaining the "rare natural beauty of the Southern Appalachian Region." George Powell, the president of the ANPA, decried the logging that had denuded mountain slopes and argued that federal protection was the only way to maintain these forests, which were especially valuable as scenery. To convince federal officials and politicians to support plans for a national park and undercut the arguments of extractive industries, the ANPA contrasted the economic and environmental permanence of tourism with the migratory nature of the lumber industry. Powell lamented that "the increasing scarcity of timber is causing large areas of forest in this part of our country to be rapidly acquired by those whose one thought will be immediate returns from a system of lumbering utterly reckless and ruinous." Tourism was a more efficient use of these forests, one that could maintain forests while still making money from them. Even reforestation was not ideal, because it was "a slow process ... for subsequent generations." In short, only federal protection could preserve the forests of the southern Appalachians, and only tourism could make money off these forests for the long haul.[101]

By advocating a national park, the ANPA and other supporters were staking out a claim that permanent uses of forests could only come through tourism and that tourist enterprises could only be protected when the federal government secured the forests and mountain scenery that were attractive to tourists from the depredations of individuals and corporations. This was a profoundly anticorporate view, though it quickly crumbled in the face of opposition from corporate leaders and federal conservationists who believed in allowing utilitarian uses of federally protected resources. Within a few years the ANPA had shifted its arguments from a national park to a national forest. This did not signal that the ANPA was abandoning permanence through tourism, simply that it was willing to balance tourism and other industries under the watchful eye of federal foresters, who made it clear that they also valued recreational uses of national forests and tourism. In the middle of the debate over the southern Appalachians, Treadwell Cleveland, a Forest Service official, even argued that national forests—"the greatest national recreation grounds in the world"—could contribute just as much to tourism while maintaining scenic resources. Although there were no national forests in the South, Cleveland predicted that "the objects for which the national forests were created and maintained, will guarantee the permanence of their resources and will bring about their fullest development for every use," because "national forests safeguard the integrity of the resources and place their use on a permanent basis." "For this reason," he concluded, "the recreation value of the national forests can never be destroyed."[102]

Attempts to convince legislators to support federal protection ran headlong into opposition from Joseph Cannon, the powerful Speaker of the House, who famously claimed that Congress should spend "not one cent for scenery." Cannon spearheaded congressional opposition to protection of timberlands in the East, and his efforts killed more than fifty proposals over ten years. It was not until 1911 that Asheville's boosters secured the passage of the Weeks Act, which allocated federal funds to purchase nearly six million acres of forestland in the East. By 1916 the Forest Service had acquired land in the southern Appalachians for Pisgah National Forest, giving forests a modicum of protection but also keeping them open to industrial use.[103]

After World War I, community boosters in North Carolina and Tennessee renewed calls for a national park in the southern Appalachians, however, arguing that it would bring an economic permanence to an area that was dwindling because of the extractive nature of forest products industries. This time, they gave no room for corporate permanence to coexist with tourism. Booster organizations in Tennessee and in North Carolina called for a national park, casting it explicitly in terms of protecting scenery to allow for the growth of tourism. In 1925 travel writer and park promoter Horace Kephart wrote to North Carolina congressman Zebulon Weaver regarding the proposed park. Kephart noted that logging operations had left land in the southern Appalachians "almost worthless" and admitted, "Many of our people fear to antagonize them lest they lose the slight income still derived from lumber operations here; but these folks do not see beyond their noses." Kephart noted that logging was not a long-term solution and that "the taxes that our counties derive from lumber companies will soon be dwindling to nothing. And then—the desert." But a national park would bring permanence to the area: "The opening of this country to millions of tourists would do for it what such trade has already done for Asheville, Hendersonville," and other places "only on a larger scale, and this income would be perpetual." He concluded that tourism "is the great commercial asset of this country" because "it lasts forever and forever grows in value."[104]

By insisting that permanence through tourism was only possible with a national park, promoters like Kephart ran into significant opposition, especially from industrialists who worried that a national park would hinder their business, and the fate of the southern Appalachians became a question of which path to permanence was more ideal: forest products or tourism. No opponents were more outspoken than the Champion Fibre Company, a paper mill constructed in Canton, North Carolina, in 1906. Champion's president, Reuben Robertson, argued that a national park would tie the hands of timber companies and would not be in the best economic interests of the area's residents. He declared that the "program for the future progress of Western North Carolina can not be complete or well-balanced if it considers only the tourist business." The company stressed that its corporate foresters would ensure the permanence of Appalachian forests through reforestation efforts and promoted its operations as just as permanent as federal regulation.[105] Robertson and other industrialists sought to use lawsuits to defeat the proposal for a national park and keep hundreds of thousands of acres of timberland in corporate hands. By the 1930s, the company's efforts had fallen short, however. Tennessee and North Carolina had both established state commissions to begin purchasing land in the Smokies, and in 1934 more than five hundred thousand acres were purchased by the federal government and made into Great Smoky Mountains National Park, which cemented the place of tourism in the economy of western North Carolina and eastern Tennessee.[106] Although scholars typically view this as a conflict between industrial development and environmental preservation, the struggle over the national park was actually about who was better entitled to bring about permanence: the federal government or private corporations.[107]

Federal protection of forests in the southern Appalachians established tourism as the leading industry in the mountain South, but it also excluded groups like poor white mountaineers from this prosperity. Although park boosters liked to refer to the Great Smoky Mountains as an unpeopled wilderness, approximately four thousand people who lived there were forced to sell their land to the federal government for the park, and thousands more were denied traditional access to forests that they had relied on for subsistence or other purposes. Even groups who remained by leasing land back from the Park Service found that their lives had been altered in dramatic fashion. Longtime modes of subsistence—hunting, gathering herbs, cutting trees—were expressly banned by the Park Service under its lease agreements. Fire had long been a traditional mountain practice, but the Park Service not only made burning illegal but also mandated that residents on leases aid in fighting forest fires.[108] One mountaineer who was "agin the Park" explained, "The Park won't do me nor my children a mite of good. They tell me I can't break a twig, nor pull a flower after there's a Park. Nor can I fish with bait for trout, nor kill a boomer, nor a bear on the land owned by my pap, and grandpap and his pap before him."[109] Local groups, according to historian Kathryn Newfont, saw federal protection of the Smoky Mountains as creating "federally funded pleasure grounds" that were only for "wealthy outsiders" and offered little to displaced residents. Although some mountaineers simply ignored Park Service regulations and continued traditional activities, Newfont also shows that later generations challenged the expansion of wilderness-designated areas as well as increased resource extraction through a "commons environmentalism." For these groups, permanence through corporate forestry or federal protection held little appeal. By ignoring Park Service regulations and fighting against the rationalization of the Appalachian landscape, they expressed a long-term vision based in traditional rights and responsibilities of commons areas.[110]

The successful creation of a national park in the southern Appalachians was concrete evidence for civic leaders that tourism was the "highest" form of development that they could pursue. During and after the controversy in the southern Appalachians, municipal boosters sought to increase tourism and preserve the scenic elements that attracted tourists by convincing the federal government to protect other unique landscapes, though few were as successful. In the late 1920s, boosters in western Arkansas worked to convince federal officials to convert Ouachita National Forest into a national park—the first park that would be accessible for residents of Oklahoma, Texas, Arkansas, and Louisiana. As a national park Ouachita would preserve scenic vistas from the lumbering allowed in national forests. Arkansas boosters were foiled, however, when federal officials and officers of the National Parks Association concluded that the area was not up to the scenic standards of a national park. What scenery it had, they concluded, would be preserved by the Forest Service's selective cutting policies, and federal officials and NPA officials successfully counseled Calvin Coolidge to veto the park bill.[111] In Florida, a booster in Wakulla County urged the federal government to take action to protect landscapes there because "no development could be more lasting or profitable than the making of it into a great national park and tourist resort." Clearly influenced by action in the southern Appalachians, the author argued that "resort centers are [the] greatest means of permanent development and that for real and abiding prosperity resort cities excel industrial ones"—a strategy that Asheville provided a "striking example" of.[112] In the 1930s community boosters in Stewart County even urged federal officials to make Providence Canyon—Georgia's "Little Grand Canyon"—into a national park, despite the fact that the canyon was actually a series of deep gullies caused by human-induced erosion.[113]

State officials also became more active in preserving landscapes for recreation and tourism. In the 1910s southern states created the first state parks to preserve scenery and promote tourism, including North Carolina's Mount Mitchell State Park in 1915, Florida's Royal Palm State Park in 1916, and Petit Jean State Park in Arkansas in 1923. Raymond Torrey, secretary of the National Conference on State Parks, reported in 1926 that population growth was making the region the "coming field for such development" and credited Texas, Florida, Alabama, Arkansas, and Tennessee with "excellent beginnings." These were just "beginnings," however. Even in 1929 John Holmes, the state forester of North Carolina, urged the formation of more state parks to promote the permanence of forests, concluding that this "system of attractive state parks will bring tourists to the state and perpetuate our scenic resources." By 1930 only a few southern states had established mechanisms for acquiring lands for parks, however, and even fewer had actually acquired land. Virginia, South Carolina, Georgia, and Mississippi had no state parks whatsoever, and the Southeast had less than 1 percent of national acreage protected in either state forests or parks. Only Texas, with fifty-four state parks totaling more than thirty-one thousand acres, could compete with states in the North and West.[114] Although the link between parks and environmental permanence was forged in the 1920s, the South's state park renaissance would have to wait for federal involvement in the 1930s.

New state parks may have preserved scenic spaces so that tourism could perpetually contribute to the South's economy, but they were also spaces that William O'Brien calls "landscapes of exclusion." Although there were rarely laws that designated state parks as exclusively white spaces, parks were segregated by long-standing tradition. Until well into the 1930s, African Americans were almost entirely excluded from state park facilities, and O'Brien explains that this "exclusive access" was even a "designed feature" of these landscapes.[115] Sociologist Forrester Washington, with the Atlanta School of Social Work, admitted in 1928 that "it is hardly necessary to state that no mixing of the races will be found" in recreational spaces. "The only interesting fact to look for," he noted, "is whether or not any accommodations at all—even segregated—are provided for Negroes."[116] Even during the state park building frenzy that accompanied the march of the Civilian Conservation Corps through the South after 1933, park infrastructure was strictly divided by race. As late as 1941, the South only had nine state parks entirely reserved for African American visitors. Even Great Smoky Mountains National Park followed local practices of segregation, and facilities were separated by race until midcentury.[117] Although state and national parks maintained scenic resources for tourism, they also helped maintain the South's exploitative racial hierarchy by strictly and unequally dividing the resources of leisure among southerners by race. Tourism did not just contribute to the physical exclusion of African Americans from white spaces of leisure, it also naturalized the separation of African Americans from nature in ways that would later write black southerners out of the narrative of outdoor recreation almost entirely.[118]

꽃

By the New Deal, tourism was well established in the South and commonly viewed as the most permanent industry of all. In many ways, New Deal planners would finally fulfill the vision of the growth coalition, which had long argued that tourism had the potential to bring permanent economic growth without environmental cost. New Deal agencies worked tourism and recreation into their plans in a more far-reaching way than ever before, though this involved a more prominent role for the federal government. TVA administrators wanted to bring permanence to the rural South, for instance, but they believed that government authority was necessary to create the "federal landscape" that used recreational imperatives to solve these problems.[119] As late as 1944 a correspondent for the *Atlanta Constitution* predicted that the "No. 1" industry for the postwar South would be recreation. After highlighting the ways that TVA officials and town boosters in Guntersville, Alabama, had created a prosperous outdoor recreation industry there, the correspondent noted that the end of the war would allow "countless communities" to "reap rich harvests from recreation." "This boom will be of permanent character," he predicted, because people would have time off for vacations and because "this country will offer the average man more attractive playgrounds than ever before."[120] As the South transitioned into the Sunbelt, even this optimistic correspondent understated how much tourism would transform the modern South, and the idea that tourism was a permanent solution to the South's environmental woes would only grow.

CONCLUSION

New South boosters, businesspeople, and public officials were remarkably successful at building a permanent economy atop the ruins of the Civil War. Natural resources were the cornerstone of New South economic growth, and in the decades after Appomattox southern leaders worked to protect resources that were valuable raw materials for a range of industries. Charles Herty worked with industry officials to develop a way to prolong the life of profitable longleaf pines for extracting resin. Pulp and paper manufacturers employed corporate foresters to regenerate forests for producing wood pulp. Commercial fertilizers allowed the continuous production of cash crops like cotton and tobacco, even in the face of declining soil fertility. Utility companies built huge dams that harnessed waterpower that had been wasted in free-flowing rivers. As the size of the cutover grew, lumber companies diversified into chemical industries that manufactured a range of wood-based products. State officials enacted regulations promoting more efficient uses of gas and mineral resources in order to limit wastes in extraction and prolong their use. Sportsmen bought up millions of acres and transformed them into private hunting grounds that maintained populations of game animals like deer and quail. Resort developers became effective powerbrokers advocating for government protection of valuable scenic resources. Conservation entwined with segregation to keep workers doing low-wage manual labor, maintain white supremacy, and undercut efforts by black and white workers to challenge exploitative living and working conditions. In the eyes of white boosters and businesspeople, these measures were a stunning success, and they kept stocks of profitable industrial and agricultural resources from being exhausted so that businesses could continue to prosper.

Boosters were also effective at reducing the strain on intensively used resources by encouraging the development of waste industries that seemed to transcend the South's limited resources. In 1937 the *Blue Book of Southern Progress*, an annual publication from the *Manufacturers' Record*, explained that the Great Depression had "brought a closer operation of agriculture and industry" that was building up manufacturing in the South and "making greater uses of its raw materials." Although cotton was still "king," it was "forced to acknowledge the power of the new Princes of petroleum, paper, chemicals, and other products and by-products from the farms, forests, and mines of the South."[1]

These and other waste industries grew quickly in the twentieth century, and by the 1930s they were major industries of their own. In 1938 twelve southern states were producing more than half of all the nation's wood veneers, which allowed low-grade wood to be used for higher-grade purposes.[2] By 1939 the cottonseed oil industry had solved its supply problems and produced more than a billion tons of cottonseed oil, drawing on a resource that had limited commercial use before oil manufacturing. Pulp and paper manufacturers continued to move into the region, and by 1940 the South had half of the nation's rayon manufacturers, which produced more than 70 percent of all the rayon produced in the nation. Furniture manufacturing, especially in North Carolina, contributed almost $150 million to the region's economy annually and drew on lower grades of wood that helped to prolong southern forests. Chemical and mineral industries were making especially big strides in diversifying the economy. By the start of World War II, the region produced nearly all of the nation's sulphur, carbon black, natural gas, crude petroleum, bauxite, fuller's earth, phosphate, kaolin, and ball clay, and the *Blue Book* reported that the region had "the indispensable requirements for success" along chemical lines.[3] The southern economy still had an extractive bent, but the goods that it was extracting were more varied than ever and reflected interest in permanence by using waste materials and resources.

Hope for permanence through technology also gave momentum to and sometimes morphed into the chemurgy movement in the 1920s and 1930s. Chemurgists sought to use applied chemical research to discover new industrial uses for agricultural goods in order to stimulate economic growth and make agriculture and manufacturing more interdependent. It is no coincidence that many of the nation's outspoken advocates of chemurgy were southerners who had long promoted permanent uses of regional resources. For instance, in 1937 a manufacturer from Florida described chemurgy in terms that could have been lifted from earlier statements about permanence when he claimed that chemurgists wanted to develop "raw materials . . . that can be perpetually produced at a profit from the soil without impairment of the soil." He concluded that "this is the only source of perpetual cumulative wealth."[4]

In the first decades of the twentieth century, then, permanence shaped everything from the decisions that municipal officials made about what industries were best for the South to the strategies used by corporations to maintain a steady supply of raw materials, though there was rarely a consensus on what was best. Competing ideas about permanent growth and strategies for maintaining stable stocks of natural resources informed efforts to rethink virtually every part of the South's economy after the Civil War, from agriculture to tourism. As southern officials and businesspeople worked to ensure that their profitable natural resources would be available to fuel lasting growth, they transformed corporate practice, the structure of the region's economy, and the southern environment in far-reaching ways.

But permanence came with a high price.

Permanent industries no doubt prolonged the life of discrete stocks of valuable resources and lined the pockets of businesspeople and boosters, but they did not offer much for the majority of working people. In fact, by adopting strategies designed to ensure resource permanence, businesspeople were able to keep low-wage industries like naval stores, lumbering, cotton cultivation, and tourism as key players in the region's economy and prevent radical changes in the labor structure and social hierarchy. Because permanent industries were almost always labor-intensive, then, they prolonged the most exploitative aspects of the New South vision. Chemurgy, for instance, promised to use chemicals to bring new dimensions to southern development, but it depended on black laborers growing cotton under exploitative labor contracts. White boosters used permanence as a way to promote exclusionary racial policies and white supremacy by chipping away at the independence of African Americans. Permanence as defined by white elites placed the responsibility for maintaining and policing resource stocks in the hands of corporations and white business and political leaders, leading the steep price of permanence to fall most heavily on black southerners.

African Americans and poor whites in the South did not simply accept these exploitative conditions. They fought back against corporate uses of timber, minerals, scenery, soils, and waters that cut off their own access to these resources, affected their quality of life, or maintained policies of white supremacy. Although they were hemmed in by the racial climate of the New South, black southerners made it clear that the brand of permanence envisioned by white boosters was not desirable. By fighting back against corporate permanence, they did manage to carve out important gains for themselves. But these gains were never enough to secure the promises of Reconstruction or to challenge the New South vision of white boosters and businesspeople.

By facilitating the continuance of manual labor, permanent enterprises also stunted the technological innovation and infrastructure that were key parts of economic growth in other parts of the country. Efficiency gains in southern industries were intended to maintain stocks of profitable resources or reduce pressure on the most-used resources through the use of by-products and wasted raw materials. These measures did not change the fact that these enterprises, from agriculture to tourism, were overwhelmingly dependent on human labor. Maintaining manual labor, in fact, was an important component of the vision of boosters, but it held back the region's economic growth. The result for most southerners—aside from urban businesspeople and professionals—was deepening poverty and economic stagnation. Even in the twentieth century, the region remained mired in a staple crop economy with exploitative labor and credit systems, and in 1930 55 percent of southern farmers were still stuck as tenants.[5] Despite urban growth, the majority of southerners continued to live in rural areas where poverty and malnutrition were widespread. Declining prices for cotton and other staples spawned waves of foreclosures and bankruptcies throughout the rural South that only exacerbated these problems. Even with its significant progress in industrial development, the South remained "a low wage region in a high wage country," and manufacturers quashed most attempts to unionize southern laborers.[6] Franklin D. Roosevelt summed up the state of the region in 1938, when he famously declared that the South was the "Nation's No. 1 economic problem." It was not until after World War II that a combination of federal defense spending, population growth, and industrial development pulled the region out of its economic torpor and refashioned it into the prosperous Sunbelt.[7]

The social costs of permanence were closely intertwined with the environmental costs. In 1938 Roosevelt pointed to "wasted or neglected resources of land and water" and "abuses suffered by the soil" as crucial problems still facing the region. The report of the National Emergency Council described forests that had been "girdled, chopped, and burned without regard for their permanent value as timber or as conservers of the soil" and decried how the "great natural resources of the South have been exploited with the traditional American regard for cream and disregard for skimmed milk."[8] Despite progress by companies in greening parts of their operations and municipal efforts to attract more permanent industries to the region, by the mid-twentieth century the region was a cautionary tale about the environmental consequences of unchecked development—a point underscored by bureaucrats from the National Emergency Council, as well as popular authors like Erskine Caldwell and Stuart Chase.

Given that corporate leaders and public officials throughout the South embraced permanence, how, then, do we explain the gullies, the exhausted fields, the dammed rivers, and the air and water pollution that have pockmarked the southern landscape for much of the twentieth century?

For one, conservation did not always work on its own terms. People and corporations sometimes continued to waste resources. Conservation may have transformed the acres owned by large firms, but it was less popular among private landowners and small companies without the money and manpower to throw at maintaining stocks of raw materials. The region's emphasis on private avenues for conservation also meant that clashing visions for what permanence was and how to achieve it were difficult to resolve because they pitted private interests against each other. Southern Democratic governments were less active than their counterparts later in the twentieth century at promoting economic development, which complicated the process of choosing between various paths. Throughout much of the New South era, Democratic state officials were content to hang back and let private interests take the lead in promoting development. A patchwork of railroad subsidies, grants of land, and tax breaks certainly did encourage economic growth, but they fell far short of the measures that active state development boards would take in the mid-twentieth century to "sell the South." By the 1920s southern states were beginning to organize state commissions that more aggressively courted new businesses—Alabama's Department of Commerce and Industries, North Carolina's Department of Conservation and Development, and Florida's Bureau of Immigration, among others.[9] Yet for most of the New South era, public officials were reluctant to engage in these active policies of industrial recruitment, and working out the right path for development was left to private interests.

The most important issue, however, was that attempts to secure permanent uses of resources were myopic, and the roots of environmental degradation in the modern South are largely a result of the particular definition of permanence that southern leaders bought into. Southern businesses may have tried to use resources more efficiently or reduce their production of wastes—and many succeeded—but these efforts never went far enough to avoid environmental problems. The very definition of permanence meant that business leaders could ensure the long-term availability of resources without ever having to radically rethink their operations. Municipal officials who hoped to attract more permanent industries to their community also never had to reconsider their obsession with industrial development. Permanence did not have a preservation component, even in the tourism industry. It was always about development through wise corporate use. Permanence, in short, never challenged the logic of capitalist development. It was just a way to cope with environmental limits through expansion. Attracting new enterprises to the region, using resources that had been idle, and eliminating waste in industrial processes all quickened the pace of development. Permanence allowed business leaders to modify their strategies in order to deal with resource depletion without cutting production. In this way, it never challenged the most exploitative uses of the South's natural resources and reinforced what Donald Worster calls the "maximizing creed," which is a key characteristic of capitalism's relationship with the environment.[10] By defining conservation as the permanent use of corporate resources, then, leaders of the New South hit on a goal that they could work toward by maintaining resource stocks without reining in development or addressing other pressing environmental issues.

Efforts to achieve permanence sometimes even made environmental problems worse by intensifying the use of certain natural resources or creating problems that could not be addressed simply by using resources more efficiently. Manufacturing paper from wood pulp, for instance, required forest management but created water and air pollution. Reforesting denuded areas with slash pine created industrial forests that simplified complex ecosystems. The region's addiction to commercial fertilizers had little effect on the long-term health of soils. Even the growth of tourism paved the way for sprawl and development that threatened natural landscapes. These issues were only defined as problems by people concerned about quality of life or ecological ethics. In the 1930s, the Vanderbilt Agrarians, a group of twelve southern poets, writers, and academics who advocated for a return to an agricultural way of life, called attention to the shortsightedness of boosters' concepts of environmental quality. In their famous volume decrying the South's industrialism, *I'll Take My Stand*, they stated that "nature industrialized, transformed into cities and artificial habitations, manufactured into commodities" was "no longer nature but a highly simplified picture of nature." All meaning associated with nature, especially "the sense of nature as something meaningful and contingent," was lost when business leaders collapsed its meaning into statistics designed to maintain economic growth, even if that growth was designed for permanence."[11] The issues that the Agrarians raised in the 1930s, however, simply did not fit into the dominant developmental calculus of public officials and businesspeople who saw permanence as a way to maintain stocks of profitable raw materials for industrial uses.

What should be clear is that environmental degradation in the modern South did not occur because New South leaders embraced growth without any thought about the environmental costs. Although scholars often read the jobs versus environment struggles that characterized the post–World War II era back into the New South, businesspeople and public officials rarely saw any conflict between jobs and their narrow version of environmental quality predicated on managing stocks of natural resources for long-term economic gain. As environmentalists tried to widen the frame and call attention to other aspects of environmental quality in the 1960s and 1970s, southern corporate officials clung to their belief that environmental permanence was simply replenishing corporate resources for continuous production.

By the mid-twentieth century, permanence as both a strategy and an ideal was deeply engrained in the corporate culture of industries throughout the South. The Southern Pulpwood Conservation Association, a group organized in 1939 by the paper industry to promote renewable uses of pine, noted that the pulp and paper industry came into the South to take advantage of "renewable" pine resources. The association's strategy was that "with reasonable care the huge Southern pine forests could be made self-perpetuating" because "the cycle of cutting and replacing can go on indefinitely . . . through adherence to the sensible and systematic reforestation program being practiced and promoted by the South's pulp and paper mills," all of which would contribute to a "stronger South!"[12] In 1965 W. D. Harrigan, the president of the Southern Pine Association, framed the history of the trade group as a pursuit of permanence. He explained that his predecessors had "envisioned a permanent source of raw material" and boasted that "the diligent application and practice of sound forest management" had made sure that southern pine "exceeds that of any other species in the nation with a permanent supply assured." This would lead to a "stable lumber industry offering a perpetual source of livelihood for hundreds of thousands of men and women," as well as an "unending flow of benefits from the forests themselves," including an array of raw and manufactured materials, landscapes for leisure activities, protection for wildlife, and buffers against soil erosion.[13] Even Jonathan Daniels, famed southern liberal, waxed poetic about the benefits that pulp and paper manufacturers—and their corporate foresters—were bringing to the South in the 1950s.[14] By midcentury companies were even using claims to environmental permanence to portray their business practices as environmentally sensitive in an effort to blunt growing critiques of their operations.

By the time the environmental movement was gaining strength, the ideal of permanence had come to represent everything that environmentalists believed was wrong with industry's relationship with the environment. Although Samuel Hays points to permanence as a key characteristic of the postwar environmental movement, it meant something for environmental activists after World War II that was very different from what it meant for corporate officials and involved a more expansive vision rooted in quality of life. Although both activists and corporate officials claimed the mantle of permanence, by the midtwentieth century the way they defined this had grown increasingly disparate.[15]

The goals of environmental permanence may have shifted dramatically even in the New South era, but they still shared a great deal with sustainable development. Although sustainability was only popularized in the 1970s and 1980s, it has roots in attempts to find solutions to localized instances of resource depletion reaching back to the eighteenth century.[16] For three hundred years people have worked to cope with environmental limits while maintaining economic growth and the use of valuable resources. Advocates now speak the language of ecology, but sustainability is just the newest strategy for using natural resources to "meet the needs of the present without compromising the ability of future generations to meet their own needs."[17] Indeed, sustainable development and permanence are both predicated on finding developmental solutions to environmental problems—solutions that do not require radical changes in corporate behavior. One proponent even recently summed up sustainability as "a lifestyle designed for permanence."[18] Because of these commonalities, understanding why southern corporate leaders embraced permanent uses of resources can help to explain the popularity of sustainability with business leaders today. It can also suggest the ways that sustainable development fails to address the issues that are at the heart of so many environmental problems.

If the history of the American South is a study in irony, as C. Vann Woodward contends, the steep environmental price that southerners paid for their efforts to achieve permanent uses of natural resources provides yet another twist.[19] Whereas Woodward uses irony to call attention to the distinctive aspects of the regional experience, the ironic implications of the southern search for permanence seem all too familiar in an era in which sustainability is heralded as the key to solving global environmental woes. Although our current struggle for sustainable uses of resources is almost a century removed from the South's struggle for permanence, the lessons from this experience should provide optimism that businesses can and will make central aspects of their operations greener. Yet the experience of the post–Civil War South also suggests that unless we conceive of environmental quality in the broadest possible terms, and unless we are open to fundamentally rethinking the relationship between business and the environment, we will have little success in heading off our most pressing environmental problems.

NOTES

Preface

1. Albert E. Cowdrey, *This Land, This South: An Environmental History*, rev. ed. (1983; Lexington: University Press of Kentucky, 1996), 215.
2. James C. Cobb, *Industrialization and Southern Society, 1877–1984* (Lexington: University Press of Kentucky, 1984), 121–22.
3. C. Vann Woodward, *Tom Watson: Agrarian Rebel* (1938; New York: Oxford University Press, 1963), 90.
4. C. Vann Woodward, *The Strange Career of Jim Crow* (1955; New York: Oxford University Press, 2002), 7–8.
5. Carl N. Degler, *The Other South: Southern Dissenters in the Nineteenth Century* (Gainesville: University Press of Florida, 1974).
6. James C. Scott, *Seeing Like a State: How Certain Schemes to Improve the Human Condition Have Failed* (New Haven, Conn.: Yale University Press, 1999).
7. Edward L. Ayers, "What We Talk about When We Talk about the South," in *All Over the Map: Rethinking American Regions*, ed. Edward L. Ayers, Patricia Nelson Limerick, Stephen Nissenbaum, and Peter S. Onuf (Baltimore, Md.: Johns Hopkins University Press, 1996), 62–82.
8. C. Vann Woodward, *Origins of the New South, 1877–1913* (1951; Baton Rouge: Louisiana State University Press, 2006); Numan V. Bartley, *The New South, 1945–1980* (Baton Rouge: Louisiana State University Press, 1995).
9. See Andrew Zimmerman, *Alabama in Africa: Booker T. Washington, the German Empire, and the Globalization of the New South* (Princeton, N.J.: Princeton University Press, 2010), 237–50; Steven Hahn, "Class and State in Postemancipation Societies: Southern Planters in Comparative Perspective," *American Historical Review* 95, no. 1 (February 1990): 75–98.
10. Wallace Stegner, *Where the Bluebird Sings to the Lemonade Springs: Living and Writing in the West* (New York: Random House, 1992), xxii, 4. See Wendell E. Berry, "It All Turns on Affection," 2012 Jefferson Lecture, National Endowment for the Humanities, 2012, http://www.neh.gov/print/3971.

Chapter 1. Nature's Bounty

1. Robert J. Lowry, "The Cry of Conservation," *Atlanta Constitution*, July 27, 1913, 5B.
2. Ibid.
3. Ibid.
4. Walter G. Cooper, *The Cotton States and International Exposition and South, Illustrated* (Atlanta: Illustrator Company, 1896), 157; Franklin M. Garrett, *Atlanta and Environs: A Chronicle of Its People and Events, 1820s–1870s*, vol. 1 (Athens: University of Georgia Press, 1969), 514.

5. Don H. Doyle, *New Men, New Cities, New South: Atlanta, Nashville, Charleston, Mobile, 1860–1910* (Chapel Hill: University of North Carolina Press, 1990), 87–110.

6. Heather Cox Richardson, *West from Appomattox: The Reconstruction of America after the Civil War* (New Haven, Conn.: Yale University Press, 2007), 17; F. Y. Hedley, *Marching through Georgia* (Chicago: R. R. Donnelley and Sons, 1887), 320.

7. "Art. VI.—Address by Col. Ben Allston," *DeBow's Review,* August 1869, 669, quoted in Paul M. Gaston, *The New South Creed: A Study in Southern Mythmaking* (New York: Alfred A. Knopf, 1970), 23.

8. "President Johnson," *Memphis Daily Avalanche,* January 1, 1866, 2.

9. J. D. B. DeBow, "The Future of the South," *DeBow's Review* 1, no. 1 (January 1866): 6.

10. John Calvin Reed, *The Old and the New South* (New York: A. S. Barnes, 1876), 13.

11. "Northern Capital and Southern Resources," *Galveston Weekly News,* August 11, 1881, 1.

12. *Boston Herald* quoted in "Resources of the South," *Clinch Valley News,* June 1, 1888, 2. See also Gaston, *New South Creed,* 55–59.

13. Gaston, *New South Creed,* 54–79.

14. Charles Dudley Warner, "Impressions of the South," *Harper's New Monthly Magazine* 71, no. 424 (September 1885): 548.

15. Megan Kate Nelson, *Ruin Nation: Destruction and the American Civil War* (Athens: University of Georgia Press, 2012).

16. Richard H. Edmonds, *The South's Redemption: From Poverty to Prosperity* (Baltimore, Md.: Manufacturers' Record Company, 1890), 3–4.

17. Edward B. Barbier, *Scarcity and Frontiers: How Economies Have Developed through Natural Resource Exploitation* (Cambridge: Cambridge University Press, 2011), 369.

18. Richard Edmonds, *Facts about the South: Promise of Its Prosperity in Light of the Past Based on Limitless Resources* (Baltimore, Md.: Manufacturers' Record Publishing Company, 1907), 63–64.

19. Edward Atkinson, *The Development of the Resources of the Southern States* (Boston, 1898), 11.

20. Andrew Zimmerman, *Alabama in Africa: Booker T. Washington, the German Empire, and the Globalization of the New South* (Princeton, N.J.: Princeton University Press, 2010), 38–40, 53.

21. Steven Hahn, *A Nation under Our Feet: Black Political Struggles in the Rural South from Slavery to the Great Migration* (Cambridge, Mass.: Belknap Press, 2003), 127–32, 214.

22. Quoted in C. Vann Woodward, *Tom Watson: Agrarian Rebel* (1938; New York: Oxford University Press, 1963), 126–27.

23. See James C. Cobb, *Away Down South: A History of Southern Identity* (New York: Oxford University Press, 2005), 98.

24. T. Thomas Fortune, *Black and White: Land, Labor, and Politics in the South* (New York: Fords, Howard and Hulbert, 1884), 40, 146. On Fortune, see K. Stephen Prince, *Stories of the South: Race and the Reconstruction of Southern Identity, 1865–1915* (Chapel Hill: University of North Carolina Press, 2014), 132–33.

25. North Carolina Farmers' State Alliance, *Proceedings of the Fifth Annual Session of the North Carolina Farmers' State Alliance* (Raleigh, N.C.: Edwards and Broughton, 1891), 7.

26. Rupert B. Vance, *Human Geography of the South: A Study in Regional Resources and Human Adequacy* (1932; Chapel Hill: University of North Carolina Press, 1935); Howard W. Odum, *Southern Regions of the United States* (Chapel Hill: University of North Carolina Press, 1936).

27. Elliott West, *The Contested Plains: Indians, Goldseekers, and the Rush to Colorado* (Lawrence: University Press of Kansas, 1998), 54, xix.

28. "The Old and the New South," *International Review* 3 (March 1876): 209.

29. John W. Johnson, "The Emancipation of the Southern Whites," *Manufacturers' Record*, July 9, 1887, quoted in Gaston, *New South Creed*, 58.

30. "Southern Development," *Tri-Weekly State Gazette*, August 24, 1870, 1.

31. Reed, *Old and the New South*, 17, 24.

32. Henry W. Grady, "The South and Her Problems," in *Joel Chandler Harris' Life of Henry W. Grady*, ed. Joel Chandler Harris (New York: Cassell Publishing Company, 1890), 120.

33. Gaines Foster, *Ghosts of the Confederacy: Defeat, the Lost Cause, and the Emergence of the New South* (New York: Oxford University Press, 1987); Gaston, *New South Creed*, 4–13.

34. Eric Foner, *Reconstruction: America's Unfinished Revolution, 1863–1877* (New York: Perennial Classics, 1988), 379–83; Mark W. Summers, *Railroads, Reconstruction, and the Gospel of Prosperity: Aid under the Radical Republicans, 1865–1877* (Princeton, N.J.: Princeton University Press, 1984), 15–18.

35. Gaston, *New South Creed*, 32.

36. James C. Cobb, "Beyond Planters and Industrialists: A New Perspective on the New South," *Journal of Southern History* 54, no. 1 (February 1988): 45–68; James Tice Moore, "Redeemers Reconsidered: Change and Continuity in the Democratic South," *Journal of Southern History* 44, no. 3 (August 1978): 357–78.

37. C. Vann Woodward, *Origins of the New South, 1877–1913* (1951; Baton Rouge: Louisiana State University Press, 2006), 20.

38. Gaston, *New South Creed*, 4–13.

39. Moore, "Redeemers Reconsidered," 368–69; Woodward, *Origins of the New South*, 115–20.

40. David L. Carlton, "Smokestack-Chasing and Its Discontents: Southern Development Strategy in the Twentieth Century," in *The American South in the Twentieth Century*, ed. Craig S. Pascoe, Karen Trahan Leathem, and Andy Ambrose (Athens: University of Georgia Press, 2005), 106–26; James C. Cobb, *Industrialization and Southern Society, 1877–1984* (Lexington: University Press of Kentucky, 1984), 6–26.

41. George Marvin, "Progress and the Parthenon," *Outlook* 139 (1925): 653, quoted in George B. Tindall, *The Emergence of the New South, 1913–1945* (Baton Rouge: Louisiana State University Press, 1967), 98.

42. "Our Future Hope," *Knoxville Daily Chronicle*, August 22, 1872, 2, emphasis in the original.

43. George Perkins Marsh, *Man and Nature; or, Physical Geography as Modified by Human Action* (New York: Charles Scribner, 1864).

44. Alfred Runte, *National Parks: The American Experience*, 3rd ed. (Lincoln: University of Nebraska Press, 1997), 33.

45. Jeremy L. Caradonna, *Sustainability: A History* (New York: Oxford University Press, 2014), 21–88.

46. Samuel P. Hays, *Conservation and the Gospel of Efficiency: The Progressive Conservation Movement, 1890–1920* (1959; New York: Atheneum, 1974), 36–37.

47. James D. Richardson, ed., *A Compilation of the Messages and Papers of the Presidents* (Washington, D.C.: Bureau of National Literature and Art, 1908), 10:432.

48. *Proceedings of a Conference of Governors* (Washington, D.C.: Government Printing Office, 1909), 12, quoted in Ian Tyrrell, *Crisis of the Wasteful Nation: Empire and Conservation in Theodore Roosevelt's America* (Chicago: University of Chicago Press, 2015), 82.

49. *Proceedings of a Conference of Governors*, viii.

50. Gifford Pinchot, *Breaking New Ground* (1947; Washington, D.C.: Island Press, 1974), 13; Char Miller, *Gifford Pinchot and the Making of American Environmentalism* (Washington, D.C.: Shearwater Books, 2001), 85.

51. Pinchot, *Breaking New Ground*, 505.

52. *Idaho Daily Statesman*, June 21, 1907, quoted in Miller, *Gifford Pinchot*, 168. See Gifford Pinchot, "Home-Building for the Nation," *Conservation* 15, no. 9 (September 1909): 521–25.

53. John Paull, "The Making of an Agricultural Classic: Farmers of Forty Centuries or Permanent Agriculture in China, Korea and Japan, 1911–2011," *Agricultural Sciences* 2, no. 3 (2011): 175–76; Paul Sutter, *Let Us Now Praise Famous Gullies: Providence Canyon and the Soils of the South* (Athens: University of Georgia Press, 2015), 40–46.

54. Ralph H. Hess, "Public Policy and Conservation," in *The Foundations of National Prosperity: Studies in the Conservation of Permanent National Resources*, by Richard Ely et al. (New York: Macmillan Company, 1918), 162.

55. "Addresses at the Southern Conservation Congress," *American Lumberman*, October 15, 1910, 53.

56. Gifford Pinchot, "Need of the South for Practical Conservation," *Lumber Trade Journal*, October 15, 1910, 122.

57. Albert E. Cowdrey, *This Land, This South: An Environmental History*, rev. ed. (1983; Lexington: University Press of Kentucky, 1996), 46–52, 55–59.

58. *Proceedings of a Conference of Governors*, xix–xxxi. On the Conference of Governors, see Hays, *Conservation*, 127–29.

59. National Conservation Commission, *Report of the National Conservation Commission, February 1909* (Washington, D.C.: Government Printing Office, 1909), 28–35.

60. "'Conservation' and—What?," *Macon Daily Telegraph*, September 22, 1910, 4.

61. "Southern Conservation" *Daily Picayune*, October 17, 1909, 9.

62. S. N. D. North, ed., *The American Yearbook: A Record of Events and Progress, 1910* (New York: D. Appleton and Company, 1911), 299; "Conservation of Forests," *Galveston Daily News*, November 1, 1909, 7; "One Thousand Delegates for Conservation Congress," *Daily Picayune*, October 29, 1909, 4.

63. "Pinchot and T. R. to Speak at South's Conservation Congress," *Des Moines Daily News*, September 21, 1910, 3.

64. *Official Proceedings at the First Session of the Southern Commercial Congress* (n.p., 1908), 5.

65. Southern Commercial Congress, *A Brief Survey of the Activities of the Southern Commercial Congress* (Washington, D.C.: National Cooperating Committee of the Southern Commercial Congress, 1922), 1–2; "Sectional Meetings of Great Commercial Congress Prolific in Weighty and Far-Reaching Discussions," *Constitution*, March 11, 1911, 4.

66. Doyle, *New Men*, 19–20.

67. Robert W. Rydell, *All the World's a Fair: Visions of Empire at American International Expositions, 1876–1916* (Chicago: University of Chicago Press, 1984), 73. See also Bruce G. Harvey, *World's Fairs in a Southern Accent: Atlanta, Nashville, and Charleston, 1895–1902* (Knoxville: University of Tennessee Press, 2014).

68. *The Official Catalogue of the Cotton States and International Exposition* (Atlanta: Claflin & Mellichamp, 1895), 191–92; "Forestry at the Atlanta Exposition," *Forest Leaves* 5, no. 6 (December 1895): 81–83.

69. Harvey, *World's Fairs*, 157; *Prospectus: The International Cotton Exposition of Products, Machinery and Manufactures* (Atlanta: Jas. P. Harrison & Co., 1881), 16; Herman Justi, ed., *Official History of the Tennessee Centennial Exposition* (Nashville: Brandon Printing Company, 1898), 180; "The Lesson of Jamestown," *Forestry and Irrigation*, June 1907, 313–25; Robert Douglas Lukens, "Portraits of Progress in New South Appalachia: Three Expositions in Knoxville, Tennessee, 1910–1913" (M.A. thesis, University of Tennessee, 1996), 16–45.

70. T. Asbury Wright, "The Exposition," *Knoxville Sentinel*, August 27, 1913, 4. See also "Conservation Show Ready," *Call*, August 31, 1913, 32; W. M. Goodman, ed., *The First Exposition of Conservation and Its Builders* (Knoxville: Knoxville Lithographing Company, 1913), 14; Lukens, "Portraits of Progress," 46–65.

71. J. L. Bowles, "What Knoxville Exposition Means to Southern States," *Atlanta Constitution*, February 9, 1913, C5.

72. "Bas-Relief Maps Southern States," *Tulsa Daily World*, June 16, 1912, 11; Goodman, *First Exposition*, 108–40; "Educational Exhibit Is Quite Creditable," *Knoxville Sentinel*, September 6, 1913, 11.

73. "Deforestation Dangers Emphasized in Exhibit," *Knoxville Sentinel*, September 4, 1913, 7.

74. "Conservation Exposition Attracts Great Interest," *Atlanta Constitution*, October 27, 1912, A8. See also "National Conservation Exposition," *Review*, October 9, 1913, 8.

75. Goodman, *First Exposition*, 342–47.

76. J. L. Bowles, "What Knoxville Exposition Means to the Southern States," *Atlanta Constitution*, February 9, 1913, C5.

77. Wright, "Exposition," 4.

78. Pinchot quoted in Goodman, *First Exposition*, 14.

79. "City Raises $100,000 to Secure Enterprise," *Knoxville Sentinel*, August 27, 1913, 14.

80. William Bruce Wheeler, *Knoxville, Tennessee: A Mountain City in the New South*, 2nd ed. (Knoxville: University of Tennessee Press, 2005), 6–56.

81. Goodman, *First Exposition*, 100–226. For an overview of exhibits, see "Southern States Rich in Big Manufactories," *Knoxville Sentinel*, September 2, 1913, 8.

82. Advertisement, *Knoxville Sentinel*, September 2, 1913, 11.

83. Advertisement, *Journal and Tribune*, September 23, 1913, quoted in Lukens, "Portraits of Progress," 59.

84. *The National Conservation Exposition: Knoxville, Tennessee, Sept. 1st to Nov. 1st, 1913* (n.p., 1913); advertisement, *Constitution*, June 4, 1913, 94.

85. Goodman, *First Exposition*, 51.

86. "Booster for Knoxville Favors Conservation," *Atlanta Constitution*, May 27, 1911, 3.

87. Goodman, *First Exposition*, 411.

88. Quoted in Ralph R. Widner, ed., *Forests and Forestry in the American States: A Reference Anthology* (Missoula, Mont.: National Association of State Foresters, 1968), 437.

89. W. H., "The Oconee Agricultural College," *Keowee Courier*, November 18, 1870, 1.

90. Henry W. Grady, *The New South* (New York: Robert Bonner's Sons, 1890), 144–45.

91. Hays, *Conservation*, 122–27.

92. "Resources and Progress of the South," *Bankers' Magazine* 65, no. 4 (October 1902): 440.

93. Woodward, *Origins of the New South*, 144–45; Gaston, *New South Creed*, 50–51, 68–69.

94. Richard H. Edmonds, "The Utilization of Southern Wastes," *Publications of the American Economic Association* 5, no. 1 (February 1904): 163–64, 166–67.

95. "Wins Title of 'The Crusader for Crops,'" *Morning Oregonian*, August 9, 1914, 3; "Cotton to Combat Boll Weevil Pest," *Charlotte Daily Observer*, December 29, 1912, 2.

96. E. L. Worsham, "No Movement Could Mean So Much for All People," *Atlanta Constitution*, October 2, 1910, 8.

97. "Southern Conservationists Tell of Needs of the South," *Lumber Trade Journal*, October 15, 1910, 121.

98. Elmo Richardson, *The Politics of Conservation: Crusades and Controversies, 1897–1913* (Berkeley: University of California Press, 1962), 100, 99–104.

99. *Addresses and Proceedings of the Second National Conservation Congress* (Washington, D.C.: National Conservation Congress, 1911), 140, 135.

100. Ibid., 138.

101. "Of Personal Interest," *Railway and Locomotive Engineering*, January 1907, 33; Burke Davis, *The Southern Railway: Road of the Innovators* (Chapel Hill: University of North Carolina Press, 1985), 45–52.

102. See Adam Rome, "Nature Wars, Culture Wars: Immigration and Environmental Reform in the Progressive Era," *Environmental History* 13, no. 3 (June 2008): 432–53; Stephen Fox, *The American Conservation Movement* (Madison: University of Wisconsin Press, 1981), 345–51; Kevin Deluca and Anne Demo, "Imagining Nature and Erasing Class and Race: Carleton Watkins, John Muir, and the Construction of Wilderness," *Environmental History* 6, no. 4 (October 2001): 541–60. See also Karl Jacoby, *Crimes against Nature: Squatters, Poachers, Thieves, and the Hidden History of American Conservation* (Berkeley: University of California Press, 2001); Mark David Spence, *Dispossessing the Wilderness: Indian Removal and the Making of the National Parks* (New York: Oxford University Press, 2000); Louis Warren, *The Hunter's Game: Poachers and Conservationists in Twentieth-Century America* (New Haven, Conn.: Yale University Press, 1999).

103. Carolyn Merchant, "Shades of Darkness: Race and Environmental History," *Environmental History* 8, no. 3 (July 2003): 386.

104. Steven Hahn, "Hunting, Fishing, and Foraging: Common Rights and Class Relations in the Postbellum South," *Radical History Review* 26 (1982): 37–64.

105. "Forcing Conservation on the Vagrant," *Atlanta Constitution*, January 18, 1911, 4.

106. Kimberly K. Smith, *African American Environmental Thought* (Lawrence: University Press of Kansas, 2007), 4–6, 68–97.

107. Mark Hersey, "Hints and Suggestions to Farmers: George Washington Carver and Rural Conservation in the South," *Environmental History* 11, no. 2 (April 2006): 239–68.

108. Gifford Pinchot, "The Growth of the Conservation Idea," *Southern Workman* 39, no. 1 (January 1910): 49–51; "Hampton Incidents," *Southern Workman* 39, no. 1 (January 1910): 65.

109. "The Tuberculosis Exhibit in Philadelphia," *Southern Workman* 38, no. 1 (January 1909): 73.

110. R. D. Doggett, "The Conservation of Our Natural Resources," *Aurora* 24, no. 6 (March 1910): 3.

111. Cobb, "Beyond Planters," 59.

112. Tindall, *Emergence*, 233, 223–53; Cobb, "Beyond Planters," 59, 56–60. See also George B. Tindall, "Business Progressivism: Southern Politics in the Twenties," *South Atlantic Quarterly* 62 (Winter 1963): 92–106.

Chapter 2. Cultivating Permanence

1. Eugene W. Hilgard, *Address on Progressive Agriculture and Industrial Education* (Jackson, Miss.: Clarion Book and Job Office, 1873), 4–6, emphasis in the original. On Hilgard, see Walter E. Pittman Jr., "Eugene W. Hilgard and Scientific Education in Mississippi," *Earth Sciences History* 4, no. 1 (1985): 26–31; Steven Stoll, *Larding the Lean Earth: Soil and Society in Nineteenth-Century America* (New York: Hill and Wang, 2002), 202–4.

2. Hilgard, *Address*, 4–6.

3. Edmund Ruffin, *Nature's Management: Writings on Landscape and Reform, 1822–1859*, ed. Jack Temple Kirby (Athens: University of Georgia Press, 2000), 323.

4. Lynn A. Nelson, "When Land Was Cheap, and Labor Dear: James Madison's 'Address to the Albemarle Agricultural Society' and the Problem of Southern Agricultural Reform," *History Compass* 6, no. 3 (2008): 917–33.

5. Pete Daniel, *Breaking the Land: The Transformation of Cotton, Tobacco, and Rice Cultures since 1880* (Urbana: University of Illinois Press, 1985), 3–5; Roger L. Ransom and Richard Sutch, *One Kind of Freedom: The Economic Consequences of Emancipation*, 2nd ed. (Cambridge: Cambridge University Press, 2001), 51; Eric Foner, *Reconstruction: America's Unfinished Revolution, 1863–1877* (New York: Perennial Classics, 1988), 125.

6. J. T. Trowbridge, *The South: A Journey through the Desolated States, and Talks with the People* (Hartford, Conn.: L. Stebbins, 1866), 427.

7. "Annual Report of the Comptroller General of the State of Georgia, Made to the Governor," *Georgia Weekly Telegraph*, November 5, 1866, 1.

8. Gilbert C. Fite, *Cotton Fields No More* (Lexington: University Press of Kentucky, 1984), 25.

9. Trowbridge, *South*, 180, 482.

10. John Richard Dennett, *The South as It Is, 1865–1866*, ed. Henry M. Christman (Baton Rouge: Louisiana State University Press, 1965), 118.

11. Edward King, *The Great South* (Hartford, Conn.: American Publishing Company, 1875), 330.

12. Quoted in Hilgard, *Address*, 6.

13. John Majewski and Viken Tchakerian, "The Environmental Origins of Shifting Cultivation: Climate, Soils, and Disease in the Nineteenth-Century U.S. South," *Agricultural History* 81, no. 4 (Fall 2007): 522–49. See also Majewski, *Modernizing a Slave Economy: The Economic Vision of the Confederate Nation* (Chapel Hill: University of North Carolina Press, 2009), 22–52.

14. "The Moral of King Cotton," *Daily Phoenix*, August 22, 1865, 2.

15. James T. Gray, "Farms, Farmers, and Farming," *Rural Carolinian* 5, no. 7 (April 1874): 377.

16. John Bankston Davis, "Practical Farming," *Carolina Spartan*, May 21, 1884, 1.

17. Paul Gaston, *The New South Creed: A Study in Southern Mythmaking* (New York: Alfred A. Knopf, 1970), 82, 64, 63–68.

18. "Annual Report of the Comptroller General," 1.

19. Alfred Huger, "The South and Her Resources," *Rural Carolinian* 2, no. 2 (November 1870): 72.

20. Henry W. Grady, "Cotton and Its Kingdom," *Harper's New Monthly Magazine* 63 (1881): 722; Gavin Wright, *Old South, New South: Revolutions in the Southern Economy since the Civil War* (Baton Rouge: Louisiana State University Press, 1986), 19, 34, vi.

21. Carville Earle, "The Myth of the Southern Soil Miner: Macrohistory, Agricultural Innovation, and Environmental Change," in *The Ends of the Earth: Perspectives on Modern Environmental History*, ed. Donald Worster (Cambridge: Cambridge University Press, 1988), 184–86.

22. Steven Hahn, *The Roots of Southern Populism: Yeoman Farmers and the Transformation of the Georgia Upcountry, 1850–1890* (New York: Oxford University Press, 1983), 239–68.

23. Steven Hahn, "Common Right and Commonwealth: The Stock-Law Struggle and the Roots of Southern Populism," in *Region, Race, and Reconstruction: Essays in Honor of C. Vann Woodward*, ed. J. Morgan Kousser and James M. McPherson (Oxford: Oxford University Press, 1982), 53.

24. J.O.R.W., letter to the editor, *Carroll Free Press*, June 12, 1885, 2.

25. Hahn, "Common Right," 56–57.

26. Shawn Everett Kantor, *Politics and Property Rights: The Closing of the Open Range in the Postbellum South* (Chicago: University of Chicago Press, 1998), 157, 168.

27. Wright, *Old South, New South*, 59.

28. Gaston, *New South Creed*, 63–68; Stephen J. DeCanio, *Agriculture in the Postbellum South* (Cambridge, Mass.: MIT Press, 1975), 94–95; Edward Ayers, *The Promise of the New South: Life after Reconstruction* (New York: Oxford University Press, 1992), 188–95.

29. DeCanio, *Agriculture*, 96–97; Willard Range, *A Century of Georgia Agriculture, 1850–1950* (Athens: University of Georgia Press, 1954), 90–91.

30. "Essay Read before the County Agricultural Society," *Orangeburg Times*, August 7, 1873, 5.

31. "Wheat," *Brenham Weekly Banner*, May 11, 1882, 3.

32. Henry W. Grady, "The South and Her Problems," in *Joel Chandler Harris' Life of Henry W. Grady*, ed. Joel Chandler Harris (New York: Cassell Publishing Company, 1890), 47–48; Harold E. Davis, "Henry Grady, the Atlanta *Constitution*, and the Politics of Farming in the 1880s," *Georgia Historical Quarterly* 71, no. 4 (Winter 1987): 572–74.

33. "Giles County Wheat Club," *Pulaski Citizen*, October 16, 1868, 3.

34. E. M. Pendleton, "The Oat Crop—Its Importance to the South," *Rural Carolinian* 2, no. 3 (December 1870): 134.

35. August Mayer, *The Cattle Tick in Its Relation to Southern Agriculture*, USDA Farmers' Bulletin no. 261 (Washington, D.C.: Government Printing Office, 1906), 21. See also Claire Strom, *Making Catfish Bait out of Government Boys: The Fight against Cattle Ticks and the Transformation of the Yeoman South* (Athens: University of Georgia Press, 2009).

36. W. M. Rowland, "Magician Cowpea Revives Soil and Swells Bank Account," *Atlanta Constitution*, January 24, 1914, 4.

37. Bill Arp, "Home and Farm," *Atlanta Constitution*, July 27, 1885, 5; Jared G. Smith, *Cowpeas*, USDA Farmers' Bulletin no. 89 (Washington, D.C.: Government Printing Office, 1899); Earle, "Myth," 205.

38. Fite, *Cotton Fields No More*, 14.

39. Quoted in "Sorghum in the South," *Knoxville Weekly Chronicle*, August 23, 1871, 3.

40. See Mark D. Hersey, *My Work Is That of Conservation: An Environmental Biography of George Washington Carver* (Athens: University of Georgia Press, 2011), 145, 124–59; Mark Hersey, "Hints and Suggestions to Farmers: George Washington Carver and Rural Conservation in the South," *Environmental History* 11, no. 2 (April 2006): 246–47.

41. E. F., "The Cotton Plant and Soil Fertility," *Southern Planter* 46, no. 10 (October 1885): 515.

42. United States Industrial Commission, *Report of the Industrial Commission on Agriculture and Agricultural Labor* (Washington, D.C.: Government Printing Office, 1901), 10:78–79; W. F. Massey, "Have We Any Worn-Out Soils?," *Southern Planter* 61, no. 4 (April 1900): 197; James R. Troyer, "Wilbur Fisk Massey (1839–1923): North Carolina Botanist, Horticulturist, and Agriculturist," *Journal of the Elisha Mitchell Scientific Society* 116, no. 2 (2000): 101–12.

43. Earle, "Myth," 206.

44. Harold D. Woodman, *New South—New Law: The Legal Foundations of Credit and Labor Relations in the Postbellum Agricultural South* (Baton Rouge: Louisiana State University Press, 1995), 68–76.

45. Wright, *Old South, New South*, 85–86.

46. D. A. Brodie and C. K. McClellan, *Diversified Farming under the Plantation System* (Washington, D.C.: Government Printing Office, 1907), 9.

47. Eugene Allen Smith, *Report on Cotton Production of the State of Alabama* (Washington, D.C.: Government Printing Office, 1884), 62.

48. United States Industrial Commission, *Report*, 907–10.

49. C. Vann Woodward, *Origins of the New South, 1877–1913* (1951; Baton Rouge: Louisiana State University Press, 2006), 297–99.

50. "Chamber of Commerce," *Memphis Daily Appeal*, November 26, 1872, 4.

51. "A Letter from South Carolina," *Southern Planter and Farmer* 3 (March 1875): 125.

52. W. B. Mercier, "Farming as a Business," *Southern Planter* 64, no. 11 (November 1903): 708.

53. See Fite, *Cotton Fields No More*, 71–72.

54. Foner, *Reconstruction*, 163–64.

55. James Giesen, *Boll Weevil Blues: Cotton, Myth, and Power in the American South* (Chicago: University of Chicago Press, 2011), 170–75.

56. United States Census Bureau, *Statistical Abstract of the United States* (Washington, D.C.: Government Printing Office, 1929), 668.

57. Scott Reynolds Nelson, *Iron Confederacies: Southern Railways, Klan Violence, and Reconstruction* (Chapel Hill: University of North Carolina Press, 1999), 170–78.

58. George B. Tindall, *The Emergence of the New South, 1913–1945* (Baton Rouge: Louisiana State University Press, 1967), 123; Fite, *Cotton Fields No More*, 68.

59. Eugene W. Hilgard, *Report on Cotton Production in the United States*, pt. 1 (Washington, D.C.: Government Printing Office, 1884), 9.

60. Fite, *Cotton Fields No More*, 72–79; Lester D. Stephens, "Farish Furman's Formula: Scientific Farming and the 'New South,'" *Agricultural History* 50, no. 2 (April 1976): 377–90; Roy V. Scott, *Railroad Development Programs in the Twentieth Century* (Ames: Iowa State University Press, 1985), 36–57, 89–103; Scott, "American Railroads and Agricultural Extension, 1900–1914: A Study in Railway Developmental Techniques," *Business History Review* 39, no. 1 (Spring 1965): 74–79.

61. Richard A. Wines, *Fertilizer in America: From Waste Recycling to Resource Exploitation* (Philadelphia: Temple University Press, 1985), 42; Rosser H. Taylor, "The Sale and Application of Commercial Fertilizers in the South Atlantic States to 1900," *Agricultural History* 21, no. 1 (January 1947): 47–48.

62. Wines, *Fertilizer in America*, 96–108.

63. Nelson, *Iron Confederacies*, 170–78; Ransom and Sutch, *One Kind of Freedom*, 162–64, 187–88; Taylor, "Sale and Application," 48–49.

64. Ransom and Sutch, *One Kind*, 102–3, 189.
65. Earle, "Myth," 206.
66. Taylor, "Sale and Application," 50–51.
67. Swift Fertilizer Works to Consumers, undated, James series C, pt. 2, reel 10, James Jonathan Lucas Papers, *Records of Southern Plantations from Emancipation to the Great Migration*, ed. Ira Berlin (Bethesda, Md.: University Publications of America, 2004).
68. Advertisement, *Progressive Farmer*, August 4, 1896, 7.
69. Ibid.
70. "What Is It Your Land Needs?," *Punta Gorda Herald*, March 23, 1916, 7; advertisement, *Manning Times*, December 25, 1918, 7.
71. *Making Soil and Crops Pay More* (Richmond: Crop Book Department, Virginia Carolina Chemical Company, 1918), 8, 2.
72. Knapp quoted in ibid., 7, 20, 14.
73. Milton Whitney, *A Study of Crop Yields and Soil Composition in Relation to Soil Productivity*, Bureau of Soils Bulletin no. 57 (Washington, D.C.: Government Printing Office, 1909), 60; Paul Sutter, *Let Us Now Praise Famous Gullies: Providence Canyon and the Soils of the South* (Athens: University of Georgia Press, 2015), 38–46.
74. Grady, "Cotton," 720.
75. Mark V. Wetherington, *The New South Comes to Wiregrass Georgia, 1860–1910* (Knoxville: University of Tennessee Press, 1994), 160–61.
76. Rupert B. Vance, *Human Geography of the South: A Study in Regional Resources and Human Adequacy* (1932; Chapel Hill: University of North Carolina Press, 1935), 95.
77. F. S. Earle, *Southern Agriculture* (New York: Macmillan Company, 1908), 275; United States Industrial Commission, *Report*, 875; James L. McCorkle Jr., "Moving Perishables to Market: Southern Railroads and the Nineteenth-Century Origins of Southern Truck Farming," *Southern Studies* 11, no. 3/4 (Winter 2004): 19–20; Mart A. Stewart, *"What Nature Suffers to Groe": Life, Labor, and Landscape on the Georgia Coast, 1680–1920* (Athens: University of Georgia Press, 1996), 225–29.
78. Mark D. Hersey, "'Their Plows Singing beneath the Sandy Loam': African American Agriculture in the Late-Nineteenth-Century South," in *African Americans in the Nineteenth Century*, ed. Dixie Ray Haggard (Santa Barbara, Calif.: ABC-CLIO, 2010), 139.
79. Theodore Rosengarten, *All God's Dangers: The Life of Nate Shaw* (New York: Alfred A. Knopf, 1974), 106–7, 155–57.
80. Ibid., 106–8.
81. Carville Earle, "The Price of Precocity: Technical Choice and Ecological Constraint in the Cotton South, 1840–1890," *Agricultural History* 66, no. 3 (Summer 1992): 28; Fite, *Cotton Fields No More*, 24–25.
82. "Fertilizing Lands, Rye, Peas," *Reconstructed Farmer*, June 1870, 57.
83. "Gov. Scales on Farming," *Progressive Farmer*, January 19, 1887, 4.
84. "Resolutions for 1891," *Weekly Telegraph*, January 20, 1892, 7.
85. "Cotton and Fertilizers," *Savannah Tribune*, February 23, 1895, 1.
86. See Connie L. Lester, *Up from the Mudsills of Hell: The Farmers' Alliance, Populism, and Progressive Agriculture in Tennessee, 1870–1915* (Athens: University of Georgia Press, 2006), 98–99; Charles Postel, *The Populist Vision* (New York: Oxford University Press, 2007), 52–56, 107–8.
87. William Warren Rogers, "Reuben F. Kolb: Agricultural Leader of the New South," *Agricultural History* 32, no. 2 (April 1958): 109–19; Ayers, *Promise*, 222–30; Lawrence Good-

wyn, *Democratic Promise: The Populist Moment in America* (New York: Oxford University Press, 1976), 190–91.

88. J. S. Newman, *Co-operative Soil Tests of Fertilizers*, Agricultural Experiment Station of the Agricultural and Mechanical College Bulletin no. 23 (Montgomery, Ala.: Brown Printing Company, 1891), 3–8, 54–61.

89. Lala Carr Steelman, *The North Carolina Farmers' Alliance: A Political History, 1887–1893* (Greenville, N.C.: East Carolina University Publications, 1985), 150–51.

90. "The State Alliance," *Newberry Herald and News*, July 30, 1891, 2; "The State Exchange," *Newberry Herald and News*, May 7, 1891, 2.

91. G. Terry Sharrer, *A Kind of Fate: Agricultural Change in Virginia, 1861–1920* (Ames: Iowa State University Press, 2000), 102–3.

92. J. W. Fitz and Josiah Ryland Jr., *Profitable Farming in the Southern States* (Richmond, Va.: Franklin Publishing Company, 1890), 76–77.

93. Daniel A. Tompkins, *Cotton and Cotton Oil* (Charlotte: D. A. Tompkins, 1901), 400–401.

94. Charles William Burkett and Clarence Hamilton Poe, *Cotton: Its Cultivation, Marketing, Manufacture, and the Problems of the Cotton World* (New York: Doubleday, Page and Company, 1906), 121.

95. South Carolina Commission of Agriculture, Commerce and Industries, *Ninth Annual Report of the Commissioner of Agriculture, Commerce and Industries of the State of South Carolina* (Columbia, S.C.: Gonzales and Bryan, 1913), 9.

96. F. Henry Cardoza, "Relation of Weather and Soil Conditions to the Fruit Industry of Southeastern Alabama," TAES Bulletin no. 11 (January 1908), 5, quoted in Hersey, "Hints and Suggestions," 252.

97. G. W. Carver, *A Study of the Soils of Macon County, Alabama and Their Adaptability to Certain Crops*, Bulletin no. 25 (Tuskegee, Ala.: Institute Press, 1913), 7.

98. George Washington Carver to Booker T. Washington, January 26, 1911, quoted in Hersey, *My Work*, 141, 134–44; Hersey, "Hints and Suggestions," 251–52.

99. Hersey, *My Work*, 156–57.

100. United States Industrial Commission, *Report*, 882–83; "Rotation of Crops," *Southern Planter* 61, no. 12 (December 1900): 643.

101. "We Must Stop Land-Robbing and Start Land-Building," *Jeffersonian*, January 30, 1908, 6.

102. Fite, *Cotton Fields No More*, 78–79; S. A. Knapp, *Demonstration Work in Cooperation with Southern Farmers*, USDA Farmers' Bulletin no. 319 (Washington, D.C.: Government Printing Office, 1908).

103. W. D. Hunter, *The Boll Weevil Problem: With Special Reference to Means of Reducing Their Damage*, USDA Farmers' Bulletin no. 512 (Washington, D.C.: Government Printing Office, 1909); O. F. Cook, *Common Errors in Cotton Production*, USDA Farmers' Bulletin no. 1,686 (Washington, D.C.: Government Printing Office, 1932).

104. M. A. Crosby, *An Example of Intensive Farming in the Cotton Belt*, Farmers' Bulletin no. 519 (Washington, D.C.: Government Printing Office, 1913), 13.

105. Roy V. Scott, *The Reluctant Farmer: The Rise of Agricultural Extension to 1914* (Urbana: University of Illinois Press, 1970), 288–313; Fite, *Cotton Fields No More*, 81–82.

106. Bradford Knapp, *Safe Farming*, USDA Circular no. 56 (Washington, D.C.: Government Printing Office, 1916), 3; "What Is 'Safe Farming' in the South?," *American Fertilizer*, March 13, 1920, 136, 138; "Safe Farming for the South," *Banker-Farmer* 7, no. 4–5 (March/April 1920): 6–7.

107. "The Central of Georgia Railway and Farming," *Right Way Magazine* 11, no. 5 (May 1921): 5; remarks of L. A. Downs, president, Central of Georgia Railway Company, at barbecue of County Agricultural Association, Pearl Springs Park, Coweta County, Georgia, Monday, April 19, 1926, box 1, folder 12, Executive Department Files, Central of Georgia Railway Records, Georgia Historical Society, Savannah; J. F. Jackson, "Ten Years of Agricultural Development Work on the Central of Georgia Railway," *Right Way Magazine* 11, no. 7 (July 1921): 6.

108. J. F. Jackson, "How the Railroad Helps the Farmer," radio talk from WAPI, Auburn, Ala., March 24, 1927, Central of Georgia Railway Records, Georgia Historical Society, Savannah; Jesse Jackson to Russell Lord, January 13, 1946, box 3, Jesse Frisbie Jackson Family Papers, Georgia Historical Society, Savannah.

109. L. A. Downs, "The Central of Georgia Makes Two Blades of Grass Grow Where but One Grew Before," Central of Georgia Railway Records.

110. James C. Bonner, "Advancing Trends in Southern Agriculture, 1840–1860," *Agricultural History* 22, no. 4 (October 1948): 258.

111. "Fertilizers," *Daily Constitutionalist*, January 9, 1866, 2; United States Industrial Commission, *Report*, 77.

112. H. C. Nixon, "The Rise of the American Cottonseed Oil Industry," *Journal of Political Economy* 38, no. 1 (February 1930): 73–85; Luther A. Ransom, *The Great Cottonseed Industry of the South* (New York: Oil, Paint and Drug Reporter, 1911), 9–75.

113. Richard H. Edmonds, "The Utilization of Southern Wastes," *Publications of the American Economic Association* 5, no. 1 (February 1904): 164–65.

114. "Two Points of Interest," *Atlanta Constitution*, October 15, 1882, 5; Wilbur Fisk Tillett, "The White Man of the New South," *Century Magazine* 33 (March 1887): 772–73.

115. Ransom, *Great Cottonseed Industry*, 23.

116. Francis Peyre Porcher, *Resources of the Southern Fields and Forests, Medical, Economical, and Agricultural* (Charleston, S.C.: Steam-Power Press of Evans and Cogswell, 1863), 97.

117. "Cotton Seed Cake, &c.," *Southern Farm and Home*, September 1872, 414–15.

118. Hilgard, *Address*, 13.

119. *Anderson Intelligencer*, January 25, 1905, 1.

120. G. H. Turner, "How Some of the Fertility of Southern Soils Slips Away," *Southern Planter* 61, no. 3 (March 1900): 134; E. N. Lowe, *Mississippi: Its Geology, Geography, Soil and Mineral Resources*, Mississippi Geological Survey Bulletin no. 14 (Jackson: Tucker Printing House, 1919), 223–24.

121. W. Scott Morgan, *History of the Wheel and Alliance and the Impending Revolution* (Fort Scott, Kans.: J. H. Rice and Sons, 1889), 346–47.

122. "The Cotton Seed Industry," *Georgia Weekly Telegraph*, November 23, 1893, 6.

123. "The New South," *Fort Worth Daily Gazette*, December 17, 1888, 2.

124. Woodward, *Origins*, 200; Matthew Hild, *Greenbackers, Knights of Labor, and Populists: Farmer-Labor Insurgency in the Late-Nineteenth-Century South* (Athens: University of Georgia Press, 2007), 127.

125. United States Census Bureau, *Statistical Abstract of the United States*, 1910 (Washington, D.C.: Government Printing Office, 1911), 220.

126. Tompkins, *Cotton and Cotton Oil*, 240.

127. United States Department of Agriculture, *Report upon the Numbers and Values of Farm Animals, and on Freight Rates of Transportation Companies* (Washington, D.C.: Government Printing Office, 1890), 27.

128. Leebert Lloyd Lamborn, *Cottonseed Products: A Manual of the Treatment of Cottonseed for Its Products and Their Utilization in the Arts* (New York: D. Van Nostrand Company, 1904), 221; "Our Cottonseed Industry," *State*, January 31, 1902, 4.

129. Lynette Boney Wrenn, "Cotton Gins and Cottonseed Oil Mills in the New South," *Agricultural History* 68, no. 2 (Spring 1994): 232–42.

130. See Henry Clay White, *The Manuring of Cotton*, USDA Farmers' Bulletin no. 46 (Washington, D.C.: Government Printing Office, 1897), 7.

131. E. H. Jenkins and John Phillips Street, "Cotton Seed Meal as a Fertilizer," *Connecticut Agricultural Experiment Station*, Bulletin no. 156 (June 1907): 156–57.

132. United States Census Bureau, *Statistical Abstract*, 1910, 220; "Wonderful Work of the South," *Dallas Morning News*, February 14, 1902, 6.

133. Quoted in Lynette Boney Wrenn, *Cinderella of the New South: A History of the Cottonseed Industry, 1855–1955* (Knoxville: University of Tennessee Press, 1995), 180.

134. Ibid., 179–80.

135. Vance, *Human Geography*, 97.

136. Ransom and Sutch, *One Kind of Freedom*, 188–89; Earle, "Myth," 207. On "corporate plantations," see Nan Elizabeth Woodruff, *American Congo: The African American Freedom Struggle in the Delta* (Cambridge, Mass.: Harvard University Press, 2003), 23–30.

137. Earle, "Price," 56; Earle, "Myth," 56.

138. See Randal S. Beeman and James A. Pritchard, *A Green and Permanent Land: Ecology and Agriculture in the Twentieth Century* (Lawrence: University Press of Kansas, 2001), 9–34.

Chapter 3. Utilizing Southern Wastes

1. Ronald D. Eller, *Miners, Millhands, and Mountaineers: Industrialization of the Appalachian South, 1880–1930* (Knoxville: University of Tennessee Press, 1982), 108.

2. J. S. Holmes, *Forest Conditions in Western North Carolina*, North Carolina Geological and Economic Survey Bulletin no. 23 (Raleigh: Edwards and Broughton Printing Company, 1911), 43, 65.

3. Margaret Lynn Brown, *The Wild East: A Biography of the Great Smoky Mountains* (Gainesville: University Press of Florida, 2000), 78–103.

4. *Delightful Drives: "Way Down in Dixie Land"* (Waterloo, N.Y.: Waterloo Wagon Company, 1910), n.p.

5. Robert W. Griffith, "Industrial Development of Western North Carolina," *Southern Tourist*, March 1926, 106.

6. See Eller, *Miners, Millhands, and Mountaineers*; Donald Edward Davis, *Where There Are Mountains: An Environmental History of the Southern Appalachians* (Athens: University of Georgia Press, 2000); Lawrence S. Early, *Looking for Longleaf: The Fall and Rise of an American Forest* (Chapel Hill: University of North Carolina Press, 2004); Robert B. Outland III, *Tapping the Pines: The Naval Stores Industry in the American South* (Baton Rouge: Louisiana State University Press, 2004); Randall L. Hall, *Mountains on the Market: Industry, the Environment, and the South* (Lexington: University Press of Kentucky, 2012).

7. Griffith, "Industrial Development," 100–106.

8. Ibid. See also Carroll E. Williams, "A Well Rounded Out Paper-Making Industry in Western North Carolina—a Marvel of Efficiency," *Manufacturers' Record*, March 29, 1923; E. Kaye Lanning, "Champion Fibre Company: Industry in Western North Carolina" (M.A. thesis, University of North Carolina, 1980), 35–45.

9. Griffith, "Industrial Development," 100–106.

10. Paul W. Gates, "Federal Land Policy in the South, 1866–1888," *Journal of Southern History* 6, no. 3 (August 1940): 303–30; Warren Hoffnagle, "The Southern Homestead Act: Its Origins and Operation," *Historian* 32, no. 4 (August 1970): 612–29; Paul W. Gates, "Federal Land Policies in the Southern Public Land States," *Agricultural History* 53, no. 1 (January 1979): 206–27; Michael L. Lanza, *Agrarianism and Reconstruction Politics: The Southern Homestead Act* (Baton Rouge: Louisiana State University Press, 1990).

11. *Congressional Record*, 44th Cong., 1st sess., 3293–94; Lanza, *Agrarianism*, 118.

12. Lanza, *Agrarianism*, 114.

13. Claude F. Oubre, "'Forty Acres and a Mule': Louisiana and the Southern Homestead Act," *Louisiana History* 17, no. 2 (Spring 1976): 148. See also Hoffnagle, "Southern Homestead Act," 620.

14. *Congressional Record*, 44th Cong., 1st sess., 850.

15. Nollie W. Hickman, *Mississippi Harvest: Lumbering in the Longleaf Pine Belt, 1840–1915* (Jackson: University Press of Mississippi, 1962), 70–71.

16. *Congressional Record*, 44th Cong., 1st sess., 850–51.

17. Ibid., 816.

18. Ibid., 1087.

19. Christie Farnham Pope, "Southern Homesteads for Negroes," *Agricultural History* 44, no. 2 (April 1970): 209. Paul Gates calculated the lower figure of 36 percent using a shorter time span. See Gates, "Federal Land Policies," 215–17.

20. C. Vann Woodward, *Origins of the New South, 1877–1913* (1951; Baton Rouge: Louisiana State University Press, 2006), 117; Gates, "Federal Land Policies," 221; Gates, "Federal Land Policy," 313.

21. Albert E. Cowdrey, *This Land, This South: An Environmental History*, rev. ed. (1983; Lexington: University Press of Kentucky, 1996), 103.

22. Edward Ayers, *The Promise of the New South: Life after Reconstruction* (New York: Oxford University Press, 1992), 124–25; Mason C. Carter, Robert C. Kellison, and R. Scott Wallinger, *Forestry in the U.S. South: A History* (Baton Rouge: Louisiana State University Press, 2015), 4.

23. Outland, *Tapping the Pines*, 98–121.

24. Woodward, *Origins*, 302–3; Albert E. Cowdrey, *This Land, This South*, 111–14, 118–24; Hickman, *Mississippi Harvest*, 44–61, 311; Eller, *Miners, Millhands, and Mountaineers*, 128–60; Ayers, *Promise*, 104–31.

25. Otis Marion Trimble, "The History and Development of the Administration of Conservation of Natural Resources in Georgia" (M.A. thesis, Emory University, 1949), 36–37.

26. "The Forests," *Memphis Daily Appeal*, May 20, 1872, 2.

27. "Awful Slaughter of Timber," *Shenandoah Herald*, May 8, 1891, 1.

28. Hickman, *Mississippi Harvest*, 84.

29. *Southern Lumberman*, August 1, 1900, 8, quoted in ibid., 154–55.

30. "Reasons Why Lumber Prices Are High," *Southern Lumberman*, December 25, 1906, 9.

31. "Florida an Arid Waste in a Few Years," *Panama City Pilot*, February 13, 1908, 3.

32. "Alabama Forestry Commission," *Southern Lumberman*, January 18, 1908, 52.

33. "Alabama Forests," *Southern Lumberman*, February 15, 1908, 39.

34. Gavin Wright, *Old South, New South: Revolutions in the Southern Economy since the Civil War* (Baton Rouge: Louisiana State University Press, 1986), 162, 158.

35. "Millview Machinery and Equipment to Be Moved," *Pensacola Journal*, June 8, 1907, 1.

36. William P. Jones, *The Tribe of Black Ulysses: African American Lumber Workers in the Jim Crow South* (Champaign: University of Illinois Press, 2005), 38.

37. *Report of the Georgia State Board of Forestry to the Georgia General Assembly of 1922* (Atlanta: Foote and Davies Company, 1922), 9–10, quoted in I. James Pikl Jr., "Pulp and Paper and Georgia: The Newsprint Paradox," *Forest History* 12, no. 3 (October 1968): 9.

38. Rupert B. Vance, *Human Geography of the South: A Study in Regional Resources and Human Adequacy* (1932; Chapel Hill: University of North Carolina Press, 1935), 124.

39. F. R. Pierce, "Past, Present, and Future of Yellow Pine," *Southern Lumberman*, January 25, 1908, 29.

40. John R. Walker, "Future of the South Atlantic Forests," *Manufacturers' Record*, January 17, 1907, 7.

41. Gifford Pinchot, "Practical Forestry for Southern Farms," *Modern Farming* 21, no. 5 (May 1908): 10.

42. Southern Pine Association, *Southern Pine: What It Is—What Is It Used For* (New Orleans: Southern Pine Association, 1923), 32, Southern Pine Association File, Forest History Society Archives, Durham, North Carolina.

43. *Brief History of Conservation in Louisiana and Facts Regarding Contract with the Urania Lumber Company* (Alexandria, La.: Alexandria Printing Company, 1928), 7–8, 10–14; Anna C. Burns, *A History of the Louisiana Forestry Commission* (Natchitoches: Louisiana Studies Institute, Northwestern State College, 1968), 13–20.

44. Alabama General Assembly, *General Laws and Joint Resolutions, 1923* (Montgomery: Brown Printing Company, 1923), 641–42.

45. Georgia General Assembly, *Acts and Resolutions, 1925* (Atlanta: Byrd Printing Company, 1925), 203.

46. Carter, Kellison, and Wallinger, *Forestry*, 7–10.

47. Jones, *Tribe*, 29–30.

48. James E. Fickle, *The New South and the "New Competition": Trade Association Development in the Southern Pine Industry* (Urbana: University of Illinois Press, 1980), 7, 18.

49. Samuel P. Hays, *Conservation and the Gospel of Efficiency: The Progressive Conservation Movement, 1890–1920* (1959; New York: Atheneum, 1974), 34–35; "Passing of Yellow Pine Manufacturers' Association—Organization of the Southern Pine Association," *St. Louis Lumberman*, December 15, 1914, 58–65.

50. Fickle, *New South*, 39, 54–56, 241–60; "Pine Association Launched," *Southern Lumberman*, January 23, 1915, 27–29.

51. Thomas D. Clark, *The Greening of the South: The Recovery of Land and Forest* (1984; Lexington: University Press of Kentucky, 2004), 30–31; Burns, *A History*, 11.

52. E. S. Murrell, "Wonderful Possibilities for Grant Parish," *Colfax Chronicle*, April 26, 1913, 4.

53. "Why Not Exempt Them?," *Bogalusa Enterprise*, November 18, 1915, 4.

54. O. H. L. Wernicke, *The Lumberman's Obligation to the South* (New Orleans: Southern Pine Association, n.d.), 13.

55. Jones, *Tribe*, 20–26.

56. Wernicke, *Lumberman's Obligation*, 16–17.
57. Jones, *Tribe*, 24–28, 28–29.
58. Clark, *Greening*, 30.
59. Carter, Kellison, and Wallinger, *Forestry*, 31–34, quote on 33–34.
60. Jones, *Tribe*, 24–28.
61. Fickle, *New South*, 259, 257.
62. Carter, Kellison, and Wallinger, *Forestry*, 47.
63. Outland, *Tapping the Pines*, 225.
64. "Demonstration Forest," *Southern Field* 18 (1928): 6.
65. Jones, *Tribe*, 30.
66. Outland, *Tapping the Pines*, 67–69, 98–121.
67. "Protection for the Pines," *Macon Telegraph*, March 10, 1899, 4.
68. "The Turpentine Men," *Wilmington Messenger*, August 20, 1901, 8.
69. U.S. Senate Committee on Interstate Commerce, *Inspection of Naval Stores* (Washington, D.C.: Government Printing Office, 1909), 128.
70. Outland, *Tapping the Pines*, 212–15.
71. "The Southern Naval Stores Industry," *Times Picayune*, August 12, 1901, 4.
72. "New Method of Turpentining Will Now Save Many Millions," *Atlanta Constitution*, September 15, 1902, 3; Charles H. Herty, *A New Method for Turpentine Orcharding*, USDA Bureau of Forestry Bulletin no. 40 (Washington, D.C.: Government Printing Office, 1903), 9.
73. Germaine M. Reed, *Crusading for Chemistry: The Professional Career of Charles Holmes Herty* (Athens: University of Georgia Press, 1995); Outland, *Tapping the Pines*, 216–24.
74. Reed, *Crusading for Chemistry*, 16.
75. Charles H. Herty, "The Role of Chemistry in the Industrial Development of the South," *Manufacturers' Record*, September 14, 1916, 55–56; Germaine M. Reed, "Charles Holmes Herty and the Promotion of Southern Economic Development," *South Atlantic Quarterly* 82, no. 4 (Autumn 1983): 424–36.
76. Quoted in Reed, *Crusading for Chemistry*, 17.
77. Ibid., 16–23.
78. Herty, *A New Method*, 43.
79. Reed, *Crusading for Chemistry*, 26–27.
80. "Industrial Notes," *Times Picayune*, October 28, 1901, 11.
81. Jacksonville Board of Trade, *Report for 1903–1904* (Jacksonville: H. and W. B. Company, 1904), 24.
82. "The Herty Turpentine Method," *Paint, Oil and Drug Review*, October 1, 1902, 11.
83. U.S. Senate, *Inspection of Naval Stores*, 58.
84. Outland, *Tapping the Pines*, 223.
85. Clyde Leavitt, "Forest Fires," in *Report of the National Conservation Commission* (Washington, D.C.: Government Printing Office, 1909), 2:414.
86. Pete Daniel, *The Shadow of Slavery: Peonage in the South, 1901–1969* (Urbana: University of Illinois Press, 1972), 36–40; Outland, *Tapping the Pines*, 162–206.
87. Daniel, *The Shadow of Slavery*, 4–18, quote on 4; Outland, *Tapping the Pines*, 236–37.
88. Fred Cubberly to the Attorney General, May 30, 1925; letter by L. L. Fabisinski, June 5, 1925, File 50-17, Peonage Files of the U.S. Department of Justice, 1901–1945, ed. Pete Daniel (Bethesda, Md.: University Publications of America, 1989).

89. Philip E. Chazal, *The Century in Phosphates and Fertilizers: A Sketch of the South Carolina Phosphate Industry* (Charleston, S.C.: Lucas-Richardson Lithograph and Printing Company, 1904), 1–3, 10–11; Nathaniel Shaler, *On the Phosphate Beds of South Carolina* (Boston: A. A. Kingman, 1870), 222–36.

90. *Journal of the House of Representatives of the State of South Carolina* (Columbia, S.C.: John W. Denny, 1870), 513–17.

91. Francis S. Holmes, *Phosphate Rocks of South Carolina and the "Great Carolina Marl Bed"* (Charleston, S.C.: Holmes' Book House, 1870), 73–74.

92. Wright, *Old South, New South*, 46; "Annual Message of His Excellency Governor F. J. Moses, Jr.," *Aiken Tribune*, January 18, 1873, 3; United States Commissioner of Labor, *The Phosphate Industry of the United States* (Washington, D.C.: Government Printing Office, 1893), 105.

93. George M. Wells, *Report of the Attorney General to the General Assembly of South Carolina Concerning the Phosphate Interests of the State* (n.p., 1877), 533.

94. William J. Cooper, *The Conservative Regime: South Carolina, 1877–1890* (1968; Columbia: University of South Carolina Press, 2005), 121–22.

95. South Carolina Phosphate Commission, *Testimony Taken before the Phosphate Commissioners at Sundry Meetings Held in Charleston, S.C.* (Columbia: Charles A. Calvo Jr., 1887), 584, 672, 653, 647–48; American Society of Mechanical Engineers, *Transactions* (New York: American Society of Mechanical Engineers, 1907), 28:961.

96. Walter Edgar, *South Carolina: A History* (Columbia: University of South Carolina Press, 1998), 430–39; "Farmers Are in Revolt," *Macon Telegraph*, March 28, 1890, 1; "Triumphant Tillmanites," *Macon Telegraph*, September 12, 1890, 1.

97. South Carolina Phosphate Commission, *Testimony*, 569–70.

98. South Carolina General Assembly, *Acts and Joint Resolutions of the General Assembly of the State of South Carolina* (Columbia, S.C.: James H. Woodrow, 1891), 691–95.

99. Quoted in Chazal, *Century in Phosphates*, 54; Tom W. Shick and Don H. Doyle, "The South Carolina Phosphate Boom and the Stillbirth of the New South, 1867–1920," *South Carolina Historical Magazine* 86, no. 1 (January 1985): 22.

100. South Carolina General Assembly, *Acts and Joint Resolutions*, 691–95.

101. Reprinted in "Coosaw Comment," *State*, March 13, 1891, 4; "Dabbling in Deep Water," *State*, February 21, 1891, 4.

102. "A State Enjoined," *Columbus Daily Enquirer*, March 7, 1891, 1; "Coosaw Phosphate Quarrel," *Macon Telegraph*, March 7, 1891, 1; "Coosaw Again!," *State*, March 22, 1891, 4; "Coosaw Gets a Little Irony," *State*, March 30, 1891, 8.

103. Coosaw Mining Company v. State of South Carolina, 144 U.S. 567 (U.S. Supreme Court, 1892).

104. "Our Phosphate Industry," *State*, November 21, 1892, 2.

105. Shick and Doyle, "The South Carolina Phosphate Boom," 21–31.

106. Ian Tyrrell, *Crisis of the Wasteful Nation: Empire and Conservation in Theodore Roosevelt's America* (Chicago: University of Chicago Press, 2015), 79–88.

107. The case was dismissed by the county court but was remanded for proceedings on appeal. Commonwealth v. Trent & Others, 117 Ky. 34, 37, 38, 46 (Court of Appeals of Kentucky, 1903).

108. Federal Oil Conservation Board, *State and Federal Conservation Laws and Regulations Relating to Production of Oil and Gas* (Washington, D.C.: Government Printing Office, 1931), 110–13.

109. Graham B. Smedley, *Oil and Gas Laws of Texas* (Dallas: Martin Stationery Company, 1921), 163–66.

110. Federal Oil Conservation Board, *State and Federal Conservation Laws*, 105–7, 16–22; Carl H. Moneyhon, *Arkansas and the New South, 1874–1929* (Fayetteville: University of Arkansas Press, 1997), 120–21.

111. Willard Rouse Jillson, *The Conservation of Natural Gas in Kentucky* (Louisville: John P. Morton and Company, 1922), 129.

112. "Carbon Black Plants Violation of Texas Conservation Statute," *Oil Weekly*, May 8, 1920, 41; William R. Childs, *The Texas Railroad Commission: Understanding Regulation in America to the Mid-Twentieth Century* (College Station: Texas A&M Press, 2005), 163–64.

113. C. A. Warner, *Texas Oil & Gas since 1543* (1939; Ingleside, Tex.: Copano Bay Press, 2007), 75; Railroad Commission of Texas, *Twenty-Ninth Annual Report of the Railroad Commission of Texas* (Austin: Boeckmann-Jones Company, 1921), 159.

114. Warner, *Texas Oil and Gas*, 230; Jacqueline Lang Weaver, *Unitization of Oil and Gas Fields in Texas: A Study of Legislative, Administrative, and Judicial Policies* (New York: Resources for the Future, 1986), 68–74.

115. Federal Oil Conservation Board, *State and Federal Conservation Laws*, 26–27, 137–38.

116. Richard H. Edmonds, "The Utilization of Southern Wastes," *Publications of the American Economic Association* 5, no. 1 (February 1904): 166–67. See also James C. Lawrence, "Utilizing Waste Materials in the South," in *Thirty Years of Southern Upbuilding* (Baltimore, Md.: Manufacturers' Record Publishing Company, 1912), 75–76.

117. J. B. White, "Utilization of Waste in Forest and Mill," in *The Forest and the Saw Mill*, Official Report of the Eighth Annual Convention, National Lumber Manufacturers' Association, 1910, p. 145, National Forest Products Association Records, 1902–86, Forest History Society Archives.

118. Hays, *Conservation*.

119. "Southern Progress," *Montgomery Advertiser*, March 7, 1903, 10.

120. National Conservation Commission, *Report of the National Conservation Commission, February 1909* (Washington, D.C.: Government Printing Office, 1909), 162.

121. *His Inspiration*, cartoon in the *St. Louis Lumberman*, March 15, 1913, 63.

122. H. S. Sackett, "Utilization of Woods and Mill Waste," in *Lumber: America's Second Manufacturing Industry*, the Official Report of the Eleventh Annual Convention of the National Lumber Manufacturers' Association, 1913, pp. 194–96, National Forest Products Association Records.

123. "The New Plant of the Forest Products Co. at Slidell, La.," *St. Louis Lumberman*, March 15, 1913, 62; "The Utilization of Yellow Pine Waste," *St. Louis Lumberman*, March 1, 1913, 56.

124. Quoted in C. F. Korstian, *The Economic Development of the Furniture Industry of the South and Its Future Dependence upon Forestry*, North Carolina Department of Conservation and Development, Economic Paper no. 57 (Raleigh: North Carolina Department of Conservation and Development, 1926), 22.

125. Quoted in William L. Hall, "A Forward Step in Forest Conservation," *American Forestry*, June 1910, 328. See also Edwin A. Start, "The New Forest Products Laboratory," *American Forestry*, July 1910, 387–403.

126. Carlile P. Winslow, *Creating New Values from Southern Woods* (Madison: U.S. Department of Agriculture, Forest Service, Forest Products Laboratory, 1929), 1–2, 1–7.

127. Quoted in "Utilizing Waste Products," *Atlanta Constitution*, January 19, 1902, 28A.

128. "American Leaders in Science and Industry Discuss the South," *Manufacturers' Record*, September 14, 1916, 46.

129. "To Vulcanize Wood," *Southern Lumberman*, December 28, 1907, 35; "Relief for Lumber Situation," *Manufacturers' Record*, October 31, 1907, 54–55.

130. "To Vulcanize Wood," 35; "To Vulcanize Wood," *St. Louis Lumberman*, April 1, 1909, 87; "To Use Vulcanizing Process," *Southern Lumberman*, February 3, 1917, 31.

131. *Proceedings of the Sixteenth Annual Convention of the American Railway Engineering Association* (Chicago: American Railway Engineering Association, 1915), 16:862.

132. W. J. Cummings, "Waste Material as a Source of Profit and Added Security on Timber Bonds," *Annals of the American Academy of Political and Social Science* 41 (May 1912): 78.

133. "New Industry," *Highland Recorder*, December 15, 1905, 2.

134. "Revival of the Potash Industry," *Morgan City Daily Review*, March 26, 1917, 4; "Potash from Sawmill Waste," *Donaldsonville Chief*, March 31, 1917, 4.

135. "Sweet Potato Products," *Southern Field*, no. 4 (n.d.): 3.

136. Quoted in *Thomasville Times Enterprise*, May 16, 1903, 4.

137. "Useful Products from Sawmill Waste," *Southern Field* 18 (1928): 16; John Hebron Moore, "William H. Mason, Southern Industrialist," *Journal of Southern History* 27, no. 2 (May 1961): 172–83; James E. Fickle, *Mississippi Forests and Forestry* (Jackson: University Press of Mississippi, 2001), 138.

138. "Furniture Industry at High Point," *Southern Field* 24 (1930): 9.

139. Korstian, *Economic Development*, 10, 15–16.

140. "President Winston's Talk," *Charlotte Daily Observer*, October 26, 1901, 14.

141. Korstian, *Economic Development*, 18.

142. Jeffrey B. Robb and Paul D. Travis, "The Rise and Fall of the Gulf Coast Tung Oil Industry," *Forest History Today*, Spring/Fall 2013, 14–19. See also Whitney Adrienne Snow, "Tung Tried: Agricultural Policy and the Fate of a Gulf South Oilseed Industry" (Ph.D. diss., Mississippi State University, 2013).

143. "Tung Oil in Florida," *Science News-Letter*, February 26, 1927, 139.

144. Mississippi General Assembly, *Local and Private Laws, Regular Session 1934* (n.p., 1934), 705; Mississippi General Assembly, *Laws, Second Extraordinary Session, 1936* (n.p., 1936), 61–62; Louisiana General Assembly, *Acts, Regular Session, 1936* (n.p., 1936), 565–66.

145. Milton I. Stewart, *A Message of Progress: The Industrial Past and Present and Its Own Home Town, Elizabeth, Louisiana* (n.p., 1923), Industrial Lumber Company (Elizabeth, La.), Forest History Society Archives; "Timber Growing at Elizabeth, LA," *Southern Lumberman*, December 19, 1925; James C. Cobb, *Industrialization and Southern Society, 1877–1984* (Lexington: University Press of Kentucky, 1984), 80.

146. "Adds Paper Mill to Industrial Community," *American Lumberman*, August 19, 1922, 56; F. Ray Marshall, *Labor in the South* (Cambridge, Mass.: Harvard University Press, 1967), 285–86; Bernard A. Cook and James R. Watson, *Louisiana Labor: From Slavery to Right-to-Work* (Lanham, Md.: University Press of America, 1985), 255–56.

147. Mississippi General Assembly, *Laws, Regular Session, 1918* (Jackson: Tucker Printing House, 1918), 201–3.

148. Mississippi General Assembly, *Laws, Appropriations, General Legislation and Resolutions, Regular Session 1926* (Jackson: Tucker Printing House, 1926), 265–66.

149. *An Annotated Supplement to Marr's Revision of the Statutes of Louisiana of 1915* (New Orleans: F. F. Hansell, 1926), 1497–98.

150. Louisiana General Assembly, *Acts, Regular Session, 1926* (New Orleans: F. F. Hansell and Brother, 1926), 246.

151. Louisiana General Assembly, *Acts, Regular Session, 1940* (n.p., 1940), 851. The state did raise the valuation to 25 percent of the total value of the property.

152. Alabama General Assembly, *General Laws, Extra Session, 1936* (Birmingham: Birmingham Printing Company, 1936), 44.

153. North Carolina General Assembly, *Public Laws and Resolutions, Public Local Laws, Extra Session, 1920* (Raleigh: Commercial Printing Company, 1920), 13.

154. "Blast Them Out," *Atlanta Constitution*, January 16, 1918, 8.

155. Georgia General Assembly, *Acts and Resolutions, 1925* (Atlanta: Byrd Printing Company, 1925), 297–98.

156. Clark, *Greening*, 52–53, 102–4.

157. William Boyd, "The Forest Is the Future? Industrial Forestry and the Southern Pulp and Paper Complex," in *The Second Wave: Southern Industrialization from the 1940s to the 1970s*, ed. Philip Scranton (Athens: University of Georgia Press, 2001), 168–73.

158. "Paper Industry Started from Wood Pile," *Fourth Estate*, January 29, 1921, 11.

159. "It's a Poor Tree That Doesn't Go to Modern Market," *Natural Resources*, July 28, 1923, 2.

160. P. L. Simmonds, *Waste Products and Undeveloped Substances: A Synopsis of Progress* (London: Robert Hardewicke, 1873), 286; "Palmetto Paper," *Charleston Daily News*, November 29, 1872, 2; "Palmetto Paper," *Paper Makers' Monthly Journal*, May 15, 1901, 141; W. M. Parsley (Carr and Carr, Inc., Realtors in West Palm Beach) to Herty, March 6, 1927, box 60, folder 4, Charles H. Herty Papers, Stuart Rose Manuscript, Archives, and Rare Book Library, Emory University, Atlanta, Ga.

161. *Paper Maker's Monthly Journal*, May 15, 1909, 170.

162. Clark, *Greening*, 102–8; Reed, *Crusading for Chemistry*, 297–333.

163. Boyd, "Forest," 173–83.

164. Pineland Bag Corporation v. Riley, Auditor, 142 Miss. 574, 582 (Supreme Court of Mississippi, 1926).

165. James C. Cobb, *The Selling of the South: The Southern Crusade for Industrial Development, 1936–1990*, 2nd ed. (Urbana: University of Illinois Press, 1993).

166. Mississippi General Assembly, *Laws, Regular Session, 1912* (Nashville: Brandon Printing Company, 1912), 103–4.

167. Alabama General Assembly, *Local, Private and Special Acts, Regular Session, 1927* (Montgomery: Brown Printing Company, 1927), 365; and *General Laws, Regular Session, 1927* (Montgomery: Brown Printing Company, 1927), 55–57.

168. *An Annotated Supplement*, 1497–98.

169. Harry B. Skillman, ed., *1932 Cumulative Supplement to the Compiled General Laws of Florida* (Atlanta: Harrison, 1932), 925.

170. *Blue Book of Southern Progress, 1930* (Baltimore, Md.: Manufacturers' Record, 1930), 234–35.

171. Susan E. Dick and Mandi D. Johnson, "The Smell of Money: The Pulp and Paper-Making Industry in Savannah, 1931–1947," *Georgia Historical Quarterly* 84, no. 2 (Summer 2000): 309.

172. *Fifty Years of Paper Making*, West Virginia Pulp and Paper Company, October 1937, p. 21, Westvaco Corporation Records, Forest History Society Archives.

173. Boyd, "Forest," 168–69.

174. Michael Williams, *Americans and Their Forests: A Historical Geography* (New York: Cambridge University Press, 1989), 265.

175. A. C. Goodyear, "Forestry," in *Reforestation in the South* (Bogalusa: Great Southern Lumber Company, 1923), 12.

176. "Bogalusa Mill Part of Utilization Plan," *Southern Lumberman*, December 20, 1924, 148.

177. C. W. Goodyear, *Bogalusa Story* (Buffalo: Wm. J. Keller, Inc., 1950), 138–39.

178. Ibid., 137–40, 160–71; Michael Curtis, "Early Development and Operations of the Great Southern Lumber Company," *Louisiana History* 14, no. 4 (Autumn 1973): 355–67; "Great Southern Outlines Reforestation Program," *Bogalusa Enterprise and American*, December 2, 1920, 8.

179. Goodyear, "Forestry," 11.

180. Jones, *Tribe*, 24–28.

181. *New Orleans Item*, quoted in Meigs O. Frost, "Wonderful Story of a Wonderful City—Bogalusa," *Bogalusa Enterprise and American*, March 31, 1921, 6; Jones, *Tribe*, 16.

182. "World's Greatest Paper Manufacturer Praises Bogalusa," *Bogalusa Enterprise and American*, April 28, 1921, 1.

183. Courtenay De Kalb, *Bogalusa: Perpetual Timber Supply through Reforestation as Basis for Industrial Permanency of Bogalusa* (Baltimore, Md.: Manufacturers' Record, 1922).

184. "Statement of Economic Conditions in the Southern Pine Region," June 11, 1931, box 71, National Forest Products Association Records.

185. *Blue Book*, 57.

Chapter 4. The Costs of Permanence

1. United States Census Bureau, Eighth Census, Agricultural Schedule, Regiment 42, Anderson County, South Carolina, p. 142, dwelling 1111.

2. "Burning of Rankin's Mills," *Daily Phoenix*, February 28, 1873, 2; *Anderson Intelligencer*, March 6, 1873, 2; "Extra Term of Court," *Anderson Intelligencer*, November 13, 1872, 2.

3. South Carolina General Assembly, *Journal of the House of Representatives of the State of South Carolina* (Columbia: John W. Denny, 1870), 227.

4. "The Court," *Anderson Intelligencer*, February 1, 1872, 2.

5. "The Court," *Anderson Intelligencer*, February 8, 1872, 2; "The Court," *Anderson Intelligencer*, February 1, 1872, 2.

6. See State v. Rankin, 3 S.C. 438 (South Carolina Supreme Court, 1872).

7. "September Term," *Anderson Intelligencer*, September 26, 1872, 2.

8. *Anderson Intelligencer*, January 16, 1873, 2.

9. Reform, "Extract from Gov. Moses' Last Message," *Anderson Intelligencer*, February 6, 1873, 2.

10. A Refugee, "Health and Drainage," *Anderson Intelligencer*, July 31, 1873, 2; A Refugee, "Health and Drainage Again," *Anderson Intelligencer*, October 2, 1873, 2.

11. "A Drainage Meeting," *Anderson Intelligencer*, December 11, 1873, 2.

12. A Refugee, "Health and Drainage," 2.

13. Thomas H. Russell, "The Spirit of the People," *Anderson Intelligencer*, November 13, 1873, 2.

14. "The Drainage Law," *Anderson Intelligencer*, March 5, 1874, 2; "Acts and Joint Resolutions Passed by the General Assembly of South Carolina, at the Session of 1873–74," *Anderson Intelligencer*, June 18, 1874, 1.

15. "The Drainage Law and the Action of the County Commissioners," *Anderson Intelligencer*, July 30, 1874, 1.

16. Larry Hasse, "Watermills in the South: Rural Institutions Working against Modernization," *Agricultural History* 58, no. 3 (July 1984): 280.

17. For an overview of resource extraction, see chapter 3. There are a few exceptions. See Tycho de Boer, *Nature, Business, and Community in North Carolina's Green Swamp* (Gainesville: University Press of Florida, 2008), 87–195; Duncan Maysilles, *Ducktown Smoke: The Fight over One of the South's Greatest Environmental Disasters* (Chapel Hill: University of North Carolina Press, 2011); Christopher J. Manganiello, *Southern Water, Southern Power: How the Politics of Cheap Energy and Water Scarcity Shaped a Region* (Chapel Hill: University of North Carolina Press, 2015).

18. Edward Ayers, *The Promise of the New South: Life after Reconstruction* (New York: Oxford University Press, 1992), 105.

19. C. Vann Woodward, *Origins of the New South, 1877–1913* (1951; Baton Rouge: Louisiana State University Press, 2006), 291–320.

20. William Gregg, "Southern Patronage to Southern Imports and Domestic Industry," *DeBow's Review* 30, no. 2 (February 1861): 223.

21. Advertisement, *Constitution*, April 8, 1876, 1; Woodward, *Origins*, 108–41.

22. "Manufactures: The South's True Remedy," *DeBow's Review* 3, no. 2 (February 1867): 176.

23. "Here's Your Cigars," *Atlanta Constitution*, December 21, 1890, 21.

24. William Irwin, *The New Niagara: Tourism, Technology, and the Landscape of Niagara Falls, 1776–1917* (University Park: Pennsylvania State University Press, 1996), 131–51.

25. Manganiello, *Southern Water*, 50.

26. August Kohn, *The Water Powers of South Carolina* (Charleston, S.C.: Walker, Evans and Cogswell Company, 1911), 5.

27. Samuel P. Hays, *Conservation and the Gospel of Efficiency* (1959; New York: Atheneum, 1974), 5.

28. On air pollution, see M. L. Quinn, "Industry and Environment in the Appalachian Copper Basin, 1890–1930," *Technology and Culture* 34, no. 3 (July 1993): 575–612; Maysilles, *Ducktown Smoke*. Water has recently attracted notice from scholars who show that it shaped the New South in important ways but do not consider how water illuminates conflicts over manufacturing. There are a few exceptions. See Craig Colten, *Southern Waters: The Limits to Abundance* (Baton Rouge: Louisiana State University Press, 2014); Manganiello, *Southern Water*; Casey P. Cater, "Regenerating Dixie: Electric Energy and the Making of the Modern South" (Ph.D. diss., Georgia State University, 2016). New Orleans and the Mississippi River have attracted attention from scholars interested in water, but most focus on how residents responded to challenges like flooding and river control. See Ari Kelman, *A River and Its City: The Nature of Landscape in New Orleans* (Berkeley: University of California Press, 2003); Craig E. Colten, *An Unnatural Metropolis: Wresting New Orleans from Nature* (Baton Rouge: Louisiana State University Press, 2005); Christopher Morris, *The Big Muddy: An Environmental History of the Mississippi and Its Peoples from Hernando De Soto to Hurricane Katrina* (New York: Oxford University Press, 2012).

29. Christopher John Manganiello, "Dam Crazy with Wild Consequences: Artificial Lakes and Natural Rivers in the American South, 1845–1990" (Ph.D. diss., University of Georgia, 2010), 58–59; Theodore Steinberg, *Nature Incorporated: Industrialization and the Waters of New England* (Amherst: University of Massachusetts Press, 1994), 30; Harry L.

Watson, "'The Common Rights of Mankind': Subsistence, Shad and Commerce in the Early Republican South," *Journal of American History* 83, no. 1 (June 1996): 13–43.

30. Colten, *Southern Waters*, 135–37.

31. South Carolina General Assembly, *Acts and Joint Resolutions* (Columbia: Calvo and Patton, 1878), 624.

32. A. J. Walker, ed., *Revised Code of Alabama* (Montgomery: Reid and Screws, 1867), 503–7.

33. *Revised Code of the Statute Laws of the State of Mississippi* (Jackson: Alcorn and Fisher, 1871), 415–16.

34. George W. Munford, ed., *Third Edition of the Code of Virginia* (Richmond: J. E. Goode, 1874), 605–6.

35. Eric Foner, *Reconstruction: America's Unfinished Revolution, 1863–1877* (New York: Perennial Classics, 1988), 210–16; Woodward, *Origins*, 1–22.

36. *Charleston News and Courier*, reprinted in "How to Make a City," *Gold Leaf*, June 27, 1895, 2.

37. Manganiello, *Southern Water*, 47–59. See also Christopher J. Manganiello, "Hitching the New South to 'White Coal': Water and Power, 1890–1933," *Journal of Southern History* 78, no. 2 (May 2012): 255–92.

38. Gavin Wright, *Old South, New South: Revolutions in the Southern Economy since the Civil War* (Baton Rouge: Louisiana State University Press, 1986), 60–64; Broadus Mitchell and George Sinclair Mitchell, *The Industrial Revolution in the South* (Baltimore, Md.: Johns Hopkins Press, 1930), 3–4.

39. Rupert B. Vance, *Human Geography of the South: A Study in Regional Resources and Human Adequacy* (1932; Chapel Hill: University of North Carolina Press, 1935), 275.

40. Christine Meisner Rosen, "'Knowing' Industrial Pollution: Nuisance Law and the Power of Tradition in a Time of Rapid Economic Change, 1840–1864," *Environmental History* 8, no. 4 (October 2003): 565–97.

41. Steinberg, *Nature Incorporated*, 16.

42. Morton J. Horwitz, *The Transformation of American Law, 1780–1860* (Cambridge, Mass.: Harvard University Press, 1977), 74–78; Rosen, "'Knowing' Industrial Pollution."

43. These conclusions are based on a database of several hundred nuisance cases relating to water and air pollution that I compiled from the former states of the Confederacy and Kentucky, all decided between 1865 and 1930. To provide a sampling from each state, I chose decisions that were appealed to a higher state court after the initial trial. Even conservatively estimating that appeals reflect only 10 percent of all cases, it is evident that legal challenges to pollution, dams, and flooding were substantial and likely numbered in the thousands. On estimating appellate rates, see Theodore Eisenberg, "Appeal Rates and Outcomes in Tried and Nontried Cases: Further Exploration of Anti-plaintiff Appellate Outcomes," *Journal of Empirical Legal Studies* 1, no. 3 (November 2004): 659–88.

44. Manganiello, "Dam Crazy," 70–71.

45. See Royal G. Shannonhouse, "Some Principles of Water Law in the Southeast," *Mercer Law Review* 13 (Spring 1962): 347. See also White et al. v. The East Lake Land Company and The East Lake Land Company v. White et al., 96 Ga. 415 (Supreme Court of Georgia, 1895).

46. Athens Manufacturing Company v. Rucker, 4 S.E. 885, 886 (Supreme Court of Georgia, 1887).

47. *Tennessee Coal, Iron, and Railroad Company v. Hamilton*, 14 So. 167, 171 (Supreme Court of Alabama, 1893).

48. *Hunter v. Pelham Mills*, 29 S.E. 727, 729 (Supreme Court of South Carolina, 1898).

49. *Hodges v. Pine Product Company*, 68 S.E. 1107 (Supreme Court of Georgia, 1910).

50. Ibid., 1109; *Pelham Phosphate Co. v. Daniels*, 94 S.E. 846 (Court of Appeals of Georgia, 1918); Christopher J. Manganiello, "Fish Tales and the Conservation State," *Southern Cultures*, Fall 2014, 46–51.

51. William G. Thomas, *Lawyering for the Railroad: Business, Law, and Power in the New South* (Baton Rouge: Louisiana State University Press, 1999), 124–29.

52. *Farley v. Gate City Gas Light Company*, 105 Ga. 323 (Supreme Court of Georgia, 1898).

53. See Maysilles, *Ducktown Smoke*.

54. Horwitz, *Transformation*, 16–30; James W. Ely Jr. and David J. Bodenhamer, "Regionalism and American Legal History: The Southern Experience," *Vanderbilt Law Review* 39 (1986): 555; Timothy S. Huebner, *The Southern Judicial Tradition: State Judges and Sectional Distinctiveness, 1790–1890* (Athens: University of Georgia Press, 1999), 2.

55. *Drake, Ex'r. v. Lady Ensley Coal, Iron & Railway Company*, 14 So. 749, 750, 751 (Supreme Court of Alabama, 1893).

56. Maysilles, *Ducktown Smoke*, 61; Horwitz, *Transformation*, 37–38; Paul M. Kurtz, "Nineteenth-Century Anti-entrepreneurial Nuisance Injunction—Avoiding the Chancellor," *William & Mary Law Review* 17 (Summer 1976): 621–70.

57. Jonathan M. Wiener, *Social Origins of the New South: Alabama, 1860–1885* (Baton Rouge: Louisiana State University Press, 1978), 182.

58. Ethel Armes, *The Story of Coal and Iron in Alabama* (Birmingham: Chamber of Commerce, 1910), 323, 477; Grace Hooten Gates, *The Model City of the New South: Anniston, Alabama, 1872–1900* (Tuscaloosa: University of Alabama Press, 1978), 50–51.

59. *Clifton Iron Co. v. Dye*, 6 So. 192, 193 (Supreme Court of Alabama, 1888).

60. *Folmar Mercantile Co. v. Town of Luverne*, 203 Ala. 363, 368 (Supreme Court of Alabama, 1919).

61. Ayers, *Promise*, 55–56.

62. Robert Weise, "Big Stone Gap and the New South, 1880–1910," in *The Edge of the South: Life in Nineteenth-Century Virginia*, ed. Edward L. Ayers and John C. Willis (Charlottesville: University Press of Virginia, 1991), 173–93.

63. "The Dam Question," *Big Stone Post*, March 6, 1891, 4.

64. "The Dam Question," *Big Stone Post*, February 20, 1891, 2.

65. "The Dam Question," *Big Stone Post*, March 6, 1891, 4.

66. "The Dam Question," *Big Stone Post*, February 20, 1891, 2.

67. Ibid. On the absentee economy, see Woodward, *Origins*, 311.

68. "The Dam Question," *Big Stone Post*, February 20, 1891, 2; "Mr. Longini's Dam," *Big Stone Post*, March 20, 1891, 2.

69. "The Dam Question," *Big Stone Post*, February 20, 1891, 2.

70. "The Dams Again," *Big Stone Post*, February 27, 1891, 2.

71. Ibid.

72. "The Dam Question," *Big Stone Post*, February 20, 1891, 2.

73. "Changes and Removals," *Clothier and Furnisher* 23, no. 11 (June 1894): 64.

74. Albert E. Cowdrey, *This Land, This South: An Environmental History*, rev. ed. (1983; Lexington: University Press of Kentucky, 1996), 104–7; David R. Goldfield, *Cotton Fields*

and Skyscrapers: Southern City and Region (Baltimore, Md.: Johns Hopkins University Press, 1982), 95–96; Woodward, *Origins of the New South*, 425–28; Colten, *Southern Waters*, 91–115. On state efforts, see John H. Ellis, *Yellow Fever and Public Health in the New South* (Lexington: University Press of Kentucky, 1992), 83–104, 125–68.

75. Edwin B. Goodell, *A Review of the Laws Forbidding Pollution of Inland Waters in the United States* (Washington, D.C.: Government Printing Office, 1904), 52–53, 45–46, 50–51, 50, 29. For a general overview, see 28–36. Colten, *Southern Waters*, 164–65.

76. Martin V. Melosi, *The Sanitary City: Urban Infrastructure in America from Colonial Times to the Present* (Baltimore, Md.: Johns Hopkins University Press, 1999), 55.

77. "The Water We Drink," *Memphis Daily Appeal*, July 1, 1881, 4; Ellis, *Yellow Fever*, 111–18.

78. Colten, *Southern Waters*, 96; Ellis, *Yellow Fever*, 113–15, 89–102, 139–42.

79. Werner Troesken, "The Limits of Jim Crow: Race and the Provision of Water and Sewerage Services in American Cities, 1880–1925," *Journal of Economic History* 62, no. 3 (September 2002): 748–49; Samuel Kelton Roberts Jr., *Infectious Fear: Politics, Disease, and the Health Effects of Segregation* (Chapel Hill: University of North Carolina Press, 2009).

80. Melosi, *Sanitary City*, 41–42.

81. Stuart Galishoff, "Germs Know No Color Line: Black Health and Public Policy in Atlanta, 1900–1918," *Journal of the History of Medicine* 40 (January 1985): 25; Bartow Elmore, "Hydrology and Residential Segregation in the Postwar South: An Environmental History of Atlanta, 1865–1895," *Georgia Historical Quarterly* 94, no. 1 (Spring 2010): 35, 38.

82. Ellis, *Yellow Fever*, 114.

83. Troesken, "Limits," 744–46.

84. Galishoff, "Germs," 25.

85. L. M. Hershaw, "Mortality of Negroes," in *Some Efforts of American Negroes for Their Own Social Betterment*, ed. W. E. B. Du Bois (Atlanta: Atlanta University Press, 1898), 62.

86. Ellen Griffith Spears, *Baptized in PCBs: Race, Pollution, and Justice in an All-American Town* (Chapel Hill: University of North Carolina Press, 2016), 26.

87. Troesken, "Limits," 735.

88. See Tera W. Hunter, *To 'Joy My Freedom: Southern Black Women's Lives and Labors after the Civil War* (Cambridge, Mass.: Harvard University Press, 1997), 187–88; Elmore, "Hydrology," 36–37.

89. Quoted in "Negro Health Week, April 21–27," *Southern Workman* 47, no. 4 (April 1918): 169.

90. *Social and Physical Condition of Negroes in Cities* (Atlanta: Atlanta University Press, 1897), 3–4, 21; Elmore, "Hydrology," 53.

91. Sandra Crouse Quinn and Stephen B. Thomas, "The National Negro Health Week, 1915 to 1951: A Descriptive Account," *Minority Health Today* 2, no. 3 (March/April 2001): 44–48.

92. "Joint Debate Is Proposed," *Columbus Enquirer Sun*, November 3, 1903, 8.

93. City of Durham v. Eno Cotton Mills, 54 S.E. 453, 454 (Supreme Court of North Carolina, 1906).

94. Ibid.

95. "Would Columbus Mills Be Liable in Damages?," *Columbus Ledger*, June 17, 1906, 7.

96. *Durham*, 54 S.E. 453, 455–56; "Report of Board of Health," *Robesonian*, August 27, 1906, 3.

97. *Durham*, 54 S.E. 453, 457, 464.

98. "Report of Board of Health," 3.

99. "Pollution of Streams," *Times-Dispatch*, February 17, 1906, 4.

100. Alexander Potter, "Advance in Sewage Purification," *Municipal Engineering* 31, no. 6 (December 1906): 439.

101. "Would Columbus Mills," 7.

102. "Pure Water Elsewhere," *Times*, August 3, 1901, 4.

103. E. C. Levy, "Report to the Water Committee on the Investigation of the Effect of Trades Wastes on the Water of James River at Richmond" (Richmond, 1905), reprinted in Earle Bernard Phelps, "The Pollution of Streams by Sulphite Pulp Waste—a Study of Possible Remedies," in *Contributions from the Sanitary Research Laboratory and Sewage Experiment Station* (Boston, 1909), 5:6–8.

104. "People Must Have Purest of Water," *Times Dispatch*, February 15, 1906, 6; "State Must Aid in Fight on Disease," *Times Dispatch*, December 30, 1907, 1.

105. Council of the City of Richmond, *Certain Resolutions of the Council of the City of Richmond* (Richmond: Clyde W. Saunders, 1912), 51–52.

106. "Protect Water in James River," *Times Dispatch*, February 8, 1912, 8; "To Protect Water in James River," *Lexington Gazette*, February 14, 1912, 1.

107. "Charter Changes Offered in House," *Times Dispatch*, January 11, 1912, 9.

108. "Business People Not Behind Bill," *Times Dispatch*, February 23, 1912, 10.

109. "Council to Urge Passage of Bill," *Times Dispatch*, February 12, 1912, 10.

110. "Charter Changes Offered in House," *Richmond Times Dispatch*, January 11, 1912, 9.

111. "Business People Not Behind Bill," 10.

112. *Annual Report of the Department of Public Utilities of the City of Richmond, Virginia* (Richmond: William Byrd Press, 1930), 9.

113. "Pine Pulp Industry Proves Fastest Growing in the South," *Atlanta Constitution*, December 9, 1945, quoted in William Boyd, *The Slain Wood: Papermaking and Its Environmental Consequences in the American South* (Baltimore, Md.: Johns Hopkins University Press, 2015), 149.

114. See T. Robert Hart, "The Lowcountry Landscape: Politics, Preservation, and the Santee-Cooper Project," *Environmental History* 18 (January 2013): 127–56.

115. Steinberg, *Nature Incorporated*, 16.

116. Gary Kulik, "Dams, Fish and Farmers: The Defense of Public Rights in Eighteenth-Century Rhode Island," in *The Countryside in the Age of Capitalist Transformation*, ed. Steven Hahn and Jonathan Prude (Chapel Hill: University of North Carolina Press, 1985); Steinberg, *Nature Incorporated*.

Chapter 5. Tourism's New Path

1. George B. Tindall, *The Emergence of the New South, 1913–1945* (Baton Rouge: Louisiana State University Press, 1967), 104–9; Paul S. George, "Brokers, Binders, and Builders: Greater Miami's Boom of the Mid-1920s," *Florida Historical Quarterly* 65, no. 1 (July 1986): 27–51.

2. Bruce Schulman, *From Cotton Belt to Sunbelt: Federal Policy, Economic Development, and the Transformation of the South, 1938–1980* (New York: Oxford University Press, 1991), 41–42; Tindall, *Emergence*, 583–86.

3. Rupert B. Vance, *Human Geography of the South: A Study in Regional Resources and Human Adequacy* (1932; Chapel Hill: University of North Carolina Press, 1935), 503–4.

4. Hal K. Rothman, *Devil's Bargains: Tourism in the Twentieth Century American West* (Lawrence: University Press of Kansas, 1998), 10. On Sunbelt tourism, see Schulman, *From Cotton Belt*, 220–21.

5. Nina Silber, *The Romance of Reunion: Northerners and the South, 1865–1900* (Chapel Hill: University of North Carolina Press, 1993); Rebecca Cawood McIntyre, *Souvenirs of the Old South: Northern Tourism and Southern Mythology* (Gainesville: University Press of Florida, 2011); Karen L. Cox, ed., *Destination Dixie: Tourism and Southern History* (Gainesville: University Press of Florida, 2012).

6. C. Brenden Martin, *Tourism in the Mountain South: A Double-Edged Sword* (Knoxville: University of Tennessee Press, 2007); Richard D. Starnes, *Creating the Land of the Sky: Tourism and Society in Western North Carolina* (Tuscaloosa: University of Alabama Press, 2005).

7. Cindy S. Aron, *Working at Play: A History of Vacations in the United States* (New York: Oxford University Press, 1999), 15–44; Martin, *Tourism*, 1–20. See also Lawrence Fay Brewster, *Summer Migrations and Resorts of South Carolina Low-Country Planters* (Durham, N.C.: Duke University Press, 1947).

8. Edward A. Pollard, *The Virginia Tourist: Sketches of the Springs and Mountains of Virginia* (Philadelphia: J. B. Lippincott and Company, 1870), 14.

9. Henry M. Field, *Bright Skies and Dark Shadows* (1890; Freeport, N.Y.: Books for Libraries Press, 1970), i.

10. Albert G. Way, *Conserving Southern Longleaf: Herbert Stoddard and the Rise of Ecological Land Management* (Athens: University of Georgia Press, 2011), 20–36; Conevery Bolton Valencius, *The Health of the Country: How American Settlers Understood Themselves and Their Land* (New York: Basic Books, 2004), 85–108; Gregg Mitman, *Breathing Space: How Allergies Shape Our Lives and Landscapes* (New Haven, Conn.: Yale University Press, 2007), 10–51.

11. Way, *Conserving Southern Longleaf*, 27–31. On the piney woods, see Vance, *Human Geography*, 109–44.

12. Way, *Conserving Southern Longleaf*, 195.

13. Advertisement, *Christian Union*, November 19, 1892, 962.

14. Lawrence S. Early, *Looking for Longleaf: The Fall and Rise of an American Forest* (Chapel Hill: University of North Carolina Press, 2004), 42; M. B. Trezevant, "The New Orleans of To-Day," *National Real Estate Journal*, January 15, 1912, 433.

15. Advertisement, *Outlook*, December 12, 1896, 1119.

16. Levi Branson, ed., *Branson's North Carolina Business Directory, 1896* (Raleigh, N.C.: Levi Branson, 1896), 8:54–56.

17. *History of North Carolina* (Chicago: Lewis Publishing Company, 1919), 6:174–76; *Southern Pines, N.C.* (n.p., 1896).

18. "In the Carolina Pine Forests, the Abode of Health and Sunshine," *Illustrated American*, February 27, 1897, 319.

19. Quoted in A. N. Bell, "Southern Pines Park; a New Winter Health Resort," in *Transactions of the Third Annual Meeting of the American Climatological Association* (New York: D. Appleton and Company, 1887), 216–17.

20. Printed in the *Southern Pines Tourist*, reprinted in "Mutual Segregation Arrangement," *Mebane Leader*, April 16, 1914, 1; Karen L. Cox, *Dreaming of Dixie: How the South Was Created in American Popular Culture* (Chapel Hill: University of North Carolina Press, 2013), 120–26.

21. W. E. B. Du Bois, ed., *Some Efforts of American Negroes for Their Own Social Betterment* (Atlanta: Atlanta University Press, 1898), 33–34; "News in Brief," *Pinehurst Outlook*,

February 9, 1900, 5; *The Pickford Sanitarium for Consumptive Negroes, Southern Pines, N.C.* (Raleigh, n.d.), 2–3; "Will You Believe It?" and "Some Facts about Our Trustees," *Southern Sanitarium*, January 1, 1897, 9–17; North Carolina General Assembly, *Public Laws and Resolutions of the State of North Carolina* (Raleigh, N.C.: Edwards and Broughton and E. M. Uzzell, 1899), 976.

22. William F. Waugh, "Southern Pines, N.C.," *Times and Register*, September 17, 1892, 392.

23. "Southern Pines, N.C.," *S.A.L.magundi* 1, no. 2 (May 1895): 1.

24. *Southern Pines, N.C.*, 12; Manly Wade Wellman, *The County of Moore, 1847–1947* (Moore County: Moore County Historical Association, 1962), 104.

25. Richard J. Moss, "Constructing Eden: The Early Days of Pinehurst, North Carolina," *New England Quarterly* 72, no. 3 (September 1999): 388–414; Larry R. Youngs, "Lifestyle Enclaves: Winter Resorts in the South Atlantic States, 1870–1930" (Ph.D. diss., Georgia State University, 2001), 176–80.

26. Joe Mitchell Chapple, "Sojourning 'neath the Long Leaf Pines," *National Magazine* 34, no. 2 (June 1911): 315.

27. "Purse, Daniel Gugel," in *Herringshaw's Encyclopedia of American Biography of the Nineteenth Century*, ed. Thomas William Herringshaw (Chicago: American Publishers' Association, 1901), 765.

28. Philip Alexander Bruce, *The Rise of the New South* (Philadelphia: George Barrie's Sons, 1905), 312.

29. McIntyre, *Souvenirs*, 7; Silber, *Romance*, 66–92. An exception is Reiko Hillyer, *Designing Dixie: Tourism, Memory, and Urban Space in the New South* (Charlottesville: University of Virginia Press, 2014).

30. Marguerite S. Shaffer, *See America First: Tourism and National Identity, 1880–1940* (Washington, D.C.: Smithsonian Institution Press, 2001), 20.

31. Martin, *Tourism*, 27; Aron, *Working at Play*, 49.

32. Thomas Curtis Clarke et al., *The American Railway* (New York: Charles Scribner's Sons, 1889), 180; John F. Stover, *The Railroads of the South, 1865–1900: A Study in Finance and Control* (Chapel Hill: University of North Carolina Press, 1955), 231; Maury Klein, "The Strategy of Southern Railroads," *American Historical Review* 73, no. 4 (April 1968): 1052–68.

33. John R. Stilgoe, *Metropolitan Corridor: Railroads and the American Scene* (New Haven, Conn.: Yale University Press, 1983), 3.

34. "Let Us Change Diet," *Florida Agriculturalist*, September 22, 1892, 616; "Tourist vs. Settler," *Florida Agriculturalist*, July 27, 1892, 472.

35. Virginia Midland Railway, *Tourist's Guide to the Virginia Springs and Summer Resorts on and Reached by the Virginia Midland Railway* (Alexandria, Va.: Robert Bell's Sons, 1881), n.p.; Seaboard Air Line Railway, *Winter Resorts Located on and Reached via the Seaboard Air Line* (Richmond, Va.: Everett Wadley Company, 1897), 46.

36. W. Raymond and I. A. Whitcomb, *A Grand Tour through the New South* (Boston: American Printing and Engraving Company, 1890), 6.

37. Rothman, *Devil's Bargains*, 12–13.

38. Harry M. Strickler, *A Short History of Page County, Virginia* (Richmond, Va.: Dietz Press, 1952), 96–121, 194–208; Elizabeth Atwood, "'Saratoga of the South': Tourism in Luray, Virginia, 1878–1905," in *Edge of the South: Life in Nineteenth Century Virginia*, ed. Edward L. Ayers and John C. Willis (Charlottesville: University of Virginia Press, 1991), 157–72.

39. Thomas Bruce, *Southwest Virginia and Shenandoah Valley* (Richmond, Va.: J. L. Hill Publishing Company, 1891), 219–23.

40. Thomas P. Grasty, "Luray, Scientific Town Sites," *Independent*, August 28, 1890, 29.

41. Norfolk and Western Railway Company, *Industrial and Shippers Guide* (Roanoke, Va.: Union Printing and Manufacturing Company, 1916), 76.

42. Edward Ayers, *The Promise of the New South: Life after Reconstruction* (New York: Oxford University Press, 1992), 60.

43. E. P. Woodward, "Life in the Turpentine Woods—Gardening for Pleasure and Profit," *Southern Planter* 46, no. 8 (August 1886): 386; Seaboard Air Line Railway Company, *The Southern Pines: The Best Resort for Those with Lung or Throat Troubles in the United States* (n.p., 1887), 25.

44. *Southern Pines, N.C.*, 8.

45. Waugh, "Southern Pines, N.C.," 329.

46. Moss, "Constructing Eden," 392–93; Youngs, "Lifestyle Enclaves," 169–80.

47. "Interesting Environs," *Pinehurst Outlook*, November 15, 1901, 12.

48. Albert Phenis, "4,000,000 Peach Trees, All in Bloom, Bring Springtime Glory to Sandhills of North Carolina," *Manufacturers' Record*, March 15, 1923, 65.

49. Earl Pomeroy, *In Search of the Golden West: The Tourist in Western America* (1957; Lincoln: University of Nebraska Press, 1990), 131.

50. John F. Sears, *Sacred Places: American Tourist Attractions in the Nineteenth Century* (New York: Oxford University Press, 1989), 182; Aron, *Working at Play*, 146–47; Irwin, *New Niagara*, 153–77; Catherine Cocks, *Doing the Town: The Rise of Urban Tourism in the United States, 1850–1915* (Berkeley: University of California Press, 2001).

51. David E. Nye, *American Technological Sublime* (Cambridge, Mass.: MIT Press, 1994).

52. Atlanta and West Point Railroad Company and Western Railway of Alabama, *The Heart of the South* (St. Louis: Woodward and Tiernan, 1898), 3.

53. Roderick Frazier Nash, *Wilderness and the American Mind*, 4th ed. (1967; New Haven, Conn.: Yale University Press, 2001), 152–54; Sears, *Sacred Places*, 122–81.

54. Albert A. Hopkins, *Our Country and Its Resources* (New York: Munn and Company, 1917), 97.

55. See Paul S. Sutter, *Driven Wild: How the Fight against Automobiles Launched the Modern Wilderness Movement* (Seattle: University of Washington Press, 2002).

56. Tindall, *Emergence*, 254–58; Howard Lawrence Preston, *Dirt Roads to Dixie: Accessibility and Modernization in the South, 1885–1935* (Knoxville: University of Tennessee Press, 1991), 39–68.

57. Anne Mitchell Whisnant, *Super-Scenic Motorway: A Blue Ridge Parkway History* (Chapel Hill: University of North Carolina Press, 2010), 20–21.

58. *Atlanta Constitution*, November 10, 1914, quoted in Preston, *Dirt Roads*, 54; "Remarks on the Dixie Highway," *Highway Engineer and Contractor* 2, no. 6 (June 1920): 58.

59. "Bring In the Tourists and Then Keep Them Here," *Anniston Star*, June 27, 1930, 4.

60. Forrester B. Washington, "Recreational Facilities for the Negro," *Annals of the American Academy of Political and Social Science* 140 (November 1928): 273.

61. "The Trip to Chattanooga," *Savannah Tribune*, August 25, 1917, 1.

62. See Andrew W. Kahrl, *The Land Was Ours: African American Beaches from Jim Crow to the Sunbelt South* (Cambridge, Mass.: Harvard University Press, 2012), 4; Andrew W. Kahrl, "The 'Negro Park' Question: Land, Labor, and Leisure in Pitt County, North Carolina, 1920–1930," *Journal of Southern History* 79, no. 1 (February 2013): 113–42.

63. Washington, "Recreational Facilities," 279–82.

64. Alex Lichtenstein, "Good Roads and Chain Gangs in the Progressive South," *Journal of Southern History* 59, no. 1 (February 1993): 91, 85–110.

65. See Gregory T. Cushman, "Environmental Therapy for Soil and Social Erosion: Landscape Architecture and Depression-Era Highway Construction in Texas," in *Environmentalism in Landscape Architecture*, ed. Michael Conan (Washington, D.C.: Dumbarton Oaks Research Library, 2000), 54–55.

66. "Beautification of Highways of the State Urged in Talk by Mrs. Lawton," *Pilot*, January 17, 1930, 3; John A. Jakle and Keith A. Sculle, *Motoring: The Highway Experience in America* (Athens: University of Georgia Press, 2009), 105–45.

67. Brewster, *Summer Migrations*, 49–51.

68. William Banks, "Aiken as a Winter Resort," *State*, March 26, 1905, 17; "South Carolina Kaolin," *Manufacturers' Record*, May 5, 1904, 349.

69. R. Bruce Stephenson, *Visions of Eden: Environmentalism, Urban Planning, and City Building in St. Petersburg, Florida, 1900–1995* (Columbus: Ohio State University Press, 1997), 16–19.

70. "What Can We Offer," *St. Lucie County Tribune*, November 9, 1906, 4.

71. *Jackson County Journal*, January 29, 1915, quoted in Stephen Wallace Taylor, *The New South's New Frontier: A Social History of Economic Development in Southwestern North Carolina* (Gainesville: University Press of Florida, 2001), 33.

72. Casey P. Cater, "Regenerating Dixie: Electric Energy and the Making of the Modern South" (Ph.D. diss., Georgia State University, 2016), 118–34; E. Merton Coulter, "Tallulah Falls, Georgia's Natural Wonder, from Creation to Destruction," *Georgia Historical Quarterly* 47, no. 3 (September 1963): 249–61. See also Andrew Beecher McAllister, "'A Source of Pleasure, Profit, and Pride': Tourism, Industrialization, and Conservation at Tallulah Falls, Georgia, 1820–1915" (M.A. thesis, University of Georgia, 2002).

73. Coulter, "Tallulah Falls," 263–71.

74. Helen D. Longstreet to the American People, n.d., Helen Dortch Longstreet Papers, Georgia Historical Society, Savannah.

75. Helen D. Longstreet, "Tallulah Falls, Switzerland of America," May 14, 1912, Longstreet Papers; Longstreet, "Tallulah, Switzerland of America to Be Included in National Park," *Atlanta Constitution*, May 12, 1912, B12.

76. Helen D. Longstreet, "Tallulah Falls Worth More Than Five Hundred Millions if Preserved by America for Its Scenic Value," *Atlanta Constitution*, June 2, 1912, B17.

77. Helen D. Longstreet, "Tallulah's Cause, Cause of American People," *Atlanta Constitution*, June 14, 1912, 16, quoted in Cater, "Regenerating Dixie," 123.

78. *Toccoa Record*, March 21, 1912, quoted in Coulter, "Tallulah Falls," 262–63.

79. *Oglethorpe Echo*, July 31, 1914, quoted in Coulter, "Tallulah Falls," 262.

80. Coulter, "Tallulah Falls," 261–62.

81. "Gigantic Power Plant at Tallulah Falls to Develop about 100,000 Horse Power," *Atlanta Constitution*, April 23, 1911, A14.

82. Coulter, "Tallulah Falls," 269–71.

83. U.S. House Committee on Public Lands, *San Francisco and the Hetch Hetchy Reservoir* (Washington, D.C.: Government Printing Office, 1909), 188.

84. Nash, *Wilderness*, 161–99.

85. Scott Giltner, *Hunting and Fishing in the New South: Black Labor and White Leisure after the Civil War* (Baltimore, Md.: Johns Hopkins University Press, 2008), 109–36; Stuart A. Marks, *Southern Hunting in Black and White: Nature, History, and Ritual in a Carolina*

Community (Princeton, N.J.: Princeton University Press, 1991), 39–61; Way, *Conserving Southern Longleaf*, 36–55.

86. Theodore S. Palmer, *Some Possibilities for Game Protection in North Carolina* (Audubon Society of North Carolina, 1904), quoted in Giltner, *Hunting and Fishing*, 143.

87. Giltner, *Hunting and Fishing*, 158–67; Frank B. Vinson, "Conservation and the South, 1890–1920" (Ph.D. diss., University of Georgia, 1971), 227–79.

88. Giltner, *Hunting and Fishing*, 158–67, 144, 138–39.

89. "State Game Law Is Used as Club," *Atlanta Constitution*, November 30, 1911, 6; Julia Brock, "A 'Sporting Fraternity': Northern Hunters and the Transformation of Southern Game Law in the Red Hills Region, 1880–1920," in *Leisure, Plantations and the Making of a New South*, ed. Julia Brock and Daniel Vivian (Lanham, Md.: Lexington Books, 2015), 166.

90. Vinson, "Conservation," 229–30.

91. "Tourists and the Game Law," *Punta Gorda Herald*, March 27, 1913, 6; *Punta Gorda Herald*, April 24, 1913, 4.

92. Way, *Conserving Southern Longleaf*, 43–55.

93. Julius W. Muller, "Wild Game Hunting in the South Is Improving," *Atlanta Constitution*, November 9, 1902, C3.

94. N. L. Willett, *Game Preserves and Game of Beaufort, Colleton, and Jasper Counties, South Carolina* (Beaufort: Charleston and Western Carolina Railway, 1927), 1–2, 4, 17.

95. "Offers Paradise to Sport Lovers," *Atlanta Constitution*, August 20, 1922, 4; Stewart F. Gelders, "South Georgia Game Preserve to Be Enlarged," *Atlanta Constitution*, August 10, 1924, 6.

96. Way, *Conserving Southern Longleaf*, 22.

97. Giltner, *Hunting and Fishing*, 109–36, 137–67; Hayden R. Smith, "Knowledge of the Hunt: African American Guides in the South Carolina Lowcountry at the Turn of the Twentieth Century," in Brock and Vivian, *Leisure*, 131–44.

98. Way, *Conserving Southern Longleaf*, 47–51; Brock, "A 'Sporting Fraternity,'" 167–70.

99. Kathryn Newfont, *Blue Ridge Commons: Environmental Activism and Forest History in Western North Carolina* (Athens: University of Georgia Press, 2012), 60–65; Charles Dennis Smith, "The Appalachian Park Movement, 1885–1901," *North Carolina Historical Review* 37, no. 1 (January 1960): 38–65.

100. Memorial from the Appalachian National Park Association, in Theodore Roosevelt, *Message from the President of the United States Transmitting a Report of the Secretary of Agriculture in Relation to the Forests, Rivers, and Mountains of the Southern Appalachian Region* (Washington, D.C.: Government Printing Office, 1902), 159–64.

101. Ibid.

102. Treadwell Cleveland, "National Forests as Recreation Grounds," *Annals of the American Academy of Political and Social Science* 35, no. 2 (March 1910): 25.

103. Ronald D. Eller, *Miners, Millhands, and Mountaineers: Industrialization of the Appalachian South, 1880–1930* (Knoxville: University of Tennessee Press, 1982), 117; Newfont, *Blue Ridge Commons*, 65–70.

104. Horace Kephart to Zebulon Weaver, January 13, 1925, box 1, folder 10, Horace Kephart Collection, Hunter Library Special Collections, Western Carolina University, Cullowhee, N.C., quoted in Starnes, *Creating*, 61.

105. Quoted in Starnes, *Creating*, 60–61.

106. Daniel S. Pierce, *The Great Smokies: From Natural Habitat to National Park* (Knoxville: University of Tennessee Press, 2000), 89–129.

107. Starnes, *Creating*, 60; Martin, *Tourism*, 74–75.

108. See Pierce, *Great Smokies*, 154–73, 176–77.

109. Laura Thornborough, *The Great Smoky Mountains* (1937; Knoxville: University of Tennessee Press, 1956), 154, quoted in Pierce, *Great Smokies*, 163.

110. Newfont, *Blue Ridge Commons*, 128, 9–14; Pierce, *Great Smokies*, 175–78.

111. Committee on the Public Lands, *Hearings before the Committee on the Public Lands on H.R. 5729* (Washington, D.C.: Government Printing Office, 1928), 1–10, 101–2; John C. Miles, *Guardians of the Parks: A History of the National Parks and Conservation Association* (Washington, D.C.: Taylor and Francis, 1995), 78.

112. *Tallahassee Daily Democrat*, quoted in "A National Park at Our Door," *Thomasville Times Enterprise*, September 17, 1930, 2.

113. Paul S. Sutter, *Let Us Now Praise Famous Gullies: Providence Canyon and the Soils of the South* (Athens: University of Georgia Press, 2015), 65–82.

114. Raymond H. Torrey, *State Parks and Recreational Uses of State Forests in the United States* (Washington, D.C.: National Conference on State Parks, 1926), 11, 16–17; J. S. Holmes, "A Forest Policy for North Carolina," *Journal of the Elisha Mitchell Scientific Society* 45 (November 1929): 30, 35; Howard W. Odum, *Southern Regions of the United States* (Chapel Hill: University of North Carolina Press, 1936), 311; William E. O'Brien, *Landscapes of Exclusion: State Parks and Jim Crow in the American South* (Amherst: University of Massachusetts Press, 2016), 23–25.

115. O'Brien, *Landscapes of Exclusion*, 26.

116. Washington, "Recreational Facilities," 274.

117. O'Brien, *Landscapes of Exclusion*, 26; Pierce, *Great Smokies*, 184.

118. On this trend more recently, see Carolyn Finney, *Black Faces, White Spaces: Reimagining the Relationship of African Americans to the Great Outdoors* (Chapel Hill: University of North Carolina Press, 2014).

119. Sarah M. Gregg, *Managing the Mountains: Land Use Planning, the New Deal, and the Creation of a Federal Landscape in Appalachia* (New Haven, Conn.: Yale University Press, 2010), 2.

120. Clarence Woodbury, "Postwar Industry No. 1," *Atlanta Constitution*, October 29, 1944, 4.

Conclusion

1. *Blue Book of Southern Progress, 1937* (Baltimore, Md.: Manufacturers' Record, 1937), 7.

2. United States Census Bureau, *Statistical Abstract of the United States, 1940* (Washington, D.C.: Government Printing Office, 1941), 747.

3. *The Blue Book of Southern Progress, 1940* (Baltimore, Md.: Manufacturers' Record Publishing Company, 1940), 10, 28, 32, 15, 10.

4. B. F. Williamson Statement on Florida Conference, box 62, Charles H. Herty Papers, Stuart Rose Manuscript, Archives, and Rare Book Library, Emory University, Atlanta, Ga.; George B. Tindall, *The Emergence of the New South, 1913–1945* (Baton Rouge: Louisiana State University Press, 1967), 465–67.

5. Tindall, *Emergence*, 125.

6. Gavin Wright, *Old South, New South: Revolutions in the Southern Economy since the Civil War* (Baton Rouge: Louisiana State University Press, 1986), 76.

7. National Emergency Council, *Report on Economic Conditions of the South* (Washington, D.C.: Government Printing Office, 1938), 1; Bruce Schulman, *From Cotton Belt to Sunbelt: Federal Policy, Economic Development, and the Transformation of the South, 1938–1980* (New York: Oxford University Press, 1991), 49–54.

8. National Emergency Council, *Report*, 1–2, 53.

9. James C. Cobb, *The Selling of the South: The Southern Crusade for Industrial Development, 1936–1990*, 2nd ed. (Urbana: University of Illinois Press, 1993), 64–65.

10. Donald Worster, *Dust Bowl: The Southern Plains in the 1930s* (1979; New York: Oxford University Press, 2004), 197.

11. Twelve Southerners, *I'll Take My Stand: The South and the Agrarian Tradition* (New York: Harper & Brothers, 1930), xlvi.

12. "In the South . . . the Woods Are Full of Prosperity," Southern Pulpwood Conservation Association, Company Files, Forest History Society Archives, Durham, N.C.; James E. Fickle, *Green Gold: Alabama's Forests and Forest Industries* (Tuscaloosa: University of Alabama Press, 2014), 210.

13. "We're Here to Stay," an Address by W. D. Harrigan, President, before the Fiftieth Annual Convention of the Southern Pine Association, April 5, 1965, Southern Pine Association, Company Files, Forest History Society Archives, quoted in John M. Collier, *The First Fifty Years of the Southern Pine Association, 1915–1965* (New Orleans: Southern Pine Association, 1965), 1–2.

14. Jonathan Daniels, *The Forest Is the Future* (New York: International Paper, 1957).

15. Samuel Hays, *Beauty, Health and Permanence: Environmental Politics in the United States, 1955–1985* (Cambridge: Cambridge University Press, 1989).

16. Ulrich Grober, *Sustainability: A Cultural History* (Devon: Green Books, 2012); Jeremy L. Caradonna, *Sustainability: A History* (New York: Oxford University Press, 2014).

17. World Commission on Environment and Development, *Our Common Future* (New York: Oxford University Press, 1987), 43; Donald Worster, "The Shaky Ground of Sustainable Development," in *The Wealth of Nature: Environmental History and the Ecological Imagination* (New York: Oxford University Press, 1993), 142–55.

18. Chris Turner, *The Geography of Hope: A Tour of the World We Need* (Toronto: Vintage Canada, 2007), quoted in Caradonna, *Sustainability*, 1.

19. C. Vann Woodward, "The Irony of Southern History," *Journal of Southern History* 19, no. 1 (February 1953): 3–19.

INDEX

African Americans: agriculture and, 43–44, 45–48, 57–58, 65; conservation and, 30–32; convict lease and, 157–58; cutover lands and, 81–82; disenfranchisement of, 126; environmental injustices and, 113–14, 132–33, 140; land ownership by, 8, 31, 37–38, 48, 72, 81–82; legal system and, 126, 129; mobility of, 45, 46, 81–82, 156–57, 164; New South Creed and, 8; public health and, 31, 132–34, 146; stock laws and, 38–39; tourism and, 146–48, 156, 164, 167–68, 173. *See also* emancipation; labor; segregation

Agricultural and Mechanical College of Alabama, 56

Agricultural Wheel, 55, 63

agriculture: antebellum reforms, 34, 36, 52; Civil War and, 35–36; conservation and, 25; on corporate plantations, 66; federal extension work, 59; fruit cultivation, 152–53; as hobby, 152; to maintain soil fertility, 33–34, 37; New South Creed and, 36–38; plantation system, 11, 26, 34, 36, 50, 60; postbellum reform of, 21, 36, 37, 38–45, 59–65; shifting ideas of permanence and, 49–50, 66; soil exhaustion, 35–36; soil science, 16, 52; truck farming, 53; of yeomen, 60. *See also* diversification; fertilizer; labor: agricultural; sharecropping; staple crops

Aiken, S.C., 157–58

Alabama: agriculture in, 43–44, 46, 53–54, 61; disease in, 133; Farmers' Alliance in, 56, 63; forestry promoted in, 75, 79; industrial promotion of, 103, 105; iron manufacturing in, 119, 123–24, 125; mill dams in, 118; naval stores in, 83; outdoor recreation in, 173–74; public lands in, 71; soil exhaustion in, 36; state forests of, 79; stock laws of, 40; tourism in, 145–46, 155–56; water pollution in, 122, 123–24, 125

Alabama Farmers' Alliance, 56, 63

Alabama Federation of Women's Clubs, 75

Alabama Forestry Commission, 75, 79

Alcorn, James, 72

Allston, Ben, 4

American Civil War: agriculture during, 50; challenges after, 3–4, 5, 35–36; economic efficiency and, 25; southern environment and, 4, 5, 11, 37; tourism and, 144

American Ornithological Union, 165

American Tobacco Company, 119

ANPA (Appalachian National Park Association), 168–69

Ansel, Martin F., 19

Appalachian Experiment Station, 82

Appalachian Exposition of 1910, 20

Appalachian Exposition of 1911, 20

Appalachian National Park Association (ANPA), 168–69

Arkansas, 71, 77, 93, 94, 171–72

Arp, Bill, 43

Asheville, N.C., 17, 149, 168, 169, 170, 172

Athens Manufacturing Company, 122

Atlanta Constitution: conservation promoted by, 21, 25, 30; crop diversification promoted by, 42; game preserves advocated by, 167; hunting favored by, 164, 167; industrial development promoted by, 21, 116; social effects of conservation described by, 164; tourism promoted by, 161, 173–74

Atlanta University, 133–34

Ayers, Edward, 115, 152

Babb, Frank, 111, 113
Babb, James, 111, 113
Baltimore and Ohio Railroad Company, 99–100
Banks, Henry, 104
Banks, William, 157–58
Barbier, Edward, 6–7
Blanchard, Newton, 19
Blue Book of Southern Progress, 109, 175–76
Blue Springs Company, 135
Bogalusa, La., 106, 107–8
Bogalusa Tung Oil, 101
Bourbons. *See* Redemption
Boyd, William, 104
Bureau of Soils. *See* United States Department of Agriculture
Butte, George, 93–94

Calcasieu Paper Manufacturing Company, 102
Cannon, Joseph, 169
capitalism, xx, 8, 12, 179
carbon black, 93–94
Carver, George Washington, 31, 43–44, 57–58
cattle tick, 43, 82
CCC (Civilian Conservation Corps), 173
Central of Georgia Railway Company, 2, 60–61, 84–85
Champion Fibre Company, 68–70, 170
Chapple, Joe Mitchell, 148–49
Charleston and Western Carolina Railway, 166
Charleston Mining Company, 90
Chattahoochee River, 132, 136–37
Chattanooga Pottery Company, 85–86
chemurgy movement, 176, 177
cholera, 132, 133
Civilian Conservation Corps, 173
Civil War. *See* American Civil War
Clarke-McNary Act (1924), 80
Clayton, Powell, 72–73
Cleveland, Treadwell, 169
Clifton Iron Company, 125
climate: conservation and, 78; economic development shaped by, 7; health and, 145, 147, 154; as renewable resource, 143, 149, 161; southern boosterism of, 1, 4, 5, 10, 36; tourism and, 148, 149, 155–56. *See also* health tourism; natural resources; tourism industry
Clyatt, Samuel, 87–88
coal, 74, 76, 117, 129
Cobb, James, 32
Cobb, Ned, 53–54
Comer, Braxton Bragg, 75
commons: definition of, 38; environmental activism and, 171; social aspects of, 30, 39–40; stock laws and, 38–40
Conference of Governors, 15, 18–19
conservation movement: advocates of, 2–3, 14–16, 18–20, 22–23, 32; African Americans and, 30–32; early history of, 14, 117; efficient use of resources and, 14–15, 95–97, 109; failure in South of, 178–80; federal initiatives during, 14–16, 28, 29–30, 167; historiography of, xv–xvi, 3; needed in South, 16–17; public health and, 21, 31, 133–34; social effects of, 29–32; southern vision of, 1–3, 24–29, 29–30, 31–32; tax reform and, 29, 104–5. *See also* wise use; *and specific industries*
Consolidated Naval Stores Company, 86
convict lease, 156–57
Coolidge, Calvin, 97, 172
Coosaw Mining Company, 90, 91–92
cotton: African Americans and, 43–44, 45–48; boll weevil and, 27, 48, 59; commons and, 38–39; diversification of, 40–45, 48–49; growth in cultivation of, 48, 53; labor for, 45–48; as permanent crop, 44–45; promotion of, 25, 44–45; soil fertility and, 44–45. *See also* agriculture; cottonseed; cottonseed oil manufacturing; fertilizer; sharecropping
Cotton States and International Exposition (1895), 2, 20
cottonseed, 26, 61–65, 84, 176
cottonseed oil manufacturing, 61–65, 84, 176
Cowdrey, Albert E., 73
cowpeas, 43, 44

cutover: forest industries and, 76–77, 80–82, 106, 175; permanence and, 80–82, 101, 102; tourism and, 145–46, 148

Daniels, Jonathan, 181
Davis, Harold, 42
Davis, J. Isom, 166–67
DeBow, James Dunwoody Brownson, 4, 116
DeCanio, Stephen, 41
Degler, Carl, xvii
Dennett, John Richard, 35–36
disease: campaigns against, 130, 133–34, 154; caused by mill dams, 111–14, 127, 129; disparities in, 132–33. *See also* public health; *and specific diseases*
diversification: arguments against, 44–45, 48; arguments for, 29, 41–44, 60–61; failure of, 48–49, 53; livestock and, 43, 60; New South Creed and, 12, 37; permanence of, 42; white supremacy and, 47–48. *See also* agriculture; cotton; fertilizer
Dixie Highway, 155
Doyle, Don, 92
Ducktown Basin (Tenn.), 123
Durham Water Company, 135
Dye, James, 125

Earle, Carville, 37
economic development: American and Prussian path of, xx; conservation and, 1–3, 24–29, 32; global resources and, 6–7; in Knoxville, 23; social inequalities created by, 7–8; in South, 5–7, 12–14, 23, 175–76, 177–78. *See also* labor; New South Creed; permanence
Edmonds, Richard Hathaway, 5–6, 26, 95, 108, 116. See also *Manufacturers' Record*
Elizabeth, La., 101–2
emancipation, 12, 35, 37, 39, 165
Eno Cotton Mills, 135–37
environmental justice, 140
environmental movement, 180–81
expositions, 20–24. *See also specific expositions*
extractive industries: conservation in, 78–80, 82, 88–92, 92–95; environmental effects of, 74–77, 110; growth of, 73–74; historiography on, 68–69, 70, 114–15; impermanence of, 76–78; regulation of, 88–92; replaced by waste industries, 95–103, 109–10, 175–76; technological innovation and, 82–87, 95–103. *See also specific industries*

Farmers' Alliance, 9–10, 54–56, 63–64
fertilizer: African Americans and, 57–58; antebellum uses of, 50; complete formulas for, 50–51; cottonseed as, 61–65; environmental effects of, 54, 180; growth in use of, 50, 52–53, 65–66, 175; opposition to, 54–59; permanence of, 49–54; promotion of, 26, 29; replacements for, 57–58, 59–65; sharecropping and, 50, 53–54, 57–58; staple crops maintained by, 66–67
Finley, William, 28–29
Fisher, Carl, 142, 155
fisheries, 122, 139
Fite, Gilbert, 43, 48
Florida: agriculture in, 150–51; destruction of forests in, 75, 76–77; industrial promotion by, 105; land boom of, 142–43; naval stores in, 75, 83, 87–88; peonage in, 87–88; phosphates and, 91; public lands in, 71; stock law of, 40; tourism in, 142–43, 149, 158, 164–65, 172; truck farming in, 53; tung trees in, 101; wildlife conservation and, 164–65
forest fires, 78, 80, 105, 171
Forest Management Act (1897), 15
forest products industries. *See specific industries*
forests: deforestation of, 21, 38, 73–76, 77, 123; hardwood, 68, 100, 109–10, 123; loblolly pine, 78; longleaf, 74, 84–85, 101, 145, 175; slash pine, xviii, 78, 103; yellow pine, 75, 77, 84, 103, 106. *See also reforestation; and specific industries*
Fortune, T. Thomas, 9–10
Fox, John, Sr., 127
Freedmen's Bureau, 48
Fullerton, Robert, 75
furniture manufacturing, 100–101, 119, 176

INDEX {219}

game preserves. *See* hunting
Gaston, Paul, 12, 36
Gate City Gas Light Company, 123
Georgia: agricultural improvement in, 37; cottonseed oil industry in, 61, 64; crop diversification promoted in, 42, 60–61; depletion of forests and, 39, 74, 77, 79, 83; disease in, 132–33; expansion of cotton in, 53; Farmers' Alliance in, 55; industrial promotion by, 103; naval stores in, 83, 84–85, 87; paper manufacturing in, 104; soil exhaustion in, 35, 36, 46; stock laws of, 39–40; tourism in, 145, 149, 156, 159–62, 166–67, 172; truck farming in, 53; water pollution in, 122–23, 132, 135, 136–37; wood wastes used in, 98
Georgia-Florida Sawmill Association, 87
Georgia Power Company, 105, 159–62
Goodman, William, 24
good roads movement, 155–57
Goodyear, A. C., 106
Gordon, Will, 87–88
Grady, Henry Woodfin, xvi; crop diversification promoted by, 41–42; development promoted by, 11, 116; on emancipation, 37; fertilizers lauded by, 52–53; opposed by Watson, 9; promotes stewarding resources, 25
Grange, 8, 55–56
Grasty, Thomas, 151–52
Great Smoky Mountains National Park, 169–71, 173
Great Southern Lumber Company, 106–9
Greeley, William, 79
Griffith, Robert, 68–70

Hahn, Steven, 38–39
Hallowell, R. M., 102
Hammond, Harry, 58
Hampton Institute, 31
Hardtner, Henry, 79
Harrigan, W. D., 181
Hays, Samuel, 95, 181
health tourism: decline of, 154; growth of, 144–49; permanence of, 148–49; in piney woods, 145–49; racial exclusion in, 146–48
Hersey, Mark, 44, 58
Herty, Charles Holmes, 84–87, 104, 105, 175
Hess, Ralph, 16
Hetch Hetchy Valley (Calif.), 162–63
Hilgard, Eugene, 33–34, 49, 62–63, 66
Hilton-Dodge Lumber Company, 99
Hopkins, Albert, 154
Hopkins, Cyril, 16
Howard Vulcanizing Company, 98–99
Hunter, Tera, 133
hunting: game preserves and, 165–67; growth in South, 163, 165, 166–67, 175; social effects of, 30, 39, 164, 167–68; wildlife conservation and, 18, 30, 39, 163–67

I'll Take My Stand, 180
immigration, 12, 13, 46–47, 81, 119
industrial development: in antebellum era, 116; applied research and, 84; conservation and, 16–17, 21, 25–28; critics of, 115; environmental effects of, 114, 117–18, 120–21, 122–30; examples of, 118–20, 175–76; game preserves as, 165–66; historiography of, 114–16; home industry and, 62, 116; law and, 123, 126; New South Creed and, 12–13; state incentives for, 13, 102–3, 105–6, 179. *See also* New South Creed; *and specific industries*
Industrial Lumber Company, 101–2
iron manufacturing, 119, 122, 123–24, 125

Jackson, Jesse Frisbie, 60–61
Jacksonville Board of Trade, 86
James B. Duke Company, 119
James River, 137–39
Jevons, Stanley, 76
Jim Crow. *See* African Americans; segregation
Johnson, Oscar, 65

Kahrl, Andrew, 156
Kali Phosphate Works, 51

kaolin, 157–58, 176
Kentucky, 13, 23, 74, 92–93, 144
Kephart, Horace, 170
King, Edward, 36
King, Franklin, 16
Kirk, J. M., 123–24
Knapp, Bradford, 52, 60
Knapp, Seaman, 52, 59
Kolb, Reuben, 55
Kulik, Gary, 140

labor: agricultural, 37–38, 39, 45–48, 53–54, 58–59, 72 (*see also* sharecropping); conservation and, 30; convict leasing and, 13, 156–57; corporate welfare work and, 81–82, 107; in extractive industries, 76, 81, 87–88; immigration and, 13, 46–47; industrial growth and, 114; low wages of, 72, 177; peonage and, 87–88; permanence and, 101–2, 107–8; New South Creed and, 7–8; in tourism industry, 146–47; unionization efforts and, 102, 107–8, 178; violence and, 102, 107–8
Lady Ensley Coal, Iron and Railway Company, 123–24
Lakeland Phosphate Company, 51
Lawton, Elizabeth, 157
Levy, Ernest, 137–38
Lichtenstein, Alex, 156
Longini, Abraham, 127–29
Longstreet, Helen Dortch, 159–62
Lopez, Moses, 90
Lord, Samuel, 90
Lost Cause, 12, 150
Louisiana: conservation in, 19, 78–79, 93, 94, 101–2; crop diversification in, 43; cutover lands and, 80–81; fertilizer required in, 66; industrial promotion by, 101–2, 102–3, 105; naval stores in, 102; public lands in, 71; timber industry in, 77; tourism in, 145–46; waste industries in, 100, 101–2, 105; water quality regulated by, 131
Louis Werner Saw Mill Company, 77
Lowry, Robert J., 1–3, 14, 77
lumber industry. *See* timber industry
Luray, Va., 151–52

Making Crops and Soil Pay More (Virginia-Carolina Chemical Company), 51
malaria, 111, 114, 130
Man and Nature (Marsh), 14
Manganiello, Christopher J., 117
Manufacturers' Record: on antebellum waste of resources, 11; background of, 5; chemical industries and, 98; efficient resource use promoted by, 26, 86, 95, 98; industry alongside tourism and, 151–52, 153; statistics on growth provided by, 76, 109, 175. See also *Blue Book of Southern Progress*; Edmonds, Richard Hathaway
Marsh, George Perkins, 75; *Man and Nature*, 14
Mason Fibre Company, 100
Massey, Wilbur Fisk, 44–45
McGee, William John, 18
McIntyre, Rebecca, 149
McSweeney-McNary Forest Research Act (1928), 83
Memphis Chamber of Commerce, 47
Memphis Water Company, 131–32
Merchant, Carolyn, 30
Mercier, W. B., 47
Merrick, George, 143
mill dams. *See* waterpower
Miller, Jonathan, 47
Mississippi: agricultural labor in, 47; agriculture in, 33; fertilizer required in, 66; industrial promotion by, 102, 105; mill dam regulations in, 118; public lands in, 71, 72; soil exhaustion in, 36; stock laws of, 40; tung trees planted in, 101
Money, Hernando de Soto, 72
Moses, Franklin, 89
Muir, John, 162–63

National Conference on Utilization of Forest Products, 97
National Conservation Commission, 19, 97
National Conservation Congress (1909), 27
National Conservation Congress (1910), 19, 28–29
National Conservation Exposition (1913), 21–24

INDEX {221}

National Emergency Council, 178
National Lumber Manufacturers' Association, 82, 97–98
National Negro Health Week, 134
national parks: in Appalachians, 68–69, 168, 169–70, 171; debates over, 68–69, 160, 163; early history of, 154; social effects of, 30, 169–70, 171; tourism promotion and, 168
National Parks Association, 172
National Park Service, 171
National Tank and Export Company, 84
National Wood Vulcanizing Company, 99
natural gas, 92–94, 175
natural resources: abundance of, in South, 1, 4–6, 7, 9–12, 12–13; antebellum uses of, 10–11, 25–26, 28; depletion of, 14, 74–76, 78–79, 83; efficient uses of, 13–14, 20, 25–28, 61, 69, 88–94, 95–98, 100, 109, 168–69, 175–76; nonrenewable, 88–95; renewable, 78, 117, 143, 158, 164, 180–81; scarcity of, 8–9; scenic, 157, 158, 159, 161, 162, 169; wasted in South, 10–11, 61, 73, 93–94, 95–109, 117. *See also* conservation movement; *and specific industries and resources*
naval stores industry: adopts efficient methods of production, 83–88, 98; degradation of forests by, 75, 104; promotion of, 26, 102, 103; replaced by tourism, 145, 146, 148, 153
New Deal, xix, xviii, 140, 172–74
Newfont, Kathryn, 171
Newlands Reclamation Act (1902), 76
New South Creed: African Americans and, 7–8; in agriculture, 36–37; boosters of, 2, 3, 12, 19–20, 31, 32; conservation and, 17, 18–20, 24–25, 29; definition of, 12–14; dissent against, 8–9, 31; environmental vision of, xv, 11–12 (*see also* permanence); historiography of, xv, 3; immigration and, 12, 46–47, 81, 119; manufacturing promoted by, 116–17; outside capital and, 12, 23, 118–19, 127, 128, 129; public lands and, 72; tourism and, 150–51, 153–54, 168. *See also* economic development

New South era, xix, 10, 37. *See also* New South Creed
Norfolk and Western Railway, 151
North Carolina: coal boom in, 74; cotton in, 53; fertilizer use in, 49, 55, 56; furniture manufacturing in, 100–101; highway beautification in, 157; industrial promotion by, 103; national parks in, 68–69, 168–71; naval stores in, 82, 83; pulp and paper manufacturing in, 68–70; soil exhaustion in, 35–36; state parks of, 172; tobacco production in, 119; tourism in, 146–48, 152–53, 158, 168–71; truck farming in, 53; water quality in, 130, 131, 135–37; wildlife conservation in, 164
North Carolina Department of Conservation and Development, 101, 104, 179
North Carolina Pine Association, 78
North Land and Lumber Company, 99

O'Brien, William, 173
oil industry, 74, 92
Ouachita National Forest, 171–72
Outland, Robert, 86

Patrick, John Tyrant, 146–47, 148, 152
Pelham Cotton Mills, 122
Pensacola Tar and Turpentine Company, 81
peonage, 87–88
permanence: as business strategy, 1–3, 24, 27, 28–29, 32, 79 (*see also specific industries*); definition of, xv, 24–29; early development of, 18, 25–26; environmental degradation and, 179–80; federal government and, 15–17; New South Creed and, 32; as private impulse, 24–25, 28–29, 79; private property and, 31–32; racial components of, 7–8, 31–32; shifting goals of, 82, 176; similarities to sustainable development, xix, 181–82; success of, 175–77. *See also* conservation movement; economic development; natural resources: efficient uses of
permanent agriculture, 16, 51, 59, 67
permanent development. *See* permanence
phosphate mining, 50, 88–92, 151, 176

{222} INDEX

Pickford Sanitarium for Consumptive Negroes, 147–48
Piedmont, 120
Piedmont Pulp and Paper Company, 105
Pierce, F. R., 77
Pinchot, Gifford: conservation and, 15, 22, 28, 29, 31, 79, 80; denied opportunity to speak, 25; promotes southern conservation, 17, 19, 22, 25, 78; "wise use" mantra of, xviii, 25, 28–29, 32, 52; works with businesses, 79; yellow pine trust and, 80.
Pine Bluff, N.C., 148
Pinehurst, N.C., 148–49, 152–53
Pine Institute of America, 82
Pisgah National Forest, 169
Pollard, Edward, 144
pollution: of air, 122–23, 140, 145, 180; control of, 130–34; by industries, 115–16, 117–18, 121–22, 127–29, 134–39; of water, 114, 117–18, 121–22, 123–26, 127–29, 134–39, 140
Pomeroy, Earl, 153
Pope, Christie Farnham, 73
Pope Clay Products Company, 157
Populist Movement. *See* Farmers' Alliance
portland cement, xviii, 96, 109
Powell, Bullard and Company, 85
Powell, George, 168–69
Powell, John, 85–86
Powell Fertilizer and Chemical Company, 51
Pratt, Joseph Hyde, 155
Progressive movement: business progressivism and, 32, 155; efficiency and, 95; public health reforms and, 130, 141; regulation of industry and, 82; road-building and, 155–56; segregation and, 30, 32, 141; social designs of, 30, 32. *See also* conservation movement
Providence Canyon (Ga.), 172
public health: conservation of, 21, 31, 133–34; municipal promotion of, 130–32, 134–39; pollution and, 111–14, 127–34, 134–39; racial disparities in, 132–34; tourism linked to, 145, 154
public lands, 71–73, 74–75

pulp and paper manufacturing: applied research and, 98, 104, 105; expansion of, 103–4, 106, 109, 175, 176; hindrances to growth of, 104–5; permanence of, 68–70, 103–4, 175, 180–81; pollution by, 137–40, 180; reforestation programs of, 69, 106, 108, 170, 180–81; state promotion of, 102–3, 105–6; as waste industry, 68–70, 97, 103–4
Purse, Daniel, 99, 149

railroad industry: conservation promoted by, 28–29, 49–50; environmental degradation caused by, 122; immigration promoted by, 46; tourism and, 150–51, 155
Raker Act (1913), 162
Rankin, George Washington, 111–14
Ransom, Luther, 61–62
Ransom, Roger, 50
Raymond, Walter, 151
rayon manufacturing, 103, 109, 176
Reclamation Act, Newlands (1902), 76
Reconstruction: African Americans during, 7–8, 30, 45, 114, 177; economic development initiatives of, 12, 116, 118, 119; failure of land redistribution and, 8, 30, 71–73; stock laws during, 38–40. *See also* Redemption
Redeemers. *See* Redemption
Redemption, 6, 12, 114, 119
redintegration, 60–61
Reed, John Calvin, 4, 11
reforestation: of cutover lands, 80–82; federal cooperation and, 80, 98; forest products industries and, 69, 86, 101–2, 103–4, 106–8; legislation promoting, 78–79; tourism and, 69, 169, 170; trade unions and, 82, 180–81
regionalism, 142–43
Richardson, Elmo, 28
Ridley, Mose, 87–88
Robertson, Reuben, 170
Roosevelt, Franklin D., 178
Roosevelt, Theodore, 15, 17, 18, 19, 163
Rosen, Christine, 121
Rowlands, Lamont, 101
Ruffin, Edmund, 34

Sackett, H. S., 97
safe farming, 60
Santee-Cooper Power and Navigation Project, 140
Savannah Pulp and Paper Laboratory, 104, 105
Schick, Tom, 92
Scruggs, Lawson, 147–48
Seaboard Air Line Railway, 146, 148, 152
segregation, 8, 32, 175; access to clean water and, 132–33, 133–34; conservation movement and, 30, 32; of parks, 173; as permanent system, xvii; public health and, 114; in tourism industry, 146–47, 156, 173; of urban areas, 126, 132–34
sewerage, 128, 131–32, 132–33, 134–39
sharecropping: African Americans and, 31, 43–44, 46–48, 57–58; continuation of cotton monoculture and, 45, 178; crop lien system and, 45, 47; education and, 31, 43–44, 57–58; fertilizers and, 50, 53–54, 57–58, 65; lack of soil conservation and, 46; opposition to stock laws and, 39–40; origins of, 45–46
shifting cultivation, 36, 50
Sierra Club, 154, 162–63
Smith, Eugene Allen, 46
Smith, Hoke, 19, 59, 95–96
Smith-Lever Act (1914), 59
sorghum, 43
South: definition of, xix; diversity of, xix, 10; in Sunbelt, 143, 174, 178; underdevelopment of, 13, 23, 177–78
South Carolina: agricultural reform in, 25, 36; agriculture in, 41, 43, 47, 48, 53, 113–14; cottonseed industry in, 63; disease in, 132–33; Farmers' Alliance and, 55, 56; fertilizers required in, 49, 55, 56, 57; flooding in, 122; game preserves promoted in, 166; industrial promotion by, 105–6, 119; kaolin development in, 157–58; mill dams regulated in, 111–14; phosphate mining in, 88–92, 151; Pinchot and, 25; pulp and paper industry in, 105–6; Reconstruction politics and, 114; stock laws of, 40; tourism in, 145, 149, 151, 157–58, 166; waterpower in, 117; wood vulcanization in, 98–99
South Carolina Board of Phosphate Examiners, 90
South Carolina Farmers' Alliance, 56
Southern Appalachian Good Roads Association, 155
Southern Commercial Congress, 20
Southern Conservation Congress, 17, 19, 28
Southern Cotton Stalk, Pulp and Paper Company, 104
Southern Cultivator, 41
Southern Forest Experiment Station, 82
Southern Homestead Act, 71–74
Southern Lumberman, 75
Southern Pine Association, 78, 80–81, 83, 109, 181
Southern Pines, N.C., 146–48, 152
Southern Pines Resort Company, 146
Southern Pulpwood Conservation Association, 180–81
Southern Railway Company, 82, 100, 119–20
Southern States Lumber Company, 76–77
Sportsman's Paradise (Ga.), 166–67
staple crops: antebellum uses of, 4, 10, 12, 26, 34, 36; concerns about, 38, 40–44, 57–58; continued cultivation of, 48, 29–50, 54, 66–67; labor and, 45; New South Creed and, 36–37; soil fertility and, 10–11, 26, 35–36, 41–42, 44–45. *See also* agriculture; diversification; fertilizer; *and specific crops*
state parks, 172–73
Stegner, Wallace, xx
Steinberg, Ted, 121, 140
stock laws. *See* commons
Straub, William, 158
Sullivan, William, 107–8
sustainability. *See* sustainable development
sustainable development, xix–xx, 181–82
sustained yield, 15, 80, 82
Sutch, Richard, 50
Swift Fertilizer Works, 51

Tallulah Falls (Ga.), 159–62, 163
Tallulah Falls Conservation Association, 159
tenant farming. *See* sharecropping
Tennessee: agricultural labor in, 47; Appalachian national park advocated by, 169–71; coal boom in, 74; crop diversification in, 42; deforestation in, 74; disease in, 132; furniture manufacturing and, 100; National Conservation Exposition hosted by, 20–24; pollution control laws of, 130–31; pollution in, 123, 132; resources of, 13–14; sewerage construction in, 131–32; underdevelopment of, 13–14
Tennessee Coal, Iron and Railroad Company, 122
Tennessee Copper Company, 123
Tennessee Valley Authority (TVA), 140, 173–74
Texas, 41, 66, 74, 93–94, 130, 172
Texas Railroad Commission, 93–94
textile industry, 76, 103, 119, 135–37
Thompson, Peter, 68
Tillman, Benjamin Ryan, 90–92
Timber Conservation Contract Act, 78–79
timber industry: conservation and, 22–23, 72–73, 78–81, 82; deforestation by, 26, 73, 74–77, 79, 80–81; as migratory industry, 69, 73, 76–78, 103–4, 168, 170; replaced by tourism, 153, 168–71; shift to South of, 73–74; wastefulness of, 68–69, 77–78, 97, 103–4, 170. *See also* forests; reforestation; waste industries
Timmons, W. W., 84
Tindall, George, 32, 48
tobacco, 35, 40, 45, 48, 119, 175
Tompkins, Daniel Augustus, 56–57
Torrey, Raymond, 172
tourism industry: African American resorts and, 147–48, 156; compatible enterprises promoted by, 149–54; conflicts with water conservation, 159–63; federal protection for, 168–71; growth of, 143, 144–45, 153, 154, 163, 166–67, 173–74, permanence of, 142–44, 148–49, 154–55, 161–62, 163–64, 168–71; promoters of, 143, 154; scenery and, 154–55, 157–63, 168–71; segregation in, 146–48, 167–68, 173; transportation in, 150–51, 155–57; as waste industry, 148–49. *See also* health tourism; hunting
trade associations, 80, 82–83. *See also specific trade associations*
Troesken, Werner, 132
Trowbridge, John Townsend, 35
tuberculosis, 133, 145, 154
Tufts, James Walker, 148, 152–53
tung oil industry, 101
Turner, G. H., 63
Turpentine Operators' Association, 84, 85
Tuskegee Experiment Station, 44, 57, 58
Tuskegee Institute, 31, 43–44, 57–58, 134
Tuskegee Negro Conference, 134
TVA (Tennessee Valley Authority), 140, 173–74
Tybee Island (Ga.), 149
typhoid fever, 133

United States Bureau of Refugees, Freedmen and Abandoned Lands, 48
United States Census Bureau, 49
United States Department of Agriculture: cotton promoted by, 45; cottonseed production surveyed by, 64; demonstration work of, 59; partnership of, with Tuskegee, 44; soil fertility debated in, 16, 52; tung trees advocated by, 101
United States Department of Justice, 88
United States Department of the Interior, 15, 162
United States Division of Forestry. *See* United States Forest Service
United States Forest Products Laboratory, 97–98
United States Forest Service: Clarke-McNary Act and, 80; cooperative work of, 79; experiment stations of, 82; exposition displays of, 21; forest research of, 97; and Pinchot, 15; recreation promoted by, 169
Urania Lumber Company, 79, 80

urban growth: conflicts with industry and, 127–29, 134–35, 135–39; environmental effects of, 117, 126–30, 132–34; as impetus for tourism, 145, 163; infrastructure for, 131–33, 134–35; lack of, 178; New South Creed and, 1, 3, 12, 13, 126. *See also* segregation

USDA. *See* United States Department of Agriculture

Valley Land and Improvement Company, 151
Vance, Rupert, 142–43
Vanderbilt Agrarians, 180
Virginia: coal boom in, 74; disease in, 132; furniture manufacturing in, 100; mill dams regulated by, 118, 127–29; pollution control laws of, 127–29, 130, 131, 137–39; railroad infrastructure in, 119; soil exhaustion in, 35; tourism in, 151–52; wood waste industries in, 100
Virginia-Carolina Chemical Company, 51–52
von Liebig, Justus, 52
vulcanization process, 98–100

Washington, Booker T., 31, 133, 134
Washington, Forrester, 173
waste industries: booster promotion of, 2, 20, 21, 26, 27, 69–70, 81, 95–100; costs of, 110, 175–76; cottonseed oil as, 61–65; development of, 109–10; industrial incentives for, 102–3, 105–6; myopic view of resources and, 110; pulp and paper as, 103–9; self-sufficiency and, 43–44, 57; tourism as, 145, 148, 149. *See also specific industries*
water law: balancing-of-interests test and, 124–26, 127, 129, 138; common law roots of, 118, 121; development promoted by, 123, 124–25, 126; navigation and, 118, 131; in New England, 121; nuisance cases and, 121–26; racial disparities in, 126; reasonable use standard, 121–22; in West, 121
waterpower: compared with coal, 117; conservation of, 117, 162; expansion of, 119–20, 140, 159–62, 175; law and, 120–22, mill dams and, 111–14, 117–19, 122, 127–29, 159–63; promotion of, 11, 23, 26, 29, 116–17, 158; as renewable resource, 117; social effects of, 126, 129
water quality, 111–14, 130–39, 162. *See also* pollution: of water
Watson, Thomas E., 9, 58
Waugh, William, 148
Wausau Lumber Company, 100
Way, Albert, 167
Weeks Act (1911), 169
Wernicke, Otto, 81
Whitcomb, Irving, 151
Whitfield, George, 139
Whitney, Milton, 16, 52
Willett, N. L., 166
Winslow, Carlisle, 98
wise use, xviii, 25, 28–29, 32, 52, 72. *See also* Pinchot, Gifford
wood alcohol, 97, 100, 102–3
Woodward, C. Vann: colonial economy and, 68–69, 74; defines Redemption, 6; Homestead Act and, 73, 74; irony in South and, 182; southern environmental degradation and, xvi
Worsham, Ernest Lee, 27–28
Worster, Donald, 179
Wright, Gavin, 37, 40
Wright, T. Asbury, 21

yellow fever, 112, 130
Yellow Pine Manufacturers' Association, 80
Yellowstone National Park, 30, 154, 168
Yosemite National Park, 30, 154, 162–63, 168

Zimmerman, Andrew, 8

ENVIRONMENTAL HISTORY AND THE AMERICAN SOUTH

Lynn A. Nelson, *Pharsalia: An Environmental Biography of a Southern Plantation, 1780–1880*

Jack E. Davis, *An Everglades Providence: Marjory Stoneman Douglas and the American Environmental Century*

Shepard Krech III, *Spirits of the Air: Birds and American Indians in the South*

Paul S. Sutter and Christopher J. Manganiello, eds., *Environmental History and the American South: A Reader*

Claire Strom, *Making Catfish Bait out of Government Boys: The Fight against Cattle Ticks and the Transformation of the Yeoman South*

Christine Keiner, *The Oyster Question: Scientists, Watermen, and the Maryland Chesapeake Bay since 1880*

Mark D. Hersey, *My Work Is That of Conservation: An Environmental Biography of George Washington Carver*

Kathryn Newfont, *Blue Ridge Commons: Environmental Activism and Forest History in Western North Carolina*

Albert G. Way, *Conserving Southern Longleaf: Herbert Stoddard and the Rise of Ecological Land Management*

Lisa M. Brady, *War upon the Land: Military Strategy and the Transformation of Southern Landscapes during the American Civil War*

Drew A. Swanson, *Remaking Wormsloe Plantation: The Environmental History of a Lowcountry Landscape*

Paul S. Sutter, *Let Us Now Praise Famous Gullies: Providence Canyon and the Soils of the South*

Monica R. Gisolfi, *The Takeover: Chicken Farming and the Roots of American Agribusiness*

William D. Bryan, *The Price of Permanence: Nature and Business in the New South*

Paul S. Sutter and Paul M. Pressly, eds., *Coastal Nature, Coastal Culture: Environmental Histories of the Georgia Coast*

Andrew C. Baker, *Bulldozer Revolutions: A Rural History of the Metropolitan South*

Drew A. Swanson, *Beyond the Mountains: Commodifying Appalachian Environments*

Thomas Blake Earle and D. Andrew Johnson, eds., *Atlantic Environments and the American South*

www.ingramcontent.com/pod-product-compliance
Lightning Source LLC
Chambersburg PA
CBHW010026150725
29538CB00051B/325